CW00889286

The Smouldering Hills

by
CELIA JONES

Celia Jones

Oct 3rd 1996

CASTAN BOOKS
Cardiff

Published in Great Britain by Castan Books, Cardiff 1996
13 Duffryn Close, Llandennis Road, Cardiff CF2 6HT
Tel: 01222 751051

© Celia Jones 1996

ISBN 0 9528416 06

All rights reserved. No part of this publication may be reproduced, stored in a retrieval system, or transmitted in any form or by any means, electronic, mechanical, photocopying, recording or otherwise without the prior permission of the author.

COVER ILLUSTRATION BY KIND PERMISSION OF THE MUSEUM OF WELSH LIFE

Printed in Great Britain by J & P Davison, 3 James Place, Pontypridd.

for

ALICE

Chapter 1

North-east winds howled across the country on that winter day in 1827. Eliza was glad that she wasn't sitting on top of the mail-coach as it rattled up the Brecon Beacons; it was cold enough behind the main carriage where she held the rail in front of her tightly as she shivered. The old man at her side had turned up the collar of his great-coat to protect his ears. Every now and then, when a wheel jolted in a cart-rut, the vehicle swung violently from side to side and the young girl threw anxious glances at her unknown companion.

"Never fear, Missy," he said eventually. "This coach was made by a company of high repute; it affords superior safety on account of its construction."

"Shall we have to get out and walk up that hill?"

"I doubt it. If the horses could get up the slope at Quaker's Yard they should manage this."

The monotonous grinding of the wheels and the cracking of hooves reverberated through the valley as the team wound its way down from the staging post at Storey Arms, the horses' nostrils pouring out dense clouds of white vapour which hung in the November air as if reluctant to disperse. Eliza tried to concentrate her thoughts, conscious of the fact that she had only one groat left out of the savings she had mustered during the two years she had worked for the Crawshays in Cyfarthfa Castle.

It was difficult to think amidst all the din and, in any case, she fought against a desperate longing to sleep because there had been little chance of rest the previous night. Mrs Howells, the cook, had insisted on everything being washed and cleaned before it was put away after the dinner party for the Foremans, the Hills, the Homfrays, Mr Brunel and the Marquis of Bute, who had dined on salmon and venison, washing it down with copious draughts of champagne.

Below stairs, tempers had been frayed; twice during the day Eliza had had to scrub the flagstoned floors leading to the garden, to remove mud left by the gardeners as they trudged back and forth with potted plants for the house. Maldwyn, one of the grooms, had been dismissed for draining the dregs of a bottle of port wine. Still, she thought, it was easier for a man - he could join the militia or go to sea if needs be. Her predicament was far worse.

When the coach drew up outside the Castle Inn at Brecon, the guard helped the passengers down.

"Did you enjoy the journey?" he asked Eliza when her turn came.

1

"Wasn't it exhilarating?"

She looked at his neckerchief and jockey boots before replying. "It was a cold day for travelling, your Honour. Perhaps in the summer it would be more agreeable. If you please, Sir, could you tell me the way to Drover Street?"

The guard inclined his head to the opposite side of the road. "Yonder," he said, as he sauntered into the inn.

"Thank you, Sir," Eliza said, with a bob.

She hesitated at the beginning of a lane behind the church before making her way slowly along a row of tall houses, checking the numbers as she passed. At 23, she paused to look over the railings at the servants' entrance before walking resolutely up the steps to the front door where she pulled the bell with both hands. After a while, the door opened to reveal a stern, middle-aged woman who wore a stark brown day dress and a frilled cambric cap.

"I want to see Mr Luke Thomas," Eliza announced, with a confidence she didn't feel.

The woman scanned the girl from head to toe, her eyes pausing at the sight of the bare feet that were blue with cold.

"Have you a card?"

Eliza wasn't deterred. "No, but if you tell him that Miss Eliza Coleman from Cyfarthfa Castle wants to speak to him, he will see me." She knew that she had to be bold.

"Bide there!" came the command as the door was firmly shut.

Eliza hung her head and waited, sick with anxiety, knowing that her future hung on a slender thread. Her face was quite plain when in repose or when she was worried, but her features could take on a different aspect when she smiled, not that there had been much occasion for that in the past few months. Normally, when she was animated, her large brown eyes sparkled and her face would be transformed into one which could almost be called pretty.

Today, she looked pale and miserable. Her auburn hair was hidden under a floppy mop-cap; her flannel skirt had lost much of its brightness as repeated wash-days had reduced its colour to varying shades of plum and pale crimson. The women in her family didn't wear shawls, they had strips of home-spun cloth fringed with tassels, but as this garment had been handed down by two of Eliza's sisters, no tassels were left.

Suddenly, the door was opened by Luke Thomas himself. He was a man of early middle years, with an abundance of fair, curly hair that made him appear taller than he really was. He wore a brown velvet jacket, pale-coloured breeches and had a cream silk cravat at his neck. He was smiling cheerfully.

"Why! Elizabeth! What a surprise!"

Eliza's response was scarcely more than a twitch.

"How did you get here?" he asked, beckoning her inside with a wave of his arm.

"On the mail-coach from Merthyr."

"You must be so cold. Come and sit by the fire." He seemed genuinely concerned as he indicated a room on the left of the hall and held the door open for her.

She was grateful for the warmth of the fire as she sat timidly on the edge of an armchair, rubbing her feet in the depth of the carpet. She glared at her host as he sat down opposite her, his eyebrows raised expectantly and his demeanour signifying that he meant her no ill will. She had forgotten the freckles that softened his otherwise sharp features and found herself staring at him. Despite all the thought she had given to this meeting, now that she was here she didn't know how to begin. She was about to speak when there was a knock on the door and a young maid entered, carrying a tray.

"Thank you, Siân," Luke said, sitting with his fingers together at his chin and his eyebrows lowered.

As soon as the maid left, Eliza crumpled. "You must know why I'm here! You must! I'm bearing your child. My Mam will kill me."

Luke pursed his lips and nodded slowly. As Eliza's sobs continued, he rose to his feet and crossed the room to the window where he stood with his hands behind his back, looking at the slight flurry of snow that had begun to fall. When eventually he turned round, his shoulders fell as he contemplated her; she was looking down at her feet and wiping her nose in one of her sleeves.

"Sunt Lacrimae Rerum!" he murmured.

"What was that?" Eliza asked sharply. "What did you say?"

"I said..er..Life is a quiet and an ageless wonder."

"What does that mean?" she demanded.

Luke returned to his chair and sat down with a gentle smile. "It means, Elizabeth that your Mam will not kill you; I wouldn't permit that. Your child will not be born a bastard; I will marry you, if you will have me," he said, extending his arms.

Eliza stared at him, transfixed, as a deep frown creased her forehead. "Marry me? Marry me!" she cried with disbelief. "You want to marry me? You a gent and me a servant?"

Of all the fates she had considered, this one hadn't occurred to her. Luke was calmly pouring tea from a silver teapot, recalling the summer when the scent of bougainvillaea and jasmine in the conservatory at Cyfarthfa Castle had suffused the evening air. Crawshay and a group of men had dined well and consumed more wine than was prudent. They had caroused far into the night with a bevy of young girls spirited up for their pleasure. He had known then what lay ahead and Elizabeth had been so merry and warm, so....vibrant. Now this!

Suddenly he spoke. "You may not know, Elizabeth, that my wife died two years ago. God rest her soul! My sons are grown men and no longer live at home. I care not what others may think or say - it can be a cruel world and I must protect you, of that I am certain. I could not...live in peace knowing that you and your child would be outcasts."

He had chosen his words with care.

3

Eliza sat back in her chair, overcome with weariness. Too much had happened that day and she felt unable to think coherently any more.

"Pray, when shall we be wed?" she whispered, not believing that he meant what he said.

"Why! With all convenient speed. I shall see the vicar tomorrow and ask him to call the banns. In the meantime you shall stay here as my guest."

He pulled the bell-cord at his side, whereupon the door opened so swiftly that Eliza wondered if the maid had been listening at the keyhole, as her friend Minnie at the castle often did.

"Siân, will you please lay another place at the table for lunch and then prepare the guest room. Miss Coleman will be staying here for some time."

Siân was a buxom, bright-eyed young girl, not much more than fifteen or thereabouts. She threw a glance at the visitor and bobbed a curtsy as she left. Eliza stared back at her like Cortez, silent on the peak at Darien.

Sitting at the oak table during the meal, Eliza knew that she should have been pleased at the course which events had taken, instead of which she experienced extreme lowness of spirits and had little zest for the broth and cold mutton placed in front of her. The strangeness of being waited upon unnerved her and she couldn't stop thinking about the staff below stairs. She imagined what they would be saying, convinced that all the conversation upstairs would be repeated later by Pugh, the butler/coachman who stood silent and impassive by the sideboard.

Luke did his best to put her at ease, but her replies to his questions were muted and monosyllabic.

"I recall your telling me that your mother had twenty-four children. How many are still at home?"

"Well, she only reared nine of them. A married brother and two bachelor brothers are left there."

"How old are the young boys?"

"Huw is sixteen and Gwilym is twelve."

"Where do they work?"

"At Cyfarthfa. Huw is a collier and Gwilym is a miner."

Luke realised that Eliza was answering as if she were in front of a magistrate. He looked at the butler with a smile. "Thank you, Pugh. There is no need for you to stay."

Pugh bowed and left in silence, closing the door behind him.

"I haven't asked yet when our child will be born," Luke said as he broke a chunk of bread.

"At the beginning of April, so the doctor told me," Eliza mumbled.

"Which doctor did you see?"

Eliza's reply was almost inaudible. "Dr Price, the Crawshays' doctor."

"William Price! I know him slightly. What did you think of him?"

"Well, he's a strange man, to be sure, but he was kind. He said that if

4

you.. ... couldn't help me I was to go back and he'd see what he could do."

"He is kind when the whim takes him. Sometimes he can be the very devil. He dislikes the rich and champions the poor, like some kind of Welsh Robin Hood. What was he wearing when you saw him?"

"He had long, plaited hair and no neck-tie. That was funny, I thought. He looked peculiar." Eliza was beginning to relax; they had found some common ground. "He said marriage wasn't important; it was only for passing on furniture and things. How can he think that?"

Luke smiled. "Well, although his father is a vicar, William is not a Christian; he worships the Druids, the old pagan gods of Wales, so I suppose there is some logic in his principles. It follows that a church wedding would have little meaning for him. Apparently he leases a woman for seven years and then, after he has given her a sum of money, they part. What do you think of that?"

Eliza was shocked. "That's wicked!" Suddenly she sat upright, remembering her own situation.

"Elizabeth dear, you have had a tiring day. Would you like to rest this afternoon?" Luke asked.

"Oooh! I would. I got up at half-past four this morning so I could run away without being seen." She also longed to be alone; conversation with the gentry was indeed a trial.

It was a relief when the meal ended and they left the dining-room. Luke went to the green baize door at the back of the hall and called down the stairs. The woman in brown appeared, still unsmiling, and stood with her hands together looking intently at the unexpected guest.

"Mrs Bessant, would you show Miss Coleman to her room and help her in every way, please." The request was a command.

Eliza followed the housekeeper upstairs in silence and found herself in a large bedroom at the back of the house. After a few murmured words Mrs Bessant left, closing the door quietly behind her.

The room was not unlike some of those at the castle, with a four-poster bed, lace-trimmed pillow-cases, Persian carpets and silver and crystal on the mahogany dressing-table. When the housekeeper's footsteps died away, the only sound came from the fire in a small hearth where flames licked gently around the coals.

Eliza leant against one of the bed-posts and closed her eyes, fighting a wave of self-pity. She reminded herself that she deserved to be punished, and that what she would have to endure now was infinitely better than she had dared to hope for, but she was alone in a place where she didn't belong and all the comfort and luxury in the world couldn't compensate for her shame.

She took a deep breath and lifted her head, but as she crossed over to the window she caught sight of herself in a long bevelled mirror that stood in one corner. After a pause, her chin wobbled and she gave a wail of despair before breaking down into paroxysms of sobbing which she made no effort to control. A long time later she climbed into the bed and lay staring at the ceiling. Eventually exhaustion took over and she sank into a deep slumber, not waking till dusk.

She was startled by a knock on the door and sat up as Siân entered breezily.

"Can I light the lamps, if you please, Miss Coleman?"

"Yes!" Eliza whispered. "Pray do," she added softly, as the maid carried in a large jug of hot water which she poured into the bowl on the wash-stand. After pulling the curtains Siân returned to the doorway to light a taper from a small lamp and when all three lamps were lit she put more coal on the fire.

"Dinner is at half-past seven. You will find Mr Thomas in the library," she announced, with a bob and a grin.

Eliza had watched every move that the girl made, at a loss for words. She remembered her mother telling her that it was rude to stare, but what else was there to do? In the castle, the family and friends hardly ever looked at the servants, pretending that they weren't there, but that was going to be difficult. Until now, she had thought that she would never learn all the do's and don'ts of waiting on the gentry; she hadn't realised that it would be more complicated to be waited upon. What a tangled world it was to be sure!

She took a closer look at her surroundings when she got up, lifting a scent bottle and holding it against one of the lamps, to catch the sparkle in its depths. She ran her fingers through the rose petals and lavender in a bowl on the table at the bedside. After she had washed her face and hands, she brushed her hair and fixed a chignon on top of her head before lifting the bowl of water and putting it on the floor, where she sat with her hands around her knees while her feet soaked in the warm suds.

Her confidence retreated as she stood at the top of the stairs, listening for sounds in the house; but the place was wrapped in silence. She tip-toed down slowly, wincing when one of the floor-boards creaked. Light was shining under a door on the right of the hall. When she turned the knob and walked in, she found herself in a warm, book-lined room filled with the smell of wood-smoke. Luke had been sitting by the log fire, but stood up as she came towards him.

"Elizabeth! That's better. You look refreshed," he said, noticing the sheen on her hair.

That evening her appetite returned and she was grateful for the meal of fowl with steaming potatoes. The butler left of his own accord after serving each course, which was a relief, but, even though Eliza had been taught how to lay a table for dinner, she was dismayed at the amount of cutlery laid out on either side of her plate. Why folk couldn't be doing with one knife, fork and spoon she could never fathom; in her family you had one of each and you had to clean your plate with bread before you had any pudding, if there was any pudding to be had. Her eyes followed Luke's hands closely.

"I think I should write to your parents to let them know where you are and that we plan to wed, do you not agree, dear?" he said after a while.

Eliza's concentration was disrupted. "Aw! You aren't going to tell them I am with child!"

"No, no, of course not, but I should ask your father for permission to marry his daughter, you know."

"He won't refuse; my mother wouldn't let him," Eliza said, not liking to tell Luke that her parents couldn't read or write.

"Well, in any case, I think we should visit them as soon as possible, does your father work?"

"He's a puddler," Eliza answered with some pride "He employs two men."

"That is a skilled trade, so since he will be in the iron works all day, we shall invite him and your mother to dine with us at the inn, where you and I shall stay overnight."

Eliza's eyes became glazed as she imagined the scene.

"First of all though, you must do some shopping, to buy warm clothes, boots and shoes. Can you think of anything else that merits our immediate attention?"

"Boots and shoes? I never had any, nor my sisters, leastways, not until they were married, and then my father bought them a pair. Well, boots and shoes!" she cried, as she was about to take a healthy bite from an apple. She stopped with her mouth wide open when she noticed that Luke was peeling a pear with a small knife, dipping his fingers in a crystal bowl and then wiping his hands with his napkin.

"What is it, dear? Don't you like the thought of wearing boots?"

Eliza swallowed. "I'll like them a lot, though I should think your feet feel heavy in them, don't they?" she said, as she examined her cutlery.

After dinner they went into the drawing-room where Eliza settled herself in an armchair and studied the figurines on the mantelpiece. Luke lit a churchwarden's pipe, tapping the tobacco softly between each puff. When he was satisfied that the pipe was alight, he leaned back and frowned.

"Elizabeth, there is something you should know; try not to distress yourself."

She sat upright, on guard once more.

"I may not live much longer; I may not be alive when your child is born." He was looking into the fire, as Eliza listened with her hands at her mouth. "I am reconciled to my fate because I have had a full and favoured life with more than my share of this world's fortunes. I am not afraid to die. You mustn't be sad on my account."

The firelight sent a medley of shadows dancing round the room. Eliza left her chair and sat at Luke's feet.

"Luke!" she gulped.

"I must ask your forgiveness for the wrong that I did you," he said in a low voice. "I must ask you to forgive me for the anguish I have caused you if I am to expect forgiveness in the next world."

"You were not alone in wrong-doing; I was as much to blame and I don't deserve the kindness you are showing me."

"Calm yourself, dear. It is only right that I should look after you and provide for you and the child after my day. I am afraid you will find it rather lonely here while I am alive, but afterwards you shall have a small house back in Merthyr, near your family and friends, and sufficient means to live a comfortable life there. I can do no less." He looked down at her and stroked her cheek. "I have to rest a good deal these days and rarely go out. You will be company for me. It is good to know that you will be at my side, you will be solace for a lonely man."

"There's sad that you may not see our child."

"We must accept our lot in life. Come, let me see you smile. Let us talk about your future."

When Eliza was alone in her bedroom that night she sat at the dressing-table with her head in her hands, drained and limp, trying to absorb all that Luke had told her. After a while she turned the lamps down and sat on the window seat. It had been a long bewildering day, but she didn't feel like sleep after the hours of oblivion in the afternoon. Gas lamps fluttering in the deserted street outside lit up the snowflakes that fell softly against the window pane as she gazed into the night with unseeing eyes

After breakfast next morning, Luke gave her a purseful of sovereigns and waved her off as she went shopping. She crossed the square quickly, feeling conspicuous and finding the quietness eerie after the tumult and clangour of Merthyr. It was some time before it dawned on her that the smell of her home town was missing too.

She stood outside a *Ladies' Fashions* shop, looking at the clothes in the window and summoning up the courage to go inside. When she did so the situation wasn't helped when a strident voice told her to go back out and find the tradesmen's entrance at the rear.

She flushed and stood her ground. "I've come to buy some clothes," she said shyly, holding up her purse.

"What clothes?" asked the imperious shop assistant.

"Three skirts, four pairs of hose, two indoor jackets, three mop-caps, four muslin scarves and anything else that takes my fancy," she answered as she emptied her purse on the counter. She had given the matter thought as she was dressing that morning.

The woman behind the counter stood non-plussed. Seeing her confusion, Eliza spoke again. "Apart from a few things that I'll take with me, could you deliver the goods to 23, Drover Street this afternoon, if you please," she said softly.

When she left half-an-hour later, Eliza was wearing hose, had a new mop-cap on her head and a Paisley shawl around her shoulders. She proceeded to the cobbler's shop, emerging in leather boots and carrying a pair of indoor shoes in a box. In the milliner's shop, the choice was difficult. She ordered two bonnets and a flat velvet hat, but was diffident about buying the tall black hat that looked like a chimney-pot. It was quite the smartest of the lot - Mrs Crawshay had one, but Eliza felt that she wouldn't have the courage to wear it.

Time was getting on, so she stayed only briefly at the haberdasher's shop to buy ribbons and the handkerchiefs that Luke had suggested. She was on her way home when she paused, turned round and went back to the milliner's to buy the tall hat. Having gone that far, she bought a silk parasol as well.

When she stood on the doorstep in Drover Street, it seemed like a thousand years since she had waited there the day before. Siân unpacked the parcels that arrived in the afternoon, after which Eliza washed her hair, sprayed some scent behind her ears and put on the eau-de-nil dress. She spent a long time deciding whether to wear the guipure lace cape or a cream silk scarf over her shoulders. She chose a narrow black velvet ribbon to tie around her neck and a wider one around her hair. When she studied herself in the mirror she reckoned that, as long as she didn't speak, she might almost be a lady.

As she walked down the stairs she listened to the rustle of her voluminous petticoats. Her eyes were sparkling and a smile lit up her face as she stood on the threshold of the library.

"Elizabeth!" Luke exclaimed, shaking his head from side to side. "You look beautiful."

Chapter 2

Eliza was glad when their visit to her home in Merthyr was over. When she and Luke reached their inn, she wasn't surprised to receive a message saying that the Colemans were unable to join them, so they went to see Mrs Coleman the following morning. Luke was perfectly at ease, unlike Eliza's mother, who seemed to have been struck dumb; not since having all her teeth pulled out by the blacksmith had she said so little.

Eliza's lowly origins embarrassed her in Brecon, but sitting in that tiny kitchen in smart clothes and bonnet, she felt ridiculous. Her heart went out to her mother who was overawed by Luke, and consequently acted in a stilted, deferential manner. Both women were relieved when the visit ended. Mrs Coleman stood in the doorway, with her hands stuffed in her mouth and her eyes standing out so far that Eliza feared they might not go back if there were a sudden gust of wind. However, in the coach on the way home, Eliza's heartache evaporated as she thought about the storm which would break when her mother discovered the real reason for her marriage - gent or otherwise. The torrent of fury would last for months, if not for ever.

The journey exhausted Luke who now looked much older than his forty-five years. He didn't complain; only when he said that he felt cold in a perfectly warm room did Eliza worry. They settled down to a quiet routine which Eliza supposed was normal for gentlefolk, but it was one which she found lonely in the highest degree. The servants treated her with respect but she reacted to them with tormented nervousness; mercifully, Mrs Bessant continued to run the household, consulting only Luke who did all that he could to encourage Eliza's confidence.

In the mornings she would sit in the drawing-room copying out letters of the alphabet that he had selected, shaking sand carefully over her work when it was finished. In the afternoons, while Luke was resting, she strolled in the town, looking in shop windows, or going round the market, envying people who were talking to each other on the road. In the evenings she showed Luke her morning's work, and he helped her to read simple verses from the Bible. Apart from Luke the only other living creature with whom she could communicate with ease was Fluff, the Persian cat who, being indiscriminate, would jump on her lap and purr like a cauldron.

Sometimes she embroidered a sampler that Luke had ordered from Manchester. The hours that passed were marked by the chimes of a musical grandfather clock in the hall. Often she would put her tapestry down and walk out to listen to the melodies, returning afterwards to her stitching.

/////////////////////////////////

* *ABCDEFGHIJKLMNOPQRSTUVWXYZ* *

ABCDEFGHIJKLMNOPQRSTUVWXYZ

ABCDEFGHIJKLMNOPQRSTUVWXYZ

Elizabeth Thomas
HER WORK
1827

BEAR THE CROSS
PATIENTLY

Three weeks after her arrival, Eliza and Luke were married in a side chapel of St. John's Church. Luke's agent and attorney, the only witnesses, returned to the house for a glass of sherry. When they had left, Luke led his wife to the drawing-room where he took a small box from the bureau and gave it to her.

"For me?" she whispered.

"For my wife," he answered.

Her eyes sparkled as she paused with an indrawn breath. "I never had a present like this before!"

Lying on a purple velvet pad was a delicate gold bar, inset with three seed pearls. Luke removed the brooch and pinned it at her throat, leading her over to the mantelpiece so that she could see herself in the mirror, while he took in her radiance.

"There's lovely it is! Thank you, Luke," she said shyly.

"Elizabeth, I wish I could be a real husband to you, but that cannot be." He seemed angry.

"It doesn't matter," she said lightly.

"It does," he said sharply. "It does," he added softly as he stroked her cheek.

A week later, Eliza went down to Merthyr to see her mother again, but on her own this time. She stayed overnight, sleeping on the kitchen settle. It was all very different from the previous visit.

"Eliza! My little Eliza! What a sight! Aw! Just look at that hat! There's smart!"

Eliza grinned. "It's good to see you, Mam."

"I can't get over it. My daughter a lady! Married to a Gent! Not that we aren't a tidy family but, well, to think of it!"

Eliza waited for the spasms to subside before sitting in the armchair by the fire. "It's good to be back. How is everybody?"

The men were at work; even Mrs Coleman's daughter-in-law, who lived in the front room, had a job in the colliery where her three children were door-boys, so they had the place to themselves. She hung the kettle over the fire and settled down for a gossip.

"Things are going from bad to worse here, indeed they are. I dunno what the world is coming to, I can tell you. Your father brought home thirty-five shillings a week ten years ago and now, twenty shillings last Saturday! For a puddler!" She was screeching by the end of her announcement. She scratched her head as she continued: "How am I going to manage on twenty shillings, pray?"

Eliza shook her head and closed her hands around her cup of tea.

"Gertie lost her baby," Mrs Coleman said quietly. "The poor dab only lived for five minutes. Still, that's one less mouth to feed, that's how I look at it. Four children to feed on Ieuan's wages is too much even though little Robert is working as a door-boy now."

"Robert? But he's only four years old and he's afraid of the dark!"

"That's as may be," said Mrs Coleman with a sniff. "Lots of children his age are underground; he's not the only one working as a door-boy."

"But the cold, and the rats, and not seeing a soul for hours on end, maybe. Poor little dab!"

"Ay! It's hard, I must say. Gertie puts him to bed as soon as he gets home but it's the Devil's own job to get him up at five the next morning."

They worked their way systematically through the brothers and sisters, aunts and uncles before starting on the neighbours.

"Dai Bennett had a short life, didn't he? But he had a grand funeral at the end of it. Two horses with plumes, and lovely ham his mother gave us. Lovely it was. Pity he was killed by that waggon underground, but there you are. The Lord giveth and the Lord taketh away. More tea?" Mrs Coleman asked idly. "What next? Aw! Yes! The smallpox took Llewellyn Tabernacle last Tuesday. Darker the draper is doing well in mourning clothes, I can tell you. I've made faggots for your dinner, I know you like them. Do they give you faggots in Brecon?" she asked as she lifted the saucepan lid and tasted the contents with a spoon, indulging in a long drawn-out hissing sound. "Another five minutes and they'll be ready."

Eliza smiled as she watched her mother laying the table with a knife and fork each. She warmed to the thought that there was another whole day before she would have to leave.

"Merthyr seems a lot more crowded than it used to be. Where do all these people come from?"

"Well might you ask," Mrs Coleman answered. "We have Italians, Spaniards and now them Irish who live in shacks under the bridge, by the canal. I don't know what the place is coming to, I really don't. This part of Merthyr isn't called Georgetown any more. Do you know what they call it, because there's so many foreigners about? *China!* That's what Mrs Evans Ebenezer told me at the well yesterday. *China!* Would you believe it? Come on, let's have our dinner," she said, as she put the faggots on the plates and continued her tirade.

"Yes indeed! A trumpery lot of ragamuffins we have around the town. No wonder the shopkeepers complain about the Poor Rate going up and up. The orphans that the Guardians put in lodgings go around begging and stealing and the women who are supposed to be their landladies - well, I don't like to say what they are doing, but you're married now so I can tell you this, - there's one slut called Halfpenny Nellie; they do say she's only thirteen. She works from that beer-house called the Patriot where all the drunks in South Wales seem to meet at night. I tell you - the place is Bedlam. It's not safe for decent people to go out after dark."

"Mam! What a cook you are! I miss faggots in Brecon," Eliza said with her mouth full.

"Yes! It's not like the old days when wages were high in the war and we were building a New Jerusalem. Most of the people round here now are either Papists or heathens. They are no better than savages; they don't know how to behave proper. You should smell the place some days," she muttered in a low voice. "All them chamber pots emptied in the gutters and no rain for a week! It's terrible!"

"I noticed the smell as soon as I got out of the coach. It's strange - there's hardly any smell in Brecon," Eliza said.

"Anyway, never mind. Tell me about your life as a lady. There's funny they don't eat faggots."

"Well, some parts are nice, but it's very quiet; I don't know many people. They keep the front door shut all the time, even though they have carpet on the stairs. You can't make a cup of tea when you want one because you can't go into the kitchen. You have to ring a bell if you want anything. You mustn't ever answer the door yourself," Eliza said sadly.

"Go on! You don't say! What are the people next door like?" her mother asked eagerly.

"I don't know. I haven't seen them."

"Get away! Oooh! I wouldn't like that."

"It's lonely at times, but Luke is learning me to read English."

"Never! That makes you a lady!" Mrs Coleman cried. "I can't wait to tell Mrs Hawkins, with her 'pennyworth-of-sprats' voice, just because her husband works behind a counter and got a top hat."

After clearing the table, they sat by the fire and talked until it was time to light the lamps. The workers returned at seven, when the kitchen bustled with activity. Eliza went to see the next-door neighbours, while the men washed in the zinc tub in front of the kitchen fire. Uncle Arthur and Kitty Jones Zion turned up as well as cousin Annie and Mr Morris Ebenezer. Mrs Coleman had made a cauldron full of cawl - never happier than when she had a table full of hungry people to feed.

They talked about the old days. "I was there when Admiral Nelson came to see the cannon they was making for his ships," claimed Morris. "Crowds there were. They gave a big display with cannons being fired into the air for everyone to see."

"I heard about that," said Mr Coleman. "A boy's head got shot off!"

"Yes, that was a pity but a Lady Hamilton who was there gave the boy's mother fifteen pounds for a good funeral. Very kind lady she was."

"Who wants more?" yelled Mrs Coleman. "Come on! Eat up, Eliza, you'll have more, I know."

"Merthyr was a good place to live, then," said Uncle Arthur wistfully. "Not like now."

"Tch! I remember you coming here from Cardigan to find work and looking for a better life," Mr Coleman said.

"All they do now is cut our wages," growled Eliza's brother, Huw.

"They wanted us in the war against Napoleon. We had good money then because they had to make cannons. We helped our side to win and now there's peace, they don't care about us," muttered Morris Ebenezer.

Uncle Arthur sighed. "I reckon I might be better off going back to West Wales and helping the farmers."

"Mr Morris, any more to eat?" demanded Mrs. Coleman, who seldom listened to any male conversation, finding it extremely boring.

Arguments ensued about the merits of the various ironmasters, while Audrey and Eliza giggled in a corner; Morris started coughing like a dog with worms while Mr Coleman and Uncle Arthur joined forces to quarrel with Huw about measures that ought to be taken to improve the lot of working people. Mrs Coleman left them all to it, while she took a bowl of cawl over the road to ninety-year-old Mrs Rees who lived on her own and was almost destitute.

As Eliza listened to the hubbub in the tiny kitchen, she thought about her other world in Brecon and her return to the lonely life of a lady.

It was early in February that Luke caught a chill and decided to stay in bed for a few days. At first he seemed cheerful enough, although he was very weak; he had little appetite, taking only sips of broth or buttermilk. After three days Eliza asked Pugh to send for a doctor. While she waited she paced up and down the hall, becoming more anxious each time the clock chimed. When she heard footsteps outside she rushed to open the door, only to have to step aside as a tall, cadaverous-looking man walked in, placing his top hat in her hands without looking at her. He proceeded to walk quickly upstairs, without a word. Five minutes later he re-appeared, walking down as quickly as he had walked up.

When he reached the bottom step he looked up and frowned. "My hat!" he snapped.

Eliza handed it to him, opening her mouth to speak.

"My gloves!"

"How is my husband, doctor?"

His eyes met hers suddenly as he took the proffered gloves. "You must know that Mr Thomas is dying; no physic can cure him. Perhaps you should send for the vicar," he said as he walked to the door and waited for it to be opened.

Eliza looked helplessly around, gripped by an elemental fear. How could the gentry lead such lonely lives? she thought. At home, people would be doing something, saying something! Never again would she envy ladies sitting at their tapestries, waiting for the clock to chime. The poor who grumbled at their lot didn't know how much easier their lives were in many ways. At least they wouldn't be alone as she was now. Her mind wandered wildly until she thought about Luke, whereupon she walked slowly up the stairs to his room and sat by his bed.

From time to time, Mrs Bessant or Siân came in to light the lamps or put more coal on the fire. Eliza preferred to have only one lamp lit so that the fire-light could flicker more distinctly; she felt that the moving shadows made up for the stillness in the bed. Toward evening Mrs Bessant suggested that she might go downstairs for a meal.

"I can stay here, Ma'am," she said gently. "I will call you if necessary." Eliza sensed warmth in the housekeeper's voice. "You should eat something, Mrs Thomas."

Eliza sat in silence at the dining-room table, where Pugh hovered as usual. She had long since grown accustomed to his presence but she was startled when he spoke.

"Perhaps you would like some bread and butter pudding, Ma'am. Mrs Bessant says it's very tasty."

Eliza had taken some broth but left most of the rest of the meal. She placed her napkin on the table. "I'm not very hungry tonight, Pugh."

"You need to keep up your strength, Mrs Thomas. I should try the pudding."

Eliza gave him a wan smile. He was a middle-aged man, with a slight stoop. She hadn't heard him string more than a few words together since she had known him. She replaced the napkin in her lap as he put the pudding in front of her.

Eliza resumed her vigil after she had eaten. Luke's breathing had become uneven; sometimes, it stopped altogether before starting once more. She was staring at the pattern in the carpet when she realised that it should have started again. She stood up, with her hands at her breasts, and waited. There came a long, slow sigh. Luke had died.

In the hours and days that followed, Eliza was grateful for Mrs Bessant's tactful guidance through the proprieties that had to be observed. "Siân has pulled down the blinds in the front of the house, Ma'am. Shall I send Pugh for the vicar and the attorney? The agent sent for Mr Thomas's sons a few days ago; they should be here at any time. Will you be going out to purchase your mourning garments, or shall I send for a seamstress?"

It had been lonely enough when Luke was there, but when two of his sons arrived, the situation became unbearable. They were not much older than Eliza and their contempt for her was ill-concealed. Henry was articled to an attorney in London; James owned a chandler's business in Bristol. Neither of them bore much resemblance to their father and certainly lacked his warmth and kindness. Most of the time they remained closeted in the library, while Eliza stayed in the drawing-room. When they met for meals the long silences were difficult for her to endure. Mrs Bessant asked if she would like to have breakfast in her room, which she accepted, realising that the staff were doing all they could to help her and had probably been doing so for a long time had she but noticed. Having grasped that, she was more able to submit to the humiliation that Luke's children heaped on her.

Henry arranged a strictly private funeral, so that only six people stood around the grave. Eliza shivered in the biting east wind, eventually following the others as they left in silence to return to the broughams. None of them spoke to her and she was the only one to shed tears. On the journey home she sat in her widow's weeds, seething with anger and resentment. Luke would have protected me from all this, she told herself.

When they entered the hall the attorney asked her to join them in the library, where the will was to be read. She sat in a daze until she realised that her name had been mentioned.

"Mrs Thomas, your husband left you a furnished house in Dowlais for your lifetime. He considered that you would wish to be near your family. You are to receive sufficient in bonds and cash to maintain you and your child in a decent state. In addition, certain items from this house are also bequeathed to you..er...let me see...the musical grandfather clock, the dining-room table, the writing desk from the drawing-room and a figurine of your choice. Money will be deposited in Messrs Wilkins' bank in Dowlais, from whence you may withdraw cash."

The attorney looked at her, pulling his spectacles lower down his nose as he waited for a response. She didn't appear to have heard him; he glanced nervously at the two sons.

"Mrs Thomas, would you like to ask any questions?" he asked.

Eliza shook her head, still trying to take in what had been said.

"The house in Dowlais is ready for you at any time. Mr Thomas's overseer has been preparing it for some weeks. He will take you there whenever you wish. Would you like to travel there next week? Next month?" he asked, nodding his head as he looked over at Henry who was fidgeting in his seat.

"Tomorrow?" he suggested with a smile.

Eliza came to life. "I'll go tomorrow," she announced, as a weight slipped from her shoulders.

"Very well. I shall ask Mr Titus Jones, the overseer, to call for you in the morning. Just one more thing - a letter which Mr Thomas left you; no doubt you will wish to read it later.

At nine o'clock the next day Eliza left the house without a backward glance.

Chapter 3

Mr Titus Jones, the overseer, arrived early and awaited Eliza in the library. As soon as she saw him she recognised him as one of the men who had been at the funeral.

He bowed as he took her hand. "I am deeply grieved by your husband's death, Mrs Thomas. Please accept my condolences."

Eliza nodded. "I'm ready to leave straight away, Mr Jones," she said quietly. "As soon as the rest of the luggage is brought down."

"Very well. I have taken the liberty of buying presents for the staff, which you might like to give them. I know Mr Thomas respected them; he would have been pleased to know that you shared his appreciation, I am sure."

"Aw! Yes, indeed! They have been so kind. I'm glad you thought of it!"

When a leather trunk, a hamper and three hat boxes had been brought into the hall, the staff lined up for the farewells. Mr Jones gave parcels to Eliza, who handed them to each recipient.

"Thank you, Mrs Bessant. I'm grateful for all your help."

Mrs Bessant inclined her head but didn't change her expression, which remained inscrutable. Siân gave an excited bob and grinned.

Pugh bowed. "We wish you well, Ma'am," he said.

"Thank you all," said Eliza, holding her arms out. "I'll never forget your kindness."

"We need tarry no longer, Mrs Thomas," Mr Jones said. "The rest of the luggage has already been taken to the coach, so the sooner we get started the better. Pugh, will you help me with these, please?"

They walked along the lane and out into the square where the coach was being loaded. Only then did Eliza recall that neither of the sons had appeared to say goodbye. A young lad, who had been hired to help with the luggage at the other end of the journey, was waiting eagerly at the entrance to the Castle Inn. He clambered up on top of the coach and leant down to take the boxes from Pugh. Having arranged them he sat back, holding the rail and looking round with shining eyes. Pugh held the door open for Eliza and Mr Jones to get inside and stood back to watch them leave, giving a wave as the carriage lurched forward. The guard blew the post-horn as they moved away with a flourish towards the Beacons.

"I'm glad you thought about those presents for the staff, Mr Jones," Eliza said as they passed through the town. "I didn't know them well but they were most respectful to me."

"You were Luke Thomas's wife and everyone respected him. He was a very fine man, with the highest principles. I worked for him and the estate for twenty years and I never heard him say an unkind word about his fellow mortals nor did he ever do a mean deed. He was the most unselfish man I have ever known."

Eliza gazed wistfully at the raindrops on the carriage window. "It was nice of him to give me a home of my own and money."

Mr Jones leant towards her. "He was most concerned about your welfare. His instructions were to give you all the support possible. My wife has been helping me to refurbish your house - being a mere man I wouldn't know half the things that you would require. I am anxious to carry out Mr Thomas's wishes in every respect. He always treated me fairly and with consideration and now I have the chance to do the same for his wife. The house is in Ivor Street. Do you know where that is?"

"Yes! I've got cousins living in Brecon Street; it will be good to have them nearby."

"It's one of the properties belonging to the estate; the tenant died before Christmas and his wife went to live with her mother. We asked the lodgers to leave, so that you'll be alone there. Will you mind that?"

"I could ask a cousin to come and live with me," Eliza answered. "If that's all right," she added quickly.

"Of course. It's your home for your lifetime. After your day it reverts to the Court estate, but you can take in lodgers, you can rent it out, you can do whatever you wish while you are alive, and the furniture is yours absolutely," Mr Jones said.

Eliza looked at the rain-swept mountains and the gloomy clouds hanging over them. She had an impulse to ask about Luke's first wife, whom she had often thought about. "Did you know my husband's first wife, Mr Jones?"

He smiled. "I did, Ma'am. A pious and virtuous lady she was. She died when her last child was born dead. Sad it was to see Mr Thomas then; he grieved sorely for a long time - and now you are mourning him. What a vale of tears this mortal life can be at times. It is piteous to see you a widow and still so young, Mrs Thomas."

Eliza threw him a fleeting smile as the coach pulled up at the staging post for a change of horses. When they arrived at Merthyr, they watched as the lad put the luggage in a brougham for the rest of the journey. Mr Jones decided that they should have a meal before going to the house so they stopped at an inn at Cwm Rhyd-y-Bedd, on the outskirts of Dowlais.

As soon as Eliza stepped down, the old, familiar stench greeted her nostrils; the stream running by the side of the inn was clogged with rotting carcasses, old boots, excrement and offal, which was jammed between the pebbles. I'm truly home at last, she thought to herself with a wry smile as she looked at the great ironworks dominating the hill. The yellow, acrid smoke that belched from its chimneys drifted slowly upwards and mingled with the dark grey clouds lingering over the dolorous town.

The landlord of the inn was standing on the steps, waiting to greet them.

"Good day to you, Titus!"

"Good day to you, Will. I trust you can give us some hot, tasty food on this dismal day. The lad can have some broth and bread in the yard."

"Come inside and welcome, Ma'am," the landlord said, bowing to Eliza. "We have a roaring fire in the parlour and a meal of cutlets and fried bacon. Would you like some steaming potatoes as well?"

He was a tall, flaxen-haired man, in his late twenties, dressed in a grey cloth jacket and maroon-coloured velveteen breeches. His black shoes were adorned with silver buckles; at his neck was a white silk cravat.

Eliza was glad to sit by the fire after the tiring journey, but although the landlord was attentive, she took little heed of him, being preoccupied with her immediate future. Will Evans, on the other hand, was intrigued by the young woman in mourning brought in by the overseer of the Thomas estate. Where is she going? Who is she? he pondered as he went to the kitchen to order their meal. When he had provided for them, he took the lad's broth out to the yard.

"Where are you heading, boy?"

"I don't rightly know, your honour. Not far now, I reckon. I was hired for the day in Brecon to look after the luggage," he replied, as he tore the hunk of bread apart and stuffed a large piece in his mouth, pushing stray bits in after it.

When the brougham left the inn, the landlord stood watching it as it lumbered up the hill, skirting the ironworks before it passed out of sight.

They stopped outside a terraced house in Ivor Street where women standing in their doorways, on the opposite side of the road, took a keen interest in their arrival. Eliza lowered her eyes as she climbed down and walked in through her front door. When she reached the kitchen she turned to Mr Jones.

"This belongs to me? This house is mine?" she whispered.

"Do you think you will like it?"

"It's lovely," she gulped. "Luke has given me this!"

An oak dresser was filled with yellow and white china; copper pans and kettles stood on the brass fender in front of the hearth; lustre jugs of various sizes stood on the window-sill behind a small table on which were two Bibles - one in English, the other in Welsh.

"We must get the fire lit," Mr Jones said. "Boy! Bring some twigs and logs in from the yard. Then take the hand-cart to the well for water. The neighbours will tell you where it is."

They went into every room. "The parlour looks bare at the moment, but when your furniture arrives next week, it should look cosy. The figurine that you chose should look well on the mantelpiece, don't you think?"

Eliza nodded, clasping her hands together, then lifting them up in the air. Upstairs in the front bedroom was a large oak coffer; a bowl of lavender stood on the dressing table.

"Your wife must have put that there."

"Yes, and spare quilts and linen are inside the coffer. Come into the back bedroom and see what is in the chest of drawers."

He stood by the door as Eliza pulled a drawer open and saw a baby's layette, with two shawls and a christening gown.

"This is all too much!" she said. "What thought you and your wife have put into my home."

"As instructed by your husband. I shall be back next week with the furniture and you can tell me if there is anything we have forgotten. I think I should go down and light the fire now. You stay here if you wish."

Mr Jones returned to the kitchen where he took the box of Lucifers from the mantelpiece. The twigs were damp, sizzling and spitting when he lit the paper underneath them. When the fire had taken hold he went to the hall to fetch the hamper which he put down by the kitchen table. He was unpacking it when Eliza came back downstairs.

"Mrs Bessant filled this for you this morning. I don't know what is in it," he said. "Let's see: cheese, a loaf of bread, a bag of flour, sugar, salt, a can of milk, a hunk of cold mutton......what else?"

Eliza watched as he put each item on the table, thinking about the planning and preparation that had gone into ensuring that she had all she could possibly want.

"Look at this delicious apple-pie! Ah! Butter, a sack of potatoes and a basket of fruit, a canister of tea - I don't think she has overlooked anything, do you?"

Eliza's features softened as she pictured Mrs Bessant and Siân preparing the hamper. She wished she could have known them as real people - very likely she and Siân could have been friends in other circumstances. It vexed her that society made things so complicated for folk.

"Ah! The water has arrived by the sound of it," Mr Jones said as he went to the hall. "Right! Fill the kettles and jugs for Mrs Thomas, and then take the rest to the buckets in the yard, there's a good lad."

He turned to Eliza. "You should find enough money in this purse to last you a week," he said quietly as he took it from his pocket. "There will always be more in Wilkins' bank. Do you know where that is?"

"Yes, my sister-in-law is a cleaner there."

Mr Jones looked at her with pity. She was so young, so alone and vulnerable. His own daughter was about the same age but much more protected and cared for.

"The boy and I will carry the rest of the things upstairs for you and then - we can leave you in peace, unless there is anything else we can do?"

Eliza shook her head. "Luke would have been so pleased with what you have done already - far more than I could have expected."

"I shall be here again next week - shall we say Wednesday, about two o'clock?"

"I'll have the kettle boiling for a cup of tea."

Mr Jones took both her hands in his. "Goodbye then, Mrs Thomas. God be with you!"

They walked out to the street, Eliza taking care not to catch the eyes of the neighbours; she wasn't ready to meet them yet.

"You will be sure to thank your wife for all that she has done, won't you?" she called out as the brougham moved off.

Eliza didn't linger outside but went straight in, through the kitchen and back kitchen to the yard where she clapped her hands when she saw the privy in the far corner, by a gate to the lane - the number of privies in that part of the world was limited, so fast had the town grown. Also outside were a mound of coal, a neat stack of logs and twigs, and three buckets near the rain barrel. In the back kitchen she opened doors to find a pile of newspapers, a box of candles, two box irons and a sleeve-iron, bars of soap and a bundle of clean rags. Five large jugs stood by the door.

She put more logs on the fire, then sat in the rocking-chair, placing a cushion behind her back before staring dreamily at the flames licking around the wood. A great weariness came over her. Five minutes later her head was resting on the side of the chair, her hands stretched over her swollen stomach and her mouth half open. How long she slept she didn't know, but the sound of children playing in the street reached her ears, and hooters blasting over the town finally brought her to her feet. She walked through the house again before putting the kettle on to boil. Colour returned to her face as she opened a drawer to find a spoon for the sugar. How marvellous to be able to make your own cup of tea, she thought.

That evening, she rocked gently in the lamplight by the side of her own hearth, more contented than she had been for a long time.

Chapter 4

Eliza lay in bed thinking about Luke in his lonely grave on the hillside. Suddenly she threw back the quilt and knelt on the floor, shutting her eyes tightly and holding her hands together at her lips. She prayed for his soul and gave thanks for his generosity and kindness. As she was about to get back into bed she remembered something else; in anticipation of her mother's wrath she whispered: "God have mercy on me, a sinner."

An hour later, she was on the floor again, this time rummaging through her hatboxes, looking for Luke's letter. Some of the words were complicated but she had hesitated to ask Mr Jones to read it for her in case there was something in it which he shouldn't see. When she found it, she crossed to the window and pulled the curtains back to get more light.

It was never dark in Dowlais, where the clinkers scattered on the mountain-side glowed like garnets. Fiery clouds of orange and red fumes spewed from the great furnaces of Cyfarthfa, Plymouth, Dowlais and Penydarren, their silent flashes illuminating the skies around like the Aurora Borealis. Not two hundred yards from Eliza's home, a thousand men sweated in front of suffocating forges; half a mile underground, hundreds of colliers hacked at the walls surrounding them in the fistulas of the earth, their ears strained for any change in the creaking of the timbers over their heads, their eyes constantly checking drips of water seeping through the coal-face. But, for Eliza, Dowlais was just home. She didn't question the light by which she tried yet again to decipher Luke's letter.

My Dear Elizabeth,

I want to say so much but words are inadequate. I have thought long and deeply about you and the future of our child and wish that I could have had a longer life to look after you both, but that was not to be.

If you find yourself in deep distress, I entreat you to seek help from my sons. I have told them to regard our child as a brother or sister. I should like the child to be brought up in the Christian faith and to be able to read and write.

Do not grieve for me, for I am in a better world.

Your devoted husband

Luke

At some time before dawn, Eliza fell asleep, oblivious to the clinking of waggons and the whinnying of horses somewhere in the night.

Despite her lack of sleep, she was up and dressed by nine o'clock the next morning. She left the house to make her way to her Aunt Bessie's home in Brecon Street, quite a hazardous journey because a layer of sleet had frozen solid. The road had a mirror-like appearance, with a rainbow-coloured surface as a result of the sludge and slime that contaminated the town.

When she reached her destination, Eliza walked in through the open door, calling as she went. "Auntie Bessie! It's me, Eliza!"

Her aunt, a large, red-faced woman with wisps of grey hair falling over her eyes, was on her knees polishing the kitchen fender. She remained motionless, with the rag in her hand, as she gawped at her niece

"Whatever are you doing here?" she asked, rubbing perspiration off her forehead, her eyes riveted on Eliza's bulging stomach which could no longer be hidden. "What a surprise!" she said slowly, her voice trailing away as she heaved herself to her feet.

"I've come to live in Dowlais, in Ivor Street. I came yesterday," Eliza said, trying to keep calm. She cleared her throat in the ominous silence which filled the house. The atmosphere had become as frozen as the road outside. "My husband died last week, did you know?" she asked casually, sitting down at the table with a thumping heart.

"Died? Died!" Aunt Bessie repeated. "But only the other day you was married!" she protested, her face becoming more and more contorted.

"That was five months ago, time flies," Eliza replied. "I'm having a baby in August," she added, as she looked at the floor.

"August, is it!" said Aunt Bessie, nodding her head. "Does your mother know this?"

Eliza pretended not to hear. "I've been left a furnished house; I suppose you could say I'm a wealthy woman. How's everybody? What's the news of Eluned and the others?" she asked brightly, wanting to change the subject.

Her aunt remained stunned, blinking several times as she tried to concentrate on the chit-chat. After a pause, she sat down opposite her niece. "Eluned?" she muttered vaguely. "She's all right."

"Is she still working in Penydarren House?"

Aunt Bessie nodded.

"Does she like it there?"

"Not much, but the pay is good, one and six a week and all found," Aunt Bessie replied grudgingly as she stared at her niece.

"I wonder if she'd like to come and work for me - I'd give her two shillings and all found. I need someone to fetch the water and carry the coal and things. It would be very little work compared to Penydarren House."

"Two shillings? You will pay Eluned two shillings!" Aunt Bessie echoed, her eyebrows shooting up into her forehead. "Well, whatever next?"

"It would be lonely on my own. Perhaps, until Eluned comes home, Mair and Myfanwy would come and stay. I'd pay them threepence a week, just to fetch the water and run messages. They could come home every day to carry water for you as well."

Aunt Bessie wrestled with the overwhelming amount of information she had been given and the decisions to be made. She writhed in the chair, torn between avarice and righteousness. Eliza had planned the situation so that her aunt wouldn't have time to collect her thoughts.

"It would help me out, I'll say that much. Aled's wages have been cut again," her aunt mumbled.

"Where are they now?"

"Gone to the well."

"Right, then. Send them over for dinner. I'll get some sprats. It's Number 7, Ivor Street. Come and see it yourself, if you like," Eliza said cheerfully as she got to her feet, taking care not to turn sideways.

"I'll see," came the muted reply.

Eliza called in the corner shop for sprats, relieved that the first hurdle had been cleared, and was pleased to hear the voices of her small cousins as they ran in quarter of an hour later, followed by their grim-faced mother, who had been unable to suppress her curiosity. Mair was nine; Myfanwy eleven.

Their excitement was uncontainable as they hopped from room to room, squealing with amazement. Aunt Bessie remained silent; when she left, Eliza realised that her reaction was only a foretaste of the cataclysm that would occur when Mrs Coleman arrived on the scene.

After dinner, Eliza sent the girls over to Georgetown to explain things to her mother and invite her to tea. While she waited, sick with apprehension and foreboding, she dusted the kitchen quite unnecessarily. She turned pale when Mair ran in to say that Mrs Coleman was coming down the street.

"What's all this, Eliza?" her mother asked anxiously when she arrived at the kitchen doorway.

Eliza looked at the floor.

"Go and play outside, you two," commanded their aunt, her eyes not leaving her daughter.

The children looked at each other in dismay as they turned to go, Mair lingering in the hall in an attempt to find out what had happened.

"Out, I said!" shouted Mrs Coleman as she gave the child a clout on the ear. "Now, Eliza, what have you got to tell me?"

Eliza looked up momentarily before retreating to the settle when her knees began wobbling. Her mother stayed in the doorway, her shawl pulled tightly around her, implacable and threatening. It was all as bad as Eliza had feared.

"August? August! Do you think I'm daft, girl? I've had twenty-four, remember! You needn't tell me when the child is coming. I can't believe this," she said as she walked over to the hearth and sank with a thud onto the rocking-chair. "Aw! The shame of it! How am I going to tell your father? What will your brothers think?"

Mrs Coleman's eyes rolled in their sockets as she rocked back and forth. What moved Eliza more than the thundering salvoes of anger was the sight of her mother's toes sticking out at the end of a shabby pair of boots, the patched and darned skirt, the fear in her mother's watery eyes, the shapeless rolls of blubber, after years of childbearing, that made her look like a broken-down mattress. While Mrs Coleman continued with the onslaught, Eliza was tormented by guilt, each lash revealing the depth of hurt and betrayal that her mother felt.

"Brought you up decent and God-fearing and now look at you; it's beyond bearing. To think that a daughter of mine could do this to me. What am I going to tell the minister? How can I go to chapel? What will people say?" Her voice rose in alarm. "Mrs Hawkins," she yelled. "Aw! That I should have lived to see this day!"

She gasped for breath before continuing, while Eliza sat with her head bowed, trying not to listen.

"How can I walk through the streets? How can I face people? Do you see what you have done to me, girl?"

Eliza moaned.

"We are a tidy family, or at least we were until now. How could you do this, Eliza? Tell me, how could you?"

No answer came.

"The shame of it! Thank goodness your grandmother isn't alive to see me now. At least she will not have to bear the degradation, God rest her soul!"

Eliza cringed as if she were being whipped.

Mrs Coleman groaned, "What will become of us now? Had you thought of that, you hussy? No! You with your fine clothes. Married to a gent, was it? A gent indeed! Auntie Bessie will be smirking now - aw! she will love this. To think that a child of mine could do this to me after all I did for you, Eliza!"

Mrs Coleman's voice cracked as she let her hands fall into her lap, staring ahead, drained and exhausted. Eliza lifted her hands to her head and gave a silent wail.

"Well, you have made your bed and you can lie on it!" her mother announced as she struggled to stand up. "Don't think you can walk in on us whenever you please, neither. You can stay here, with all your fine furniture - the wages of the Devil, that's what it is," she spat out as she walked to the door, where she turned round, making herself as tall as she could manage. "This will bring me with sorrow to my grave," she said.

Eliza didn't move.

Her mother looked briefly around the kitchen before speaking again. "I don't want you darkening my door, Eliza. You are no daughter of mine," she said lightly, as if it were of no consequence. "Do you hist me?"

Eliza nodded.

"After all I did for you!" Mrs Coleman whispered, looking with disdain at her daughter who was cowering on the settle. "May God forgive you, Eliza, I never will. Just keep out of my way, that's all."

Eliza heard the front door slam. When the cousins tip-toed in a few minutes later, they found her slumped over the table, refusing to respond when they called her name. They tried shaking her, but she was as limp as a rag doll. For the rest of the day she moved about in silence, with a swollen face and blood-shot eyes.

A subdued Eliza woke up the next morning. The house itself seemed to need recuperation after the thwacks of Mrs Coleman's tongue; the impact of the salvoes that had bounced off the walls had an effect from which recovery could only be slow and painful. However, it was impossible not to respond to the bright eyes and smiles of the young cousins, who were enjoying the adventure of sleeping in a different house, away from the daily chores that they found irksome and tedious in their own home. After they had opened every cupboard and examined the contents, Eliza was able to establish some discipline, and allocated tasks for the day.

Some consolation came from other incidents, too. When Eliza opened the door in the morning, she was greeted by a voice from the other side of the road.

"Good day to you! I saw you coming Tuesday!"

"Good day to you, too," Eliza answered with a smile.

"Have you come to live here?" the woman asked. "I know you, don't I? Alwyn Coleman the puddler's daughter? I thought so. You used to go to Sunday School with my daughter Tanwen. Tanwen Morgan. Morgan the sawyer from Cyfarthfa."

"Tanwen! Of course I remember her."

The woman crossed the road. "We wondered who was coming here. A man and woman have been visiting for a few weeks but they never said nothing."

"I came from Brecon," Eliza said. "My husband died last week."

"Aw, there's sad! I heard that you had married a toff and gone away to live. Well, I never!"

Another neighbour appeared from nowhere. "Mrs Richards, this is Coleman the puddler's daughter, come here to live. Her husband died only last week," Mrs Morgan announced.

"A widow already!" said Mrs Richards. "You hadn't been married long either, had you?"

"No. Only seven months. I'm having a baby in August."

There was a distinct pause. "Well, that will be a consolation for you," Mrs Morgan said eventually.

"Have you got all you need in there?" Mrs Richards asked.

"Yes, thank you. Would you like to come in for a cup of tea?"

No sooner were the words uttered than the two women trooped into

26

the hall, followed by a third who didn't want to be left out of things. "I'm Mrs Jones. My husband is a miner at Cyfarthfa. How do you do? Aw! There's lovely!" she cried when she saw the china on the dresser.

"Just look at those jugs!" said Mrs Richards.

There was much clucking of tongues and appreciative comment as the women satisfied their pent-up curiosity. Eliza felt in the mood for company after the misery of the previous day and, as the children had gone to the well, it was as good a time as any to meet the neighbours, who were impressed with Mrs Bessant's apple-pie.

Later in the day, Mair came running in with a bundle in her arms. "I've got something for you for when your Mam scolds you," she said, as she unfolded the rags to reveal a tabby kitten.

"Aw! There's lovely! Where did you get it?"

"In Brecon Street. Let's give it some milk."

"Who does it belong to, I wonder."

"No one," Mair said. "Look how it gulps the milk; it hasn't been fed for a long time."

"I shall call it Fluff," Eliza said without hesitation.

That evening the kitchen rang with chatter and laughter as the two small cousins played with the kitten on the hearth rug. Eliza comforted herself by making a mound of 'potch' like the one they used to make in the castle. The children took turns to beat the mashed potatoes, swedes and carrots until the mixture was smooth. It tasted good with the bacon that Myfanwy had been sent out to buy that morning.

When they sat around the table for supper, the girls imparted family gossip that Eliza hadn't heard before and which did little to lift her spirits. "Elvira, that's Bernard's wife's sister, has been sent to the Poor House in Llanfyllin because she had a babby and she wasn't married," Mair whispered.

Eliza's heart missed a beat as she listened.

"The babby lived for five days and then it was buried in a field, in unblessed earth, because it wasn't christened because it was a bastard."

"Does that mean it will burn in hell-fire?" Myfanwy asked.

"No, of course not," Eliza answered crossly. "The poor dab hadn't done anything wrong."

"Dada knows someone who is going to hell-fire. He says that Dr Price who never goes to chapel and never says his prayers is going to go to hell-fire."

"Eat your supper or it will get cold," said Eliza, not enjoying the conversation.

Mair elbowed her sister. "Tell about Jane Howells!"

"Aw! Yes!" Myfanwy said eagerly. "Jane Howells was sick in her stomach and wasting away. Her gran asked Dr Price what they could do because the doctors around here were no good," she explained as she stuffed a heap of potch in her mouth. The story was accompanied by much waving about of her knife and fork as she went on. "Well, he told

Mrs Howells, who's the cook in Cyfarthfa castle where you used to work, that she should buy some Franklin's tobacco and put it in a pipe and give it to Jane to smoke! Mrs Howells passed the message on but her daughter was shocked. She said: 'I'm not having my child smoking like a gypsy.' So Jane died. When they opened her stomach afterwards, do you know what they found in her inside?" Myfanwy asked, taking another mouthful and pausing for breath.

"Worms! Hundreds of little tiny worms all wriggling about!" Mair cried with delight.

Myfanwy all but choked. "I'm telling this story, so shut your gob!" she shouted, dropping her knife and fork and putting a hand over Mair's mouth. "Dr Price was there when she was cut up and he lit a pipe and blew the smoke in her stomach and guess what happened?"

"Let Mair alone!" Eliza shouted.

Myfanwy complied and shovelled more food in her mouth before continuing. "The worms all died. Dr Price told Mrs Howells that Jane wouldn't have died if only her mother had done what he told them."

Eliza had long since put down her knife and fork. "Ych-y-fi! That's an awful story."

"It's true!" Myfanwy protested, disappointed at the effect that her dramatic monologue had had.

That night, when Eliza went to close the door, she heard voices calling softly: "Goodnight, Mrs Thomas!"

She answered them each in turn. "Goodnight, Mrs Richards! Goodnight, Mrs Jones!"

As she walked upstairs there was a trace of a smile on her lips. The neighbours didn't seem to share her mother's concern, or if they did, they didn't show it. As like as not they knew the situation and were basking in their proximity to such a source of gossip.

She took stock of things when she lay in bed. The confrontation with her mother was over; the neighbours so far were friendly; Eluned would be home next Sunday. If her own family ignored her, she would have Luke's child to cherish, please God, if they both survived its arrival - and typhoid, dysentery, diptheria, smallpox, measles and cholera permitting.

While she waited for Eluned's arrival, Eliza concerned herself with finding a mid-wife and in the process was surprised to see how much Dowlais had grown in the short time she had been away. She ventured round new roads and alleyways where shacks and hovels were jammed so closely together that it was easy to get lost. The stench from some of the back-yards was such that she often held her breath as she walked past and the constant clanging of hammers in the iron works could not have been more of a contrast with the quiet streets of Brecon where she had heard her own footsteps.

The people who were about during the day were mostly women and children who worked for Crawshay. Many of them pushed carts filled with cinders or slag; some were old and bent, swaying laboriously from side to side as they struggled along. They wore men's caps, back to front, and had sacks tied around their waists with string. All were covered with layers of dirt and grime.

After a depressing search Eliza chose a Mrs Llewellyn who had the cleanest home, which wasn't saying much but at least it was a house where Eliza didn't feel sick with the smell.

"Don't worry about a thing, dear. I'll look after you and the baby. It won't be long now by the look of you. Just send for me and I'll be there. If I'm laying-out or delivering another one, my daughter will come instead. She's just as good."

Eliza didn't share the woman's confidence but felt that there was no choice in the matter.

She busied herself making Welsh cakes and currant loaf as she had been taught in the castle. Myfanwy and Mair took some home to their mother and a milk pudding was sent in to the family next door where the children were all suffering from a fever.

On Sunday afternoon, when her two young sisters had gone to the well, Eluned walked in. "Eliza! What on earth is going on?" she cried. "I can't believe what Mam told me."

"It's true, whatever she said," Eliza answered with a grin. "Aw! There's good it is to see you, 'Luned."

"Mam said you were a rich widow. I don't understand."

"I've got a lot to tell you, all in good time. How are you? You haven't changed a bit."

Eluned was a tall, pretty eighteen-year-old with curly brown hair swept back with a ribbon. Her eye-brows arched high above luminous eyes and her nose was formed to perfection. What Eliza liked about her cousin was her vivacity and impetuosity, her capacity for enjoying life.

"Mam said you wanted me to be your housekeeper for two shillings a week, all found. Is that right?" Eluned asked incredulously.

"Yes. I don't want to live all by myself here and as you can see, I can't carry coal or scrub floors or fetch water, so - why not?" Eliza answered. "Let's have a cup of tea, the kettle has boiled."

Eluned sat down and stared at her cousin. "You're having a babby!" she cried, raising her eyebrows.

"That's right. Do you still take sugar?"

"Well, I never did!"

"'Luned, I've got so much to tell you, things that I haven't been able to tell anyone else," Eliza said, filling the teapot. "You'll never know how miserable I've been. It will be good to tell you about everything."

"All I know is that you married a wealthy gent in Brecon who learned you to read and write and bought you fine clothes, and Mam says you are a widow and even your mother doesn't know your husband is dead."

"She does now," Eliza said ruefully.

"Well, what happened?"

"All in good time. First, you will come and live here, won't you?"

"Of course. I brought my things," Eluned answered, pointing to a paper bag on the floor. "When do I start work?" she asked with a grin. "Oooh! That apple-pie looks nice! Can I have a bit?"

It had been some years since they had last seen each other. As they sat at the table having tea, Eliza told her cousin the truth about Luke Thomas and her life in Brecon. Eluned listened spell-bound, fascinated and horrified. When Eliza described her mother's tirade, Eluned threw her apron over her head and kept it there until the story ended.

"Aw! Eliza! What a time you've had of it! I had no idea what you've gone through. There's terrible!"

"I brought it all upon my own head. Take heed and don't fall like I did. The shame of it will never leave me," she said, pouring out another cup of tea.

"But everything is all right now. You've got this lovely home and money," Eluned said brightly.

"My Mam has finished with me. Your mother was shocked when I told her. People know. They must be talking."

"Your Mam will get over it, and my Mam has let me come here to work for you, hasn't she?"

"Tch! How much have you got to hand over to her?" Eliza asked.

"One and six a week."

"Well, that explains it, doesn't it. Mind you, she's right to be disgusted with me. Is she going to let Mair and Myfanwy come back now?"

Eluned's face fell. "She said they had plenty of work to do in their own house...she slapped them both when they argued with her. Well, I am staying here and that's that. When do I start?"

"You don't start till tomorrow morning and then not till eight o'clock!"

Later on they cooked a meal of sausages and the potch that Eluned had seen them make in Penydarren House, with cooking-apples mashed with potatoes and chopped onions. When it was dark they lit the lamps and piled more logs on the fire.

"So far we've talked only about me," Eliza said. "Now, what about you?"

"There isn't much to tell. I thought that working in that grand mansion would be fun, but I had to slave from morning to night and I never saw anything but the kitchen and the servants' staircase. I don't know what the Foremans look like. I never even saw the footmen in their livery. It wasn't a bit like I thought it would be. I had no life at all really."

"Well, that will change from now on. Tell me, what about that boy from Cefn who fancied you?"

"Arthur Davies? Aw! He was nice. Didn't you hear about him? He died of a fever two years ago. There's another fellow I used to fancy, but I haven't seen him for a long time. He goes to Caersalem; works as a shingler here in the foundry, or he used to. I wonder if he's still there."

"Well, you'll have to go to Caersalem and find out, won't you."

"What a different life I shall have now, and all thanks to you!"

"All thanks to Luke Thomas," Eliza said quietly.

They talked far into the night. After explaining everything to her cousin, Eliza felt a sense of relief. At last, someone knew the whole truth and didn't judge or condemn. From now on she felt she would have an ally, as well as someone to help with the housework. They had always been friends, sharing secrets as children, sliding down coal-tips on tin trays, giggling together on top of the mountain as they shouted the worst swear words they knew in Welsh, chasing dragonflies that hovered near stagnant ponds, mimicking superior ladies who queued at the well, sharing dreams of a bright future when they would be courted by rich, handsome gentlemen and carried away to far-off mansions. Eliza was glad to be able to help her cousin and enjoy her company again now.

For her part, Eluned insisted on working so hard and doing so much that Eliza protested. "Stop it, for goodness' sake, sit down!"

Eluned took little notice, being delighted with her new life. She went to Caersalem the Sunday after arriving at Ivor Street, and saw David Jones sitting in the gallery with the other tenors. When the service ended, she hung around nonchalantly, pretending to bump into him accidentally as he came out.

"Eluned!" he cried.

"Hello!" she said casually, looking bored.

"Fancy seeing you again!"

She looked round at other people. "I've come to live in Ivor Street. I'm sharing a house with my cousin, Eliza Thomas."

"I thought you were in Penydarren House."

"I was, but I didn't like it, so I left. Where are you working?"

"I was in the foundry till last week but they sacked thirty of us, so I'm looking for other work. Can I walk you home?" he asked cheerfully.

"If you like," Eluned answered, with a shrug of the shoulders.

When they reached the house, David hung about, kicking an imaginary stone with his feet.

Eluned looked up at the sky. "Do you want to meet my cousin, Eliza?"

"Yes."

"Then you'd better come in, I suppose. Eliza! Are you there?"

Eliza appeared at the kitchen door.

"This is David Jones, from Caersalem," Eluned explained. "He walked me home."

"Hello, Mr Jones," Eliza said warmly. "Come in."

It was the first, but not the last, time that David found himself in the kitchen at Ivor Street. When he had gone, Eluned hopped up and down with pleasure. "What do you think of him?"

"He's nice," Eliza answered, as Eluned turned round and round with her arms in the air.

From then on they organised their lives so that they each went to their respective chapels on Sunday mornings, leaving two large potatoes and a joint of meat to bake by the time they returned; Eliza had decided to go to Soar chapel because it had the best choir and she enjoyed the choir practices there on Wednesday evenings. While Eluned went to the well or did housework, Eliza went shopping or baked bread and cakes; between them they spent a considerable time making a dress for Eluned, while they gossiped and assessed the merits of the neighbours.

For Eliza it was a time of healing and restoration, of forgetting and renewal, of adjustment and anticipation. The baby was beginning to kick inside her.

Chapter 5

Mary Thomas was born on April 8th, 1828. As soon as Eliza took Luke's daughter in her arms nothing else mattered. Her shame evaporated and her own mother's disgust became irrelevant. Whatever the world did or said was immaterial; the vulnerable mite in Number 7, Ivor Street was all-important. Eliza experienced a new emotion, having its origin in a surge of love and a reserve of strength with which she would challenge anyone or anything that dared to hurt her child. If people said something disparaging now or in the future it wouldn't matter in the least, as long as the insult wasn't aimed at Mary. If it were, then Eliza's fury would know no bounds.

As soon as she was able to get up and about again, she used to wrap the baby in the Paisley shawl, fix it tightly around the two of them and join the other women standing in their doorways, rocking gently back and forth, tapping Mary's bottom as she did so. Before long, nothing happened within a mile of her home that she didn't know about.

Letters had been sent to Titus Jones as well as Luke's sons, informing them of Mary's arrival. Mr Jones sent a charming letter in response, as well as a silver spoon. A parcel from Henry Thomas contained a silver napkin-ring and a card which said 'With Best Wishes'. It was the last communication ever received from Mary's step-brothers.

Eliza had been a member of Soar chapel for several weeks, enjoying choir practice on Wednesday evenings and much appreciated in the advanced reading class in Sunday School. Mary's christening ceremony, after the morning service one Sunday, was attended by Eluned and her two young sisters, who were jubilant. Neighbours and friends crowded round the small family group afterwards and Eliza presided at a tea-party in the afternoon. After the tumult of the previous year, she had settled down into a pattern of quiet domesticity in which she was serenely happy.

She was now baking more bread and making more cakes than they could eat, even after most of it was given away to neighbours whose husbands were on reduced wages or injured. Life in the kitchen at Cyfarthfa was standing her in good stead; she knew that she made a tasty loaf and was proud of it. Eluned it was who thought of selling a few loaves to the hostelry at Cwm Rhyd-y-Bedd. Eliza warmed to the idea when she recalled the friendly landlord who had welcomed her on her first day in Dowlais. It wasn't long before she decided to try the idea out.

She set off one September morning carrying a basket containing two loaves, wrapped in a warm cloth. She picked her way through the muck on the road, holding the hem of her dress in one hand. As she skirted the ironworks, she could see the army of sack-clothed women in hobnail boots emptying their waggon-loads on the hillside, looking like the bluebottles that buzzed over the putrefaction and litter scattered everywhere. She wove her way through ragged, barefoot children and mangy dogs on her way down to the inn, which lay in a small valley at the foot of the mountain. At one stage, she had to wait while a hand-cart was manoeuvered around a mound of coal; it was laden with bedding and chairs tied precariously together with rope to prevent it toppling over. A group of angry women waved their fists and shouted obscenities as the cart trundled along, pushed by two grim-faced bailiff's men. It wasn't the first time she had witnessed such a scene, indeed it was becoming an almost daily occurrence.

Eliza reached the threshold of the cobbled courtyard where a handful of old men sat on a bench sipping tankards of ale in the sun. The landlord had his back to her as he chatted to his customers. A sheepdog panted in the shade of the doorway; the horse tethered to the wall surrounding the hostelry flicked its tail to ward off flies. A few chickens strutted fitfully about, pecking at bits of dirt on the ground.

She bided her time, waiting until the men had finished their discussion. Some were gazing at her with interest, and eventually Will Evans turned round to see what was claiming their attention.

"Why, good day to you, Ma'am," he cried warmly.

"Good day to you, Sir! Can I speak a few words, if you please?" she asked.

Will Evans could scarcely believe his luck when he saw Eliza standing before him. She was wearing a silver-grey gingham dress and a yellow bonnet which framed her glowing cheeks and brown eyes. The difference between her appearance that morning and the pale widow in black who had been there in the winter could not have been more striking. He had ascertained her identity and had been wondering about her ever since. Now here she was, standing in a shaft of sunlight, as pert and pretty as any girl in the district.

"I wondered if you would like to buy some bread for the hostelry, Sir. I learned to cook in Cyfarthfa Castle and I bake bread twice a week."

Will didn't hear what Eliza said; he was concentrating on the lilt and cadences in her voice which reminded him of a linnet. The sparkle in her eyes so distracted him that when she finished speaking, he was at a loss.

"Bread? Bread?" he repeated as he tried to recall her words.

"I bake on Tuesdays and Fridays. I could bring the loaves here before eight in the morning, if you like. I thought I'd charge twopence a loaf, if you agree."

"You want to sell me bread!" Will cried, pulling himself together at last. "Why, yes Ma'am. I am in need of all the bread I can get." He was delighted at the prospect.

Eliza took one of the loaves from the basket. "I brought this with me in case you'd like to try some."

"It looks very tasty. I have no need to try it. I will buy bread from you whenever you like."

Eliza beamed. "I'll bring some next Friday, then."

She was quite elated as she swung the basket through the air on her way home, unaware that Will Evans stood watching her until she was out of sight. When she had gone, he looked down at the loaf in his hand and went inside to the kitchen where his mother did the cooking and baking.

"Mother," he said absently, "you don't have to bake as much bread on Tuesdays and Fridays. I shall be buying two loaves twice a week from now on."

Mrs Evans rubbed her hands in her apron. "Whatever has come over you, boy? We don't need to buy bread elsewhere. I bake as much as we want. Have you taken leave of your senses?"

"I think I have, Mother *fach*, I think I have."

Eliza decided to call at the butcher's shop on her way home. "Good day, Mr Jones!" she cried as she saw the butcher standing dolefully on the pavement. "Have you got a whole pig's fry? I'm feeling energetic today; I'm going to spend the afternoon cooking."

Mr Jones's eyes lit up. Not many people could afford meat now, so that a whole pig's fry was a rare request. He went inside eagerly.

"It's a pleasure, Mrs Thomas. I saw you coming with a basket and I hoped you were heading for my shop," he said as he gathered the offal on the counter.

"I'm going to make faggots to take to Mrs James, Soar - do you know the family?"

"John James, is it? The pig-weigher?"

"That's the one. He's been sacked, along with twelve others."

"I heard about that. Times are getting very hard now. They do say that even more Dowlais furnaces might be shut down soon," he said gloomily.

"That would mean a lot of suffering for families. Surely that won't happen - hundreds would be out of work, without enough money to live on."

The butcher wrapped the meat up and wiped his hands with a cloth. "So many people are destitute that I have to pay more and more for the Poor Rate while fewer and fewer can afford to buy meat. I don't know what I am going to do. I will be destitute myself before long, if this goes on."

"It's a grievous state of affairs," Eliza said quietly.

"It is indeed. Will that be all, Mrs Thomas?"

"Yes, thank you, but I'll be back soon," she replied in a low voice, feeling guilty.

"I'm much obliged, Ma'am."

Eliza's cheerfulness had evaporated by the time she reached home. She reminded herself that she had more than her share of money; she didn't have to take in lodgers like most people, she had all the food and clothing she needed, the house was warm and she could even afford a housekeeper. So much, while the town seemed to be falling apart around her. She had forgotten about the landlord at the inn.

She set out for choir practice early that evening. This time her basket was full of hot faggots destined for the James family, who lived next door to Soar. Walking at night was difficult as so many people thronged the streets that it wasn't easy to avoid bumping into them. After dark Dowlais became a human ant-hill.

"Good evening all!" she called out as she walked through to the kitchen.

Mrs James was lying on the settle, holding a piece of newspaper to her mouth; her husband sat opposite.

The gloom in the house hung like a pall.

"I'm on my way to choir practice," Eliza said, trying to sound cheerful. "I wondered if you would like to have some faggots."

"That is kind of you, Mrs Thomas," Mr James said.

Eliza felt wretched. "I'm truly sorry about you losing your job. You must be so worried."

Mr James nodded. "Twelve of us got sacked; I don't know what to do. The minister was here but all he could say was 'Wait on the Lord'"

"The Lord has sent you some faggots at least. That will keep you going for one more day," she said in desperation.

Mrs James's coughing broke the silence that followed. The situation was beyond words. Mr James stared into the embers; his wife closed her eyes.

"Will you eat the faggots tonight?" Eliza asked.

"I expect so, at least the children will," Mr James said. "I don't know what will happen to them. My sister in Merthyr will take the youngest girl, she says, but the rest will be taken by the Guardians and put in lodgings in *China*. That's what my wife is thinking anyway."

"No! That would be terrible," Eliza whispered. "Aw! I'm distressed to find you in such penury and want," she cried as she pulled at her hands and shook her head.

On her way home she called once more and left afterwards holding seven-year-old James James by the hand. "You can stay with me until your mother gets better, James," she said brightly. "I don't live far away and you can go home whenever you like."

"People don't call me James, that's my father's name. I'm called Jimmy. My friends call me Jimmy Twice."

Eliza and Jimmy Twice walked into the kitchen in Ivor Street where Eluned was singing a lullaby to Mary, who was cradled in her arms.

"We have a lodger," Eliza announced. "This is Jimmy, Jimmy Twice to his friends. Jimmy, this is my cousin, Miss Eluned Mathias."

Eluned looked from one to the other in silence as Eliza took Mary and held her up in the air.

"Jimmy can sleep in the small room at the top of the house. Would you put a brick in the oven to warm his bed, 'Luned *fach*?"

Eluned took a deep breath. "Yes, of course. Hello, Jimmy. You had better call me Auntie Eluned, I think. Are you hungry?"

The boy nodded.

"Right. We've got lovely faggots for supper. Go and wash your hands in the back kitchen."

As soon as he had gone, Eliza lifted her shoulders in a gesture of despair. "What could I do? The family have no money; I think his mother is dying and the Guardians are going to put the children in lodgings in *China*. I've got a spare bed and money. I had to, 'Luned, didn't I?" she pleaded in a whisper.

"Yes, of course. Anything to save a child from *China*. Don't look so worried; it will be all right. I'll get the brick and then we'll have supper. You know, it will be nice to have a little boy to look after."

The women sat at the table later on, trying to get used to the new situation; Jimmy concentrated on the meal, not taking his eyes off his plate.

"Now, I've got some news," Eluned told her cousin. "Myfanwy has been here. She's going to start work as a scullery maid in Dowlais House on Monday. What do you think about that?"

"Dowlais House!" echoed Eliza. "I wonder what it's like there."

"It all depends on the housekeeper; now that Josiah Guest is a widower, the ones in charge of the staff can have a lot of power."

"Yes, indeed. But she'll be able to run home on her afternoon off. She could even come here for a short time when she's finished work."

"I'm sorry for Mair though. The two have always been inseparable."

"Yes, poor dab. She will be lonely."

"How did choir practice go?"

"We started a new piece by Franz Schubert. It's his version of the 23rd Psalm. Beautiful it is! The piano part is like running water all the time. We shall be singing it in the Anniversary. Do you sing, Jimmy?"

"Only if I have to," he vouchsafed. "Can I have some more?"

"If you say 'please'", Eluned answered with a smile.

Later that night Eliza went to Jimmy's room before going to bed. He was fast asleep, lying on his back, with his hands raised above his head. She pulled the quilt up over his shoulders and looked out of the window at the lights shining from Dowlais House. She could never understand why Josiah Guest built a grand house in the middle of an ironworks, but supposed it didn't matter when he could get away to his London home in Pall Mall.

By Christmas, three furnaces in Dowlais had been blown. Twenty puddlers, catchers, springers, gate-boys and pig-weighers were out of work. The bailiff's cart rattled round the streets, groaning under the weight of mattresses, chairs, grandfather clocks and other treasures seized under the orders of Mr Coffin, the President of the Court of

Requests. Each night, when Eliza went to tuck Jimmy up in bed, the skies seemed darker. His mother had died a week after he left home; his father had gone to West Wales to look for work. Four brothers and two sisters were somewhere in *China* being looked after by some slut, no doubt. Her pimp had probably taught them how to steal by now and, like others who had shared the same fate, they would probably not be found if their father looked for them later.

It took a while for Jimmy to settle down in his new surroundings and for the women to get used to looking after a seven-year-old boy. The very first day had been baffling. Eluned called him from the bottom of the stairs when she got up but there was no response. Finally, she went up to his room, to find it empty. She told Eliza before going out to the street where she walked up and down calling his name. He had vanished.

A worried Eliza returned to the James household where the news didn't come as a surprise. His father thought that Jimmy had gone to work as usual, creeping out of the house at half-past five. They decided to wait until the evening when they hoped he would come back, which he did. He walked quietly into the kitchen, holding his cap in his hand.

"Jimmy *bach*! We've been worried about you! We didn't know where you were," Eliza cried.

He looked surprised. "I've been to work."

"Where?" Eluned asked.

"In the foundry."

His clothes were damp with sweat; one shirt sleeve had a large hole with scorch marks around it.

"What happened to your shirt?"

"Aw! I got burnt. I often get burnt, but it wasn't my fault this time."

The women were appalled to see that Jimmy's arm was raw from the elbow to the wrist.

"That must have hurt," Eliza said. "Never mind. I'll mash some potatoes and wrap that around your arm; it will take the pain away. That's how Dr Price treated burns in the castle."

She peeled three large potatoes in the back kitchen while Jimmy sat in the rocking-chair. Before long he asked Eluned when they would be eating. He had had no food to take to the foundry and apart from a small piece of cheese that one of the men gave him, had eaten nothing since the previous night.

Eluned was distraught. "Aw! You should have told us! You must always take food with you. I'll leave some bread and cheese in a tin on the table every morning."

"I don't see why you have to go to work at all while you live with us, Jimmy," Eliza called out from the back kitchen. "How much do they pay you?"

"Fourpence a day. I got to go to work to give money to my mother and, anyway...." he left the sentence unfinished, looking at the floor sheepishly.

"Would you like some cold sausage to eat to keep you going till supper?" Eluned asked him.

"Yes, Ma'am," he answered eagerly. "Please!" he added in a hurry.

He chewed savagely at the sausages hoping to eat them undisturbed before more questions were fired at him.

Later, Eliza knelt on the floor to take a closer look at his arm. "Now, I'm going to put some potato on that burn and wrap it round in a cloth. You'll find it feels better straight away. It will get rid of the stinging."

Jimmy gritted his teeth while Eliza carried out the task, not feeling too good herself.

"That's better!" the boy cried with delight afterwards. "Thank you, Missus!"

"I'm Auntie Eliza to you, remember that."

Jimmy looked at the floor. "I got to go to work to pay for these lodgings," he whispered.

"Aw! You aren't a lodger, Jimmy *bach*! I was joking! You don't have to pay me anything. We'll enjoy having you here, and for nothing."

"I still have to give money to my mother," he argued.

"Of course you do," Eliza said, turning her back and rolling her eyes at Eluned who wasn't far from tears. "Now, it's time we had supper and afterwards I'll find a tin for your food at work."

Eliza and Eluned took turns to deliver the bread to the hostelry. Eluned enjoyed her visits because the landlord seldom failed to make her laugh. With Eliza, he was circumspect, concentrating on his manners and his words. Whenever Eliza carried Mary in her shawl he payed attention to the child, commenting on her good looks and intelligence. It was impossible not to like the man.

Chapter 6

As far as Will Evans was concerned, his plans regarding Eliza were no nearer fruition than they were when he first saw her. Autumn merged into winter and he still hadn't deemed it fit to speak to her about the true nature of his feelings. It was Jimmy Twice who oiled the wheels. When the lad was sacked, along with ten others, Eliza used to take him with her when she went to the inn. Once, he took the bread on his own. Will Evans and his mother got to know and like him.

The opportunity for a big step forward presented itself when the town was all but obliterated by one of the worst blizzards it had experienced for many years. During the week before Christmas, the skies darkened before filling with swirling flakes of snow which fell for three days and nights. Icicles glistened on the tops of roofs and window ledges; lace-like patterns appeared on window panes and a muffled silence fell upon the streets. People were cut off from each other, almost like the gentry, Eliza thought.

"No one will be in chapel this morning, I should think. How are you faring, Mrs Thomas?" yelled Mrs Morgan from her doorway.

"I'm all right, but Mrs Richards is stuck at the end of her back yard."

"Tell her to stay there. I'll send our Basil over to fetch her. BASIL!" Mrs Morgan's voice cleft the air. "Go and help Mrs Richards over her back yard."

Mrs Jones shouted from her front door. "How will they bury old Penry Morris tomorrow morning?"

"All them potted shrimps his wife bought and no one there to eat them. What a shame!" responded Mrs Morgan.

Eliza smiled as she scooped snow into a bucket and walked back to the kitchen. Jimmy was filling jugs in the yard. Mary cooed and kicked her legs happily in her basket on the low table by the fire.

"Right! Two eggs boiled for three minutes, one for four and one for five," Eluned cried as she threw snow into the saucepan. "Jimmy! Breakfast!"

Eluned stuck slices of bread on the ends of two toasting forks and sat on the floor holding them in front of the fire.

When they sat down to breakfast, Jimmy prattled away about the scene he had witnessed in the neighbouring back yard as Basil Morgan struggled to lift Mrs Richards to her feet, falling down himself in the process. Suddenly there was a scraping noise at the front door. Eliza and Eluned looked at each other for a second before Eluned got up, stuffed a piece of toast in her mouth, and went to investigate. Sounds of laughter reached Eliza's ears as she cleared bits of egg from Mary's chin.

"Go and see for yourself!" Eluned said when she returned. "I'll feed Mary."

When Eliza walked into the hall she saw Will Evans labouring like Hercules to clear the path outside, hurling mounds of snow into the road with an enormous shovel.

"Bracing weather, Mrs Thomas!"

"Mr Evans! Well, Bless my soul! This is uncommonly kind of you."

"It's a privilege, Ma'am."

"How did you get here from the hostelry?"

"My top-boots helped me; men going to work have made a thoroughfare down the middle of most roads."

"You must come in and have a cup of tea with us; we're just having breakfast."

"Gladly! Let me finish this bit and I'll join you," said a delighted Will, who cleared the path at the front in no time and walked into the kitchen, where he put his feet firmly under the table. "Well! This is a cosy home, I must say. I envy you, Jimmy, living here," he said as Eluned poured his tea. "I came not only to see how you were managing, but to pick up the bread," he lied. "I didn't want you trying to make your way down to the inn."

When Eluned and Jimmy started clearing the table and carrying things out to the back kitchen, Will lowered his voice and leaned towards Eliza. "Actually, what I really called for is this - I know that Jimmy is trying to find a job, and as it happens, a vacancy has just occurred at the inn for a boots boy. Do you think he would like that?"

Eliza lowered her eyes and frowned. "He would I'm sure, but...."

"But?" Will repeated.

Eliza paused when Jimmy came back in for the rest of the dishes. When he had left she continued. "The Jameses were chapel people. I don't know what his father would think about his son working in a tavern."

"My mother will look after him; she's chapel too. We don't drink anything but tea, unless it's some peppermint wine at Christmas. You need have no fear about Jimmy. I run an orderly tavern; it's not like some of the beer-houses around the place."

Eliza hesitated. "He would live in, wouldn't he?"

"Oh, yes! The 'Boots' lives in. To be precise, he would sleep in the loft over the stable, which is warm and snug. He can keep a penny from each tip that he is given and if he gets less than ninepence a week, that will be made up."

Eliza looked at the door to the back kitchen. "Do you know, we have become very fond of him. He's a nice lad, Mr Evans. If I agree to this, you would treat him kindly, won't you?" she said quietly.

"Ma'am! How could you suggest anything else," Will said, with a broad smile. "Anyway, when you deliver the bread you'll be able to see him and judge for yourself."

Eliza relaxed. "Can I call to take him to Sunday School?" she asked. "I'd like him to continue with his reading lessons."

"Of course!" Will answered, seeing his future getting brighter every minute.

"Well then, ask him yourself. Let's see what he thinks."

Will sat back, concerned by Eliza's expression. "You will miss him, won't you?"

She nodded sadly.

Jimmy could hardly contain his excitement when Will Evans left shortly afterwards. .

"Whoa, there!" Eliza said. "Do you know how to clean a pair of boots?"

Jimmy looked at her feet. "Will you teach me?" he asked anxiously.

Eliza laughed. "With the greatest of pleasure, young man. You can start this minute," she said as she led him to the back kitchen.

Jimmy left two days later, running down the hill, turning briefly when he reached the corner to wave back to Eluned and Eliza who stood on the doorstep looking miserable. Once he had gone, Eliza felt that there was no reason why one or two of his brothers and sisters couldn't come and live in Ivor Street. Although she didn't relish the idea of going to *China*, Eluned urged her on. They decided to go down to Merthyr, buy a perambulator for Mary and then proceed to the lodgings where the children had been placed.

The following Tuesday, they delivered bread to the hostelry, saw Jimmy, who obviously was happy and well cared for, and then left for Merthyr, not telling Will Evans the purpose of their mission. It was a tiring trudge down the mountain for Eliza, who was carrying Mary in a shawl, and, for both women, walking past the beer-houses and other places of ill-repute was an experience they would rather have done without.

Eliza had ascertained the address of the landlady from Mr Hughes, next door down but one, who was a member of the Board of Guardians, but she was appalled when they found a stinking hovel at the far end of an alley, next door to a noisy tavern.

They waited a long time for the door to open; when it did, a thin, slatternly woman who leant against a mildewed wall, tried with some difficulty to focus her eyes on them. Her matted hair stuck to the side of her face, her clothes were stained and she didn't appear to have washed for many a day. Eluned held a handkerchief to her nose to stifle the stench. She was glad that all she had to do was to wait outside and look after Mary.

Eliza found some children in a small unfurnished room. Their clothes were little more than rags; their feet were blackened by cinders which spread from the grate and covered most of the floor.

"Have you come to fetch us?" one of the urchins asked eagerly

"What's your name?" Eliza asked gently.

"John Jones. This is my brother, Dai. That's our sister over there. Can we come with you, lady?"

Eliza shook her head. "I'm sorry, I really am. Where do you sleep?"

"In them boxes in the corner."

The slattern was leaning against the door. "It's 'ard to keep a child on one and six a week, Ma'am," she said.

"You are paid two and six a week. I'm looking for the James children from Dowlais," Eliza said frostily. "I want to see them."

"James? James. I 'aven't got any by that name."

"They was here," shouted the small girl, looking at the landlady. "They wasn't here long though. Remember?"

"Aw! Them poor dabs! They died of a fever. They wasn't well when they came 'ere."

Eliza stumbled out of the house in a daze of indignation. "They're not there! The woman said they died."

Eluned turned pale. "Let's get away from here."

They walked home in silence, sadder but not much wiser.

Will Evans now started calling at Ivor Street once or twice a week. Sometimes he brought a dozen eggs; once, he arrived with a chicken and on New Year's Day he turned up with a shoulder of ham. He would sit drinking tea, regaling the women with tales brought to the inn by travellers, or news of the happenings in the markets in Abergavenny and Newbridge. His world extended far beyond Dowlais and his humour and mimicry made him a natural story-teller.

When he arrived with a brace of pheasants Eliza felt embarrassed. "This is too generous, Mr Evans. We shall feel indebted to you. I don't know that I can accept this gift."

"Why! Ma'am. Think nothing of it! I won these in a wager last night."

Eliza was shocked. "A wager, Mr Evans?"

"Ill-gotten gains!" Eluned said, grinning.

Will hesitated. Should he admit to the bare-knuckle fight in the yard at the inn on Tuesday or the cock-fight on Saturday? He chose the former.

"Then, we certainly can't accept," Eliza said firmly. "You are welcome to come inside but the pheasants must stay in the hall."

"I abhor fighting of any kind, between any species, human or otherwise, Mrs Thomas, but you know, when it takes place in my back yard, it looks churlish for the landlord to be the only man not contributing to the proceedings. In truth, I find it as repugnant as yourself, Ma'am," he said, cursing himself for his stupidity.

Before he left, however, he had so charmed the women that Eliza relented and hung the pheasants on a hook in the back kitchen.

After another visit the following week, Eluned stood with her hands on her hips, looking at the hall and waiting for his footsteps to die away. "Eliza, you realise that Will Evans fancies you."

"Nonsense! What a thing to say!"

"You mark my words. He will be courting you before long."

"He comes here to give us news of Jimmy. He likes us both. I certainly haven't encouraged him," Eliza snapped.

"Eliza! It's obvious. How can you be so blind?"

Eliza looked worried. "I don't want anyone courting me. I've no wish to marry again. I have my home and my child, and I lack nothing."

"Come! You can't go on like this for ever. One day I'll be wed, I hope. What will happen then? One day Mary will be wed and then you'll be all alone. Is that what you want?"

"I warrant that it would be preferable to slaving for a man and having children every year and not being able to do as I like."

"But being married to Will Evans! Just think of it! That would be a good life. Everybody likes him. His hostelry is always full; people come from far and wide to stay there. It would be an interesting life," Eluned persisted.

"'Luned, stop it! The man has given us a chicken and some eggs, that's all. Perhaps he fancies you!"

"And that ham and a brace of pheasants. Anyway, he knows about me and David Jones and he doesn't look at me the way he looks at you," argued Eluned, determined that her cousin should face the situation.

"I haven't invited him here once - and here you are marrying me off! The thing is ridiculous," Eliza said crossly as she sat down, not noticing that the cat was on the chair. The squeals of anger from Fluff diverted them both from a conversation which Eliza found disconcerting.

She dismissed the subject from her mind, so that Will Evans really did take her by surprise when he knocked on the door a few evenings later. Eluned had gone for a walk with David Jones. Eliza had put Mary to bed and was about to settle down to write a letter to Titus Jones in Brecon. Will was wearing a snuff-coloured suit, a white silk cravat and a grey top hat. He carried an ebony walking-stick with ornate silver carving on it. Even his sartorial elegance didn't alert her.

Will had ordered his suit from a tailor in Pont-y-ty-pridd a few weeks previously, following a particularly successful game of cards with old friends at the New Inn. He doubled the stakes the next week and spent his winnings on the walking-stick, telling his mother that the pigs he sold in the market had fetched a good price.

"Why, Mr Evans! Pray do come in. What a fine evening it is."

"Thank you, Mrs Thomas. I have come here because there are things I wish to discuss with you that I can contain no longer," he announced with unusual pomposity.

Eliza was puzzled. "Come and sit down," she said, walking into the kitchen.

"I would rather stand, if you please. Eliza! I must tell you what is in my heart and has been for many a month gone. Ever since I saw you in the sunlight last summer, in that yellow bonnet, I knew there was no other woman for me. I am asking you to be my wife. All that I have will be yours if you will consent to have me as your husband. I would look after you and Mary as long as I live, that I vow," he said, hardly pausing for breath.

When he had finished he walked over to the kitchen door and turned to face her, his head almost touching the lintel. "I have waited till now as I thought you might still be grieving for Luke Thomas, but that time has surely passed. If you would share your life with me I would count myself one of the luckiest men in Wales."

Eliza was looking at her hands, hardly believing her ears. Her mind seemed to be in splinters, so that she couldn't think coherently. "I......er, this has taken me by surprise. Marriage is a very serious business, Mr Evans, um....I should need time to think, indeed I should."

Her thoughts raced around in her head. She hadn't admitted, even to Eluned, that she found Will Evans attractive, considering that no one would offer marriage if they knew of her shame. She certainly didn't want to enlighten him and risk his contempt, thereby losing contact with Jimmy. In any case, did she want to live in a tavern - was it the sort of place to bring up Mary? True, life would be interesting, but.....

"Think about it, Eliza. No man will love you more than I do and I would love Mary as if I were her own father." He spoke softly, disappointed at seeing her in such a turmoil. "Shall I return this time next week for your answer?"

Eliza could think of no words to give him; she merely gave a wobbly smile, lifted her hands and let them fall to her side.

"I love you, dearest Eliza. Don't break my heart," Will said quietly as he bent his head to go into the hall. "I shall be back," he called out as he shut the front door.

When Eluned returned, she stopped at the kitchen doorway looking startled. "Eliza! What's the matter? Why haven't you lit the lamps? Why are you sitting in the dark?"

Eliza didn't lift her eyes from the hearth. "Will Evans has been here; he's asked me to be his wife."

For the rest of the week, she remained in a state of muddle and uncertainty; she was short-tempered with Mary, she scalded her wrist, broke one of the cups and saucers, and pummelled the dough so hard that the bread was not the best she had made. She told herself that she needed more time to get over the troubles she had had, that it was better to be alone and in charge of her own life. Misery often results when people are too close, she thought, with her mother in mind, and her bruised spirit didn't dispose her to rush intemperately into a situation where she could be exposed to more hurt. Reason told her to refuse Will Evans's offer, but whenever she came to that conclusion, the sun seemed to go behind a cloud and she would start ruminating again. By the time Will returned she had decided to decline him, telling him of her shame so that he wouldn't feel too badly about the matter. But, one smile from him, and she was as flustered as she had been the previous week.

"Will, there are things which you cannot know about me, which have

45

to be said. I..er...well, the fact is...um.." She took a deep breath. "Mary was born not long after I married Luke Thomas," she blurted out. "I have reason to be ashamed of myself and the disgrace that I brought on my family. If the truth be known, they haven't been here to see me or Mary, not since they found out." She was pulling at her hands, angry and downcast.

"Eliza!" Will cried. "Don't distress yourself on my account. I've known about your situation from the beginning and it doesn't deter me in the slightest. What was between you and Luke Thomas was none of my affair, and is over."

Eliza looked up quickly. "How could you know, Will?"

"Well, I knew him; he owned the inn - at least the Court estate does. He was a cousin of Thomas the Court. Titus Jones comes here every quarter to collect the rent; I knew that Luke married a young woman shortly before he died, then you came to the inn, in your widow's weeds - it was obvious," he said with a smile, not adding that he had questioned Titus closely when he last stayed at the inn.

"You knew Luke? "Eliza asked incredulously.

"Yes, though not well. His family own a good deal of property in these parts. Didn't you know that?"

Eliza looked down once more. "I didn't know much at all about Luke but he was a good man, and kind to me," she said, shaking her head.

"Well, now that we have disposed of that matter, what is your answer, Eliza? You weren't going to refuse me on those grounds, were you?"

Will's warmth and reassurance unsettled her but she continued to fight her emotions. "I don't think I'm ready to settle down yet, Will. I have a nice home and furniture and I want for nothing," she went on in a low voice, looking miserable.

"You want to live alone for the rest of your life?" he asked softly as he knelt down in front of her, taking one of her hands in his. "Don't you wish to be loved and cared for? Do you want Mary to grow up without a father?" He paused between each question. "Do you want to spend the rest of your life repenting in solitude? Would that be better than being cherished?"

There was a long silence.

"You have been truly hurt, haven't you, dear," Will said gently.

Eliza looked at him intently; she hadn't realised the depth of his understanding. "Perhaps that's it. I'm afraid of what life can do to a mortal."

Will took her hand and put it against his cheek. "Life without love or hope is lonely, dear one. In the end, you have to go on trusting. There has to be trust."

Eliza lowered her head.

Will spoke again, quietly. "If you would only trust me, Eliza, I would protect you from more hurts. Wouldn't that be worth more than facing the future on your own?"

Eliza's expression told Will that he was almost there; he had only to find the right words to overcome her hesitation.

"You are young and life has been cruel to you; your fears are greater than your hopes. Come, if you will be my wife, I'll show you how beautiful life can be; we shall laugh together and share any sorrows that may come our way. Whatever befalls us, we shall be all right, so long as we are together."

She was smiling.

Will continued eagerly. "You can bring all your furniture with you to the inn; you could rent this house out and buy pretty bonnets for Mary and she shall always have ribbons in her hair. The sun will shine on us, Eliza, believe me, and you shall never be afraid again. No one shall harm you or little Mary while I am alive."

Will Evans returned to the hostelry soon afterwards, striding along like a conqueror. When he reached the doorway he called out: "Drink up with me, my friends, I am to be wed to the prettiest girl in all Glamorgan before Michaelmas!"

Chapter 7

"It's not only me that Will loves, 'Luned. He's so good with Mary, have you noticed? She runs to him as soon as he arrives and he lifts her up in his arms and swings her around. It's lovely to see them together." Eliza was leaning against the wall of the back kitchen looking into the distance. "He's going to take me to a beautiful place for our honeymoon but he won't tell me where it is."

Eluned grinned as she struggled to her feet. "Do you think you could stop talking about Will Evans long enough to help me carry this tub to the yard? You've talked about nobody else for the past half an hour!"

"Well, you've talked about no one but Dai for the last twelve months, be fair!" Eliza said, as they put the washing down in front of the mangle.

Eliza held each garment at the edge of the wooden rollers and waited while Eluned turned the handle. "You know, I've only been half-alive till now. It's as if......as if I have woken up and seen the world around me for the first time. I hadn't noticed how beautiful ordinary things are. I blew some bubbles into the air this morning when I washed my hands and do you know, they shone like diamonds. I want to run outside when it rains and take all my clothes off and turn my face to the sky and feel the raindrops falling all over me, and last night I swear I heard the stars singing - they sounded like a million tinkling bells."

"How about putting that pillow-case through the mangle, cousin *fach*?"

Eliza guffawed. "I remember Minnie at the castle - you know, the one who listened at keyholes, she heard Dr Price telling Josiah Guest that females were quite mad when they fell in love; he said that it was a dangerous state for them to be in!"

"He's right! You are going to lose some fingers in a minute if you don't watch out."

Will visited every morning and Jimmy often came running up the hill in the afternoon to deliver a love-letter. Will's mother radiated goodwill towards her prospective daughter-in-law, delighted that her youngest and wildest son was to settle down at last. The two women used to sit together in the large Meeting Room in the hostelry, sipping glasses of peppermint while they listened to travelling gypsy harpists or local musicians.

The Dowlais Eisteddfod held there that year was a particularly good one, ending on a high note when four adjudicators failed to decide which was the better of the two bards who had submitted entries for the

Poetry prize. Since Dr William Price happened to be in the vicinity at the time, he was asked to arbitrate. Unfortunately, he decided that the prize should be divided. Although the decision was greeted with applause, the two poets were not amused when it was announced that the trophy consisted of a fine pair of leather boots.

One evening, Eliza was surprised to see her brother Huw coming into the inn with a group of men. She went over and tapped his shoulder.

"Hello Huw," she said quietly, waiting for his reaction.

"Eliza! What brings you here?"

She smiled. "It's good to see you."

"Upon my life! What a beauty you have become," he said, as he looked her up and down. "How are you faring? How's your baby?"

"Mary is lovely. I wish you would come and see her sometimes. I wish you would, Huw."

"Ay! Well, yes, perhaps I shall; I have to come here once a week for a bit."

"How is Mam and Dada?"

"Tolerable well, considering the times we live in."

"Have they heard that I'm to be wed again?"

His eyebrows shot up. "Married? Well, that's great news! I'm glad for you Eliza. Who's the lucky man?"

"Why, the landlord here - Will Evans."

"Will Evans?" he exclaimed. "You don't say! Aw! Wait till I tell Mam and Dada. They'll be pleased. Well, I can't get over it! Fancy that!"

Will approached, having seen them in animated conversation; he placed a proprietary arm around Eliza and looked keenly at Huw.

"Will! This is my brother, Huw. It's many a day since we met."

"Huw, is it?" Will said, removing his arm and extending it towards his future brother-in-law. "I'm delighted to make your aquaintance."

Huw grinned. "I'm honoured, Sir! Very happy to hear Eliza's news."

"Let's celebrate with a mug of ale."

Huw looked embarrassed. "Can I have one after the meeting? I need a clear head."

"Of course. I understand."

"What meeting are you going to?" Eliza asked.

Huw gave his sister a nervous glance. "It's men's business. Nothing to worry your pretty head about, Eliza. You wouldn't understand."

"Eliza has more important matters to consider, is that not so, my pet?" Will said.

"I look forward to seeing you afterwards, Mr Evans. Congratulations though on getting betrothed to my sister," Huw called over his shoulder as he disappeared into the Meeting Room.

"Will, what is Huw up to in there?" Eliza asked.

"Oh! The men have been meeting here for some time now. I know little about it; something to do with the Reform Bill, I think," he said casually.

"Look! Dic Dywyll is going in there. Is he interested in Reform?" she

49

persisted.

"He will probably write a ballad about it and sell copies for a penny next Saturday night. Dic likes to know what is going on."

The chance encounter with her brother crowned Eliza's happiness. His pride at the prospect of being related to the landlord was plain to see and Will went out of his way to make him feel an honoured guest.

When Huw arrived for a further meeting the next week, in Eliza's absence, Will discussed the wedding plans with him, stressing that it would add to Eliza's happiness if her father were to give her away. Huw wasn't sure that he could persuade his father to agree, not because of the break in the relationship with Eliza, but on account of Mr Coleman's shyness and unease when put in the limelight. When his other daughters had married, an older brother did the honours. Certainly there could be no question of making a speech, but Will wasn't bothered about that. In the end, they left the matter unresolved, but Huw promised to let his father know how Will felt, not mentioning the fact that it was Eliza's mother who made all the decisions in the family and that if she told her husband to give Eliza away, then he would have to, whether he liked it or not.

Eluned meanwhile worked on her mother. "Mam, Will Evans comes from a highly respected family; his first cousin could soon be Lord Mayor of London, no less. Many gentlefolk have been invited and Eliza wants Mair to be her bridesmaid!"

"Eliza is getting above her station in life again. No good will come of it," her mother said warily, being careful not to say Yes or No.

"We've been to Darker's to order the wedding dress and Eliza wants to buy a pink muslin dress for Mair. Phelps the cobbler has measured my feet for shoes and Eliza will buy Mair a pair too. Aw! Mam, please."

"This needs careful thinking about," Aunt Bessie said warily. "Is her mother going to be there?"

"We certainly hope so. People will think the Coleman family ignorant if the bride's parents are absent."

Eluned returned to Ivor Street in a state of high excitement. "Mam didn't say No, so that means Yes. The prospect of Mair having a dress and a pair of shoes was irresistible, as I knew it would be," she told Eliza.

"Wonderful!" Eliza cried. "If your mother comes, my mother won't want to be left out!"

When the day came, Eliza was expecting Huw to arrive to give her away and still wasn't sure whether her parents would be in the chapel or not. It was therefore a surprise when Mr Coleman walked into the house carrying a large paper bag.

"Uncle Alwyn!" Eluned cried. "You *are* coming to the wedding! Eliza will be so happy. She and Mair are upstairs getting dressed."

He was wearing a grey stuffed coat, two sizes too big for him, a white linen shirt, a red neckerchief, yellow corduroy breeches and a pair of blue worsted stockings.

"I feel as trussed as a Michaelmas goose; why Eliza's mother thinks it matters what I wear I can't understand. She got this coat from Jinkins the deacon, and these breeches from her brother-in-law's nephew. I can hardly breathe."

"Well, this will be the last daughter you'll be marrying off, and it's cause for celebration, isn't it?" said Eluned. "I think you look very smart."

"If Blodwen thinks I'm going to wear this top hat, she's mistaken," he said, pulling it out of the bag. "It's too big; it wobbles around my ears. I'll carry it in my hand and that's all."

"Where did you get it from?"

"Mrs Hawkins; her husband works in the grocers," he explained. "Look at it!" he said, putting it on his head.

Eluned suppressed a giggle; Mr Coleman's eyebrows had all but disappeared.

"I can't see where I'm going, but Blodwen says that doesn't matter! 'Hold on to Eliza, let her guide you,' she says."

Eliza came to the top of the stairs. "Who's down there?" she called. "I am only half-dressed so I have to stay up here."

"Your father is here!" Eluned shouted from the hall. "He's come to give you away!"

"Dada? Dada's here? That's wonderful! I'll be down in ten minutes. Aw! This is too much."

Eluned smiled as she went back to the kitchen. "Would you like a cup of tea, Uncle Alwyn? The brougham won't be here for another half an hour. What a pity Mary isn't here for you to see - I took her to the inn early this morning; a neighbour of the Evanses is going to look after her there."

Mr Coleman replaced the top hat and loosened his neckerchief. "I'd rather have a glass of ale, if you got any."

"No, but there'll be plenty when you get to the inn."

He sighed.

Will gasped when he saw Eliza walking into Soar chapel on her father's arm in a pale-blue satin wedding-dress with lace trimmings, her face framed by a matching bonnet trimmed with pink velvet roses. The aisle was narrow and Eliza's dress so wide that there was scarcely room for her father at her side. Mair walked behind them carrying a posy, her cheeks flushed with excitement and her eyes fixed on the top hat that Mr Coleman carried behind his back.

The conviviality at the reception afterwards was such that no one could remain uninvolved, least of all the parents of the bride. Will set out to charm Mrs Coleman, attending to her every wish and whim and praising her up to the skies in his speech. His elation was infectious; he made it impossible for her not to respond to the goodwill that emanated from him. Mr and Mrs Coleman returned home well pleased with themselves. When Mrs Coleman called on Mrs Hawkins to return the top hat the next day, she described the Evanses of Llantwit as 'a tidy lot'.

Eliza and Will had made a handsome pair as they stepped into the brougham that took them away at tea-time. Even Eliza didn't know where they were going until they boarded the mail-coach at Merthyr. Will had reserved a room at the Duke of Bridgewater inn at Newbridge.

"What a lovely place!" Eliza whispered when they arrived. "It's so quiet and peaceful and look at those green hills and this wide, clean river!"

"I knew you would like it, Mrs Evans."

After a meal that evening they strolled along the bridle-path by the canal, saying very little as they watched the sun go down. At sunrise, Eliza held Will in her arms, aware of his heart-beat as he slept with his head across her shoulder. In the days that followed their eyes would soften when they looked at each other, remembering the words they whispered when they were alone in the darkness.

Eluned took in lodgers - a married couple and a widow. Eliza would accept only a nominal rent in return for helping out at the hostelry on Saturday evenings, a prospect that pleased them both.

As far as Eliza was concerned, the hostelry was the centre of the universe. Most evenings, it was full of iron-workers, slaking their thirst on the way home. The Commercial Room was frequented by travellers or tradesmen while the Meeting Room was booked for weeks ahead by groups of men who had formed associations of some sort or another.

The inn was renowned for its food. Since most of Will's brothers were butchers, he had the first choice of cuts; mutton, steaks, cutlets, boiled beef, bacon and fowl were served with Glamorgan sausages or steaming potatoes. Afterwards, the menu included fruit pie and custard, blancmange or pancakes, depending on the time of year. Besides the usual spirits, the cellar stocked ale, elderberry wine and ginger beer, which old Mrs Evans claimed was the finest in the district.

Will insisted that the inn carried on with its routine as before, leaving Eliza to look after Mary. Mrs Jones, who lived in the cottage next door, scrubbed the floors in the public rooms twice a week; her daughter Matilda cleaned the family rooms and the kitchen, scattering clean sand on the floor every morning.

Jimmy fed the animals, emptied spittoons and chamber pots, brushed boots, collected used tankards, ran errands and fetched water from the well three times a day. When the inn was quiet, Eliza would take him into the little parlour, off the kitchen, and give him reading and writing lessons, sitting at the desk that had been brought over from Ivor Street. The one room that Eliza and Jimmy rarely entered was the Saloon, which Will managed with Trevor, a deaf and dumb man who shared the loft with Jimmy. Trevor had a remarkable talent for communication, when he chose; he had worked at the inn before Will's time but who his family were or where he came from nobody knew. Normally, he was a gentle, kindly person who was popular with the customers but if any trouble arose, he would await a signal from Will and go after the ringleader, lift him up by the collar and breeches and throw him outside, returning with a look of triumph.

Eliza and her mother-in-law often laughed about the bread from Ivor Street that Will used to buy. Mrs Evans baked in a stick oven in the yard. It required a skill which came after years of practice. On baking days, Mrs Evans would fill the large oven with twigs and logs, lighting them with a taper. An hour later she scattered the ashes around the sides of the oven and left them for another hour, by which time the bricks inside had become white-hot. After a few weeks, having watched several times, Eliza asked if she could help.

Old Mrs Evans stood back while Eliza scraped out the embers and attempted to wash the oven with a long-handled mop.

"Wring the mop much harder first," her mother-in-law told her, "lest the oven cools down too much."

Having cleaned the oven, Eliza rolled up her sleeve in order to test the heat, which had to be just right.

"You had better do the counting, Mother. Let me concentrate on this part," she said. "It might be dangerous."

Mrs Evans counted up to thirty while Eliza held an arm inside the oven. At twenty-nine she pulled her arm out with a cry of anguish and hopped round the yard on one leg.

"Jeremiah!" she cried as she plunged her arm into one of the water barrels.

Mrs Evans smiled. "Well, you must needs learn. I'll put my arm in and if I can't keep it there until I reach thirty the oven is too hot."

"And if you can keep it there after thirty the oven is too cold," Eliza added, wanting to show that she had grasped the routine.

Mrs Evans removed her arm at twenty-seven. "We must wait a while before trying again."

When the temperature was exactly right, Eliza put the dough inside, placed a large brick at the entrance and sealed it with clay.

"I was clumsy," she said. "You make it seem so easy!"

Mrs Evans grinned. "Well, you have a tolerable command of the skill. It takes a long time to bring it to perfection."

"I'm fortunate to have the chance of learning. No bread in the district is tastier."

Eliza counted her blessings. She liked to watch Mary's expression when they followed Jimmy, hand in hand, as he fed the horses and pigs and scattered grain for the chickens. Trevor idolised the child, lifting her up to look at the piglets in the sty or holding her in front of him when he rode the old cob-horse around the yard.

"How could I ever have thought that a hostelry might not be a suitable home for a child," she said to Eluned one Saturday evening when they were skinning rabbits for a pie.

"I envy you. I'm beginning to think that Dai might never find work and we might never be wed," Eluned said. "Indeed, I fear that I shall sink under the weight of my melancholy. I don't know what I shall do if Dai has to go far afield to find a job."

"There's no cause for despair, 'Luned. They must surely start building this railway line that people keep talking about and then they will need hundreds of men to put down the tracks."

"I've heard that the strange new road won't work; they say it could all come to grief," Eluned answered. "I don't understand how it is supposed to work."

Eliza smiled. "Will has told me about it. The iron-masters want to get coal down to the sea as fast as possible - canals are too slow and it's not much faster when horses pull waggons on iron rails so they've made huge engines that have coal fires which will boil water and give off steam which will turn the wheels, so the waggons will rush along at great speed."

"It sounds perilous."

"They'll have to put down wooden tracks to hold the new rails, all the way from Dowlais to Cardiff. They'll want a good many men to do that," Eliza said. "You might not have to wait much longer."

"I truly hope not. Dai is so despondent."

In fact, Dai was taken on as a ganger three weeks later. Eluned ran into the hostelry on Saturday evening to tell Eliza. "I'm going to be wed, Eliza! I'm going to be wed!"

"Aw! I'm happy for you. That's good news, indeed."

"Where's Will? I must tell him!"

"He isn't back from the market in Pont-y-ty-pridd, but he should be here soon."

"Dai starts work on the railway next week. Aw! we're both so pleased."

Will returned home half an hour later, in a particularly happy mood himself. "What's all this jollity and rumpus? Pray tell me so that I can join in!"

"Dai and I are to be wed. He's found work on the railway," Eluned cried.

"Upon my soul! This is cause for celebration."

"Eliza's going to lend me her wedding dress and Mair will be a bridesmaid again. I think I shall die of happiness."

"And we'll all meet here after the wedding and have a feast. That will be my contribution," Will said.

"You'll pay for a reception, Will?" Eluned whispered in amazement. "That's exceeding generous of you." She looked at Eliza with raised eyebrows.

"He must have had a good day at the market. Accept before he changes his mind, 'Luned."

On the evening before the wedding, Eliza returned to Ivor Street to discuss arrangements with Eluned while David went to the inn to spend his last evening as a bachelor with a few of his friends, including Huw. Will spent as much time as he could with them, leaving Trevor to cope with the Saloon. The locals knew how to order their ale by gesticulating, and Trevor was meticulous in counting the money which he insisted on having before he would pour out the drinks.

"It's time you were thinking of getting wed, Huw," David said. "Chasing girls would be a better pastime than attending all these political meetings."

"I've got the rest of my life to choose a wife. I value my freedom too much to rush into wedlock, anyhow. Once a woman has you in her clutches you are a prisoner for life, by my reckoning."

David shook his head and raised his tankard. "Wait till you find the right one. You'll be as daft as the rest of us then. I want nothing more than to spend the rest of my life in Eluned's clutches."

Huw was not impressed. "You mean you're prepared to spend the rest of your life living in the arse-hole of Wales?"

"I don't care where it is as long as Eluned's there. That's all that matters."

"But you only got one life; if I can't do something about the state of Merthyr and Dowlais, then I'll go somewhere else, where the air is fit to breathe. I'm not prepared to get married until this cesspit is cleaned up; I can't fathom why people want to have children when more than half the babies are dead before they are a year old," Huw said savagely.

A friend of David's joined in. "It's pretty terrible, I must say. Two or three families living in one house, slaving all day in the mines or at furnaces and dying like flies from fever or consumption. I'm thinking of going to work as a navvy in Birmingham. The wages are good."

Will hovered round them for a moment. "Well! What a cheerful conversation! I thought this was supposed to be a celebration."

David smiled. "Huw needs the love of a good woman to take his mind off rabble-rousing. He's spent too much time with that crazy Dr Price. Can you find him a wife, Will?"

Will grinned. "The trouble is that Dr Price has persuaded Huw that men shouldn't bother to get married and that virginity is old-fashioned and against the laws of nature. Isn't that so, Huw?"

Huw glowered. "A lot of what the doctor says makes sense to me. He doesn't believe in the divine right of landlords and ironmasters - he calls them blood-sucking Pharaohs. He's right, too, when he says that preachers go round shouting about predestination so that people will think their lot in life is ordained. The clergy are on the side of the wealthy, that's what he says, and I agree with him." He drained his glass and looked at his companions. "You got to admit it makes sense."

"But what can we do about it?" David asked.

"Everyone must press for Reform and for Merthyr to have its own Member of Parliament. We are the biggest town in Wales, and we haven't got a representative in Westminster. We shan't get anything done until that's put to rights."

Will collected their empty tankards. "You'd make a good Member of Parliament, Huw."

"Aw! No one takes me seriously," he muttered.

"Cheer up, lad. This is my last night with the boys, let's talk about something less serious. Tell me something funny to say in my speech tomorrow," David pleaded.

"I'm sorry, Dai," Huw said. "Er....It's love that makes the world go round; too large a mouthful of horseradish has the same effect."

David grimaced.

Huw looked at the ceiling. "How about: 'A wise woman will let her husband have her own way?'"

"That's better! Keep going."

The family gathered once more for the wedding at Caersalem the next day; since Mr Guest wasn't staying in Dowlais House at the time, Myfanwy was able to get away for half an hour for her sister's wedding and she persuaded another kitchen maid to do her washing-up after the staff supper, so that she could join the last of the festivities at the hostelry. When the bride and groom left under a hail of rice, friends lingered on, singing hymns and songs.

David's parents and other relatives had arrived early in a waggon, hired in Cefn where they lived; they could have walked but when they heard that there was to be a reception at the inn, Auntie Ella decided to bring her pedal harp. Since that necessitated transport, the rest of the family clambered on board with it. Travellers in the Commercial Room marvelled at the singing; men in the Saloon joined in some choruses and, for a few hours, the troubles of the outside world were forgotten as the warm summer night was filled with harmony.

Chapter 8

When Eliza told Will that she was carrying his child, he fussed and cosseted her like an old apple-woman. She was happier than she had ever been. It was very different from the anxious and lonely days when she had waited for Mary. By Christmas, Eluned confided that she too was expecting, so that they knitted and twittered and planned their children's futures together. Eliza always called in Ivor Street for an hour or so before choir practice and they both looked forward to Saturday nights, when Eluned came to the inn.

That year the meeting room was booked regularly by the Sons of Vulcan, the Rechabites, the Ancient Britons, the Odd Fellows or the secret group that Huw belonged to - Eliza never found out its name. Sometimes, if too many turned up, they would adjourn to the mountain-side when it wasn't raining. Huw was now spending every spare minute in his favourite pastime - stirring up support for the Reform movement, trying to channel the dispirited workers into what he termed "positive directions". He and his friend Dic Dywyll, the blind ballad singer, attended meetings at Abercanaid and *China* as well as Dowlais.

He surprised Eliza when he arrived early for a meeting in March. "I want to copy some pamphlets. Can I sit in the kitchen?"

"Of course, Jimmy can put those boots on the floor, can't you, dear?" she said, going to the dresser for a quill and a bottle of ink. "What are you up to now, if I may be so bold?

"Just something I promised Lewis Lewis I would do for him," he muttered, looking at Jimmy and then at his sister.

Eliza followed his gaze before speaking. "Jimmy, perhaps it would be better if you took the boots to the yard. There won't be a lot of room in here once I start plucking this chicken."

After Jimmy had disappeared Eliza sat down on the settle, placed a sack at her feet, and lifted the chicken on to her lap. She could pluck a chicken in seventeen minutes, but it was taking longer now that her stomach was getting in the way.

Huw dipped the quill in the ink. "Where is Mrs Evans?"

"Gone to Prayer Meeting," Eliza answered. "So you can talk freely." He wrote laboriously, his mouth open and moving silently as he copied letters from a small piece of paper on to one which was half the size of the table.

"I hope you won't get into trouble, Huw. I worry about you sometimes. I've heard about men roaming the streets and burning effigies down in Merthyr," she said quietly as she plucked the fowl.

"It's a troubled world, Eliza," he murmured.

"It isn't just here in Merthyr and Dowlais that people want a decent Reform Act, surely to goodness. If it's right, it will come, in time."

"What do you mean - if it's right, girl?"

"Well, Reform won't make the world perfect, will it? It won't give us a pure water supply. It won't stop people emptying chamber pots in the stream, it won't stop babies dying like flies."

Huw was exasperated. "So you think I shouldn't bother, is that it?"

"I just think you should be careful. Even if you do get this place its own Member of Parliament, he wouldn't be a collier or a miner, would he? More likely he would be an ironmaster or a landowner; what difference will it make whether he's here or in London?" Eliza asked brightly, as she stuffed stray feathers into the sack.

"I grant you that the town is in the hands of a few powerful, rich men and only a rich man can be a Member of Parliament, but we must be represented. How many people in Parliament know about conditions here? Does the Duke of Wellington know? Our Member would have to tell the world what it's like, because he will be responsible to us. Now, let me get on with this - it isn't easy."

Eliza smiled and wiped the feathers off her apron. "How can he represent the workers, when only people who own property worth more than ten pounds a year can have the vote, tell me?" she persisted.

"The workers might not have a vote, but they can make their voices heard, mark my words. You can't have five thousand men out of work or on cut wages, without food and without hope and expect them not to make their voices heard. It won't be long before they take matters into their own hands and when that happens, I'll be there, and proud of it!" he spat out, as he stood up to look at the finished pamphlet.

Their conversation stopped temporarily when Jimmy came back in. "I expect Trevor will want you to take him some clean tankards, *bach*. Would you go and see?" Eliza asked.

"You'll get into real trouble, Huw. There's such a thing as the law, you know. You could get deported, anything could happen," she said when Jimmy had gone.

"Real trouble!" scoffed her brother. "Don't you realise that there's real trouble already? Aw! Women!" he cried, as Jimmy and Will came in with trays of dirty tankards. He threw his arms in the air. "Will! Women are daft, I tell you."

"That's half their charm, Huw my lad," Will replied, as he pecked his wife on the cheek. "A traveller has just come in. Would you go and welcome him, dear? Jimmy, see to his clothes and boots, there's a good boy."

When they left, Huw pushed his hand through his hair. "Eliza riles me at times. I wish she wouldn't argue about men's business. She doesn't know what hardship is and she talks a lot of nonsense. By the way, I haven't told her that Dada has been sacked along with eighty one other puddlers."

"Your father? God! How will your family manage?"

Huw sat back and looked into the fire. "I don't know. Dada has been saving, but there's not much; Mam says she'll take in washing; we've got lodgers but their wages have been cut like mine. I got eight shillings last Saturday. Little Robert had a hiding yesterday for begging! We haven't paid last week's rent. I know one thing though, the bailiffs aren't going to take our furniture; I'll barricade the door first." He got to his feet. "I must go; the meeting is at seven. Is Dic Dywyll out there?"

"Yes. He's been calculating how many workers an ironmaster could support on seventy thousand pounds a year. He's going to speak, I gather."

Huw smiled. "He's good; it's amazing how many facts he can keep in his head."

"Come back afterwards. You must take some food home. Your family won't starve as long as I can help," Will said. "What do you think your mother would like?"

Huw smiled ruefully. "Mam would be precious glad of a loaf of bread, I know that."

On a quiet morning in late May the sky over Merthyr was festooned with wisps of cloud drifting slowly over the sleepy town. Blodwen Coleman had almost finished washing the dishes after the first decent breakfast the family had had for a while. Huw had arrived home with a dozen slices of bacon and half-a-dozen eggs as well as a large loaf of bread the previous night, otherwise it would have been bread and dripping.

Suddenly a neighbour ran in. "Come quick! Bailiffs are in Mrs Rees's house!"

"Mrs Rees's! Never! The poor dab is dying," Mrs Coleman cried.

Edna Phillips had run back out. In no time Mrs Coleman dried her hands and took her apron off.

Coffin's henchmen had started out early, hoping to complete their grisly task before the neighbours could do much about it. They planned to clear the ground floor and proceed upstairs, having guessed that there would be little furniture in the place.

Edna Phillips entered the hallway. "What do you think you are doing here? You must know that Mrs Rees is dying. How can you be so heartless?"

Mrs Coleman arrived breathless. "I don't believe it!" she whispered, as the men came down the stairs carrying a table and two chairs which they stacked on the cart outside the door. As soon as they could, they ran back in. "You wicked men! That poor old woman never did you any harm!" she yelled.

Other neighbours trickled out of their houses and added their own invective.

"You will burn in hell-fire for this, you bastards," a youth shouted.

"Leave the poor soul be," pleaded a female voice. "This is beyond all reason. You will not get away with it!" Mrs Coleman spat out.

The men emerged again, edging their way through the small crowd that had gathered. They carried a copper cauldron, a poker, a Bible, a box containing a broken mirror and a teapot without a lid. The waiting women studied each item as it was loaded on to the cart.

"A curse on you and your children's children!" someone shouted.

A young man appeared, stuffing his shirt into his trousers. "You filthy bastards! You've gone too far this time," he shouted. "Coffin shall suffer for this, do you hear me?" he cried, as he pushed against the cart, knocking it over and tipping the contents into the street. "I'm going to report this," he yelled, elbowing his way through the neighbours and disappearing down the nearest alley.

The men appeared with some worn carpet, a pair of curtains, a mangle and the kitchen bellows. "We are only carrying out orders," one of them said.

"If you cause any more trouble, you will be reported to the Magistrates," his mate threatened, looking anxiously around before he righted the cart and tied a rope around Mrs Rees's household possessions. "If this cart is tipped once more, the persons concerned will be arrested."

When the bailiffs came out the next time, they carried an old bedstead, a threadbare quilt, a bundle of knives and forks, a candle stuck to a saucer, a bag of pegs and a chamber-pot. The crowd was subdued.

"Aw! I can't believe this is happening. The poor dab hasn't touched a morsel of food for two days. They are robbing a dying woman," Mrs Coleman whispered, rubbing her breasts in anguish.

Suddenly one of the upstairs windows was pushed open. Mrs Rees's sister leaned out with a look of horror. "They are in here!" she shouted. "They are pulling the mattress out from under her!"

A roar went up from the onlookers who now packed the street from end to end. Mrs Rees's sister stumbled out through the passage way, one arm outstretched for support.

"This is an outrage! It cannot be allowed in a civilised country," a deacon from Ebenezer said.

"Filthy pigs! Never had a father or mother of your own, did you?" a woman yelled from an upstairs window opposite.

The bailiff's men, having completed their task, started to push the cart up the street, followed by the crowd, who hurled abuse, jeered, taunted and threatened; some of them continued the chorus all the way to the Debtors' Court.

Mrs Coleman stayed behind, tip-toeing into the house with Mrs Rees's sister. They stood on the threshold of the bedroom where the old woman was lying on the bare floor, looking already like a corpse. Her sister knelt down and gently stroked her cheeks.

"It's all right, Sis. I'm here," she whispered.

The old lady didn't respond.

Mrs Coleman took one of Mrs Rees's hands in hers; the fingers were like claws, and cold. "We can't leave her like this. Shall I go and get some straw to put under her?"

An hour later Mrs Rees died.

That night, the glow from the cinders on the mountain was pale when compared with the lights that flickered from the torches of a thousand men who had gathered in anger. Mrs Rees's death was the spark that kindled the flames of revolt.

At about eleven o'clock the men left the mountain and roamed the town aimlessly, united in their exhilaration and determination to seek revenge for their pent-up grievances. Some sang hymns, a few blew hunting horns, others shouted slogans:

REFORM! REFORM! WE WANT REFORM!

Tom Llewellyn, a puddler, led the men to the house of Stephens, the wealthy Tory trader, where they stood outside shouting taunts and abuse. Someone set an effigy alight, bringing cheers from the onlookers. Tom and his friend William Jones stayed but others moved on shouting: "REFORM! REFORM!" Many carried sticks which they rattled on the doors of people they hated most, like Coffin, who sent his loathsome bailiffs around spreading despair and misery; Darker, the Overseer of the Poor, was another one, and Jones, the money-lender, who owned the meat market.

All the windows in the Debtors' Court were smashed that night and it wasn't surprising that the authorities moved swiftly; by eleven o'clock the next morning, Tom Llewellyn and William Jones had been arrested and locked up in the Bush Inn, having been committed to prison by Bruce, the Stipendiary Magistrate who was a worried man; he spent the afternoon writing to the Marquis of Bute, the Lord Lieutenant of Glamorgan and Colonel-in-Chief of the Royal Glamorganshire Militia.

After dark, Huw was out early for another meeting on the mountain, where Lewis Lewis the haulier spoke to the men in anger. One purpose only was now uppermost in their minds - the release of Tom Llewellyn and the collier, William Jones. A scheme had been worked out which Lewis explained slowly and with deliberation.

At the end he paused: "Are there any questions?"

None came.

"Right! blow out the lights. Now, remember - no sound until you get the signal."

Lewis jumped down from the boulder on which he had been standing and started to move swiftly. As the silent throng followed through the darkness, they represented a more sinister sight than they had the night before. The mob divided at the Bush inn; some men crept down side-streets to guard the rear, others stayed at the side; most stood in the front.

Suddenly a terrifying sound erupted as the men shouted in unison and swarmed inside. The rooms on the ground floor were swamped immediately, while a dozen men rushed upstairs. A guard sitting outside a door at the end of a corridor sprang to his feet, dropping a large bunch of keys. He put his hands above his head as he stood against a wall, petrified.

Huw picked up the keys, tried them in the lock and finally found one that opened the door. "Quick! Run!" he shouted.

There was no time for greeting or exultation then, but the moment that the two prisoners appeared outside, a huge roar went up. Tom and William were carried shoulder-high in jubilation. The previous night the mob had been surprised by their power; now they rejoiced in it. They went to the Debtors' Court and burned it down to the ground before dispersing.

Huw, Lewis Lewis, William Williams, a puddler, and Dic Dywyll didn't join the crowds that roamed the town the following night; they were conferring at an inn at Abercanaid, though 'conferring' was hardly an accurate description of the arguments and squabbling that occurred. Huw wanted to wait for the annual Waun fair in June, by which time they would be more organised and could mobilise support from further afield. Lewis favoured a march on Cardiff immediately, before the authorities could act. They agreed that Reform was not enough on its own but Dic wanted to demand higher wages. In the end they backed Huw.

They decided to organise a mass meeting where Dic would make a speech demanding the abolition of the Debtors' Court, abolition of imprisonment for debt and the vote for every man over the age of twenty-one. After the fair they would march on Cardiff.

Ten thousand men were at the fair; Dic had never had such an enthusiastic audience. William carried a huge flag bearing the words 'REFORM'. Huw suggested dipping it in the blood of a dead calf which was lying with its feet in the air in a ditch near the entrance to the field. As they were doing that, someone stuck a loaf of bread on top of the flag-pole.

They were an awesome sight as they streamed away from the field after dusk, inspired and united, rank after rank shouting out in unison at the tops of their voices. They set off in high spirits, lingering near Coffin's house, where the leaders waited for the rest of the marchers to catch up. Some men hurled stones through the windows to pass the time. A hush fell when the front door opened a few inches.

Coffin stayed hidden. "What do you want of me?" he shouted in a hoarse voice.

"My grandfather clock - the one you bought from the Debtors' Court last week," cried one wit.

"Very well. If you promise not to harm me and you go away afterwards, I shall bring it out."

A roar went up. Lewis Lewis looked around, grinning with amazement. Shortly afterwards, the door opened again to reveal Coffin standing in the hall, holding the clock. Its owner came to the front, walked up to Coffin and took it from him.

"Thank you, Sir!" cried Lewis, bending low and sweeping his cap along the ground.

Another voice shouted in the night: "I want my oak table back from Darker. He got it from the Court of Requests last week. My sister saw it in his house."

"I'd like my gold watch and tea set!"

"What about my rocking-chair?" called a man at the back of the crowd.

"One at a time, boys!" Lewis shouted. "Let's start with Darker."

They gathered outside the draper's house, where Huw and another man rattled on the front door with sticks.

"Do you want us to break the door down, Darker?" Lewis cried, signalling to the crowd to be quiet.

An upstairs window opened and a figure leaned out. "I have nothing here for you. Go away!"

"Oh yes, you have; that oak dining table you got last week. Bring it out and we won't harm you."

The table was eventually carried out to the street where a spontaneous cheer greeted its recovery.

"Right! Where next?" shouted Lewis. "Come on! The town is ours."

When Huw tried to explain the night's events to his mother the next day, he was at a loss to describe the scenes that followed. The crowd split up into small groups, some went home to get their wives and children who gathered stones to throw through windows; others rattled on doors with sticks. Most of the traders were forced to give up something or other, and whether it had been confiscated by the Court or whether people just fancied some items, Huw couldn't say. In a short time the town was crammed with families carrying furniture or clocks, bedding or settles, brass fenders, coal-scuttles, sofas, hat boxes and goodness knows what else besides. Such was the pandemonium that people bumped into each other in their excitement, laughing or crying and shouting and cursing.

"Look out, you clumsy old fool! You just trod on my foot!"

"Hold on to them drawers, you idiot. They will fall out and break."

"Aw, not so fast. It's all right for you at the back, but you'll run over me in the front if you aren't careful."

Mrs Coleman leaned out of the window to see what all the noise was about. Her head was covered in small bits of rag, tied here and there in an effort to produce curls the next day. When she realised what was happening she threw herself into the spirit of things with gusto, directing the flow of traffic, issuing orders and generally joining in the rumpus.

"Tell Mrs Harris, Zion to go to Rees's place for that chest of drawers. What have you got, Mrs Williams? Aw! There's lovely! I hear Mrs

Harries, Caersalem's, got her brass bedstead back. Have you seen Huw or Alwyn anywhere?"

Tables and chairs flowed down the street, precious things were dropped, groans and cheers echoed through the night air.

"Wait a minute, Bert. I must get my breath."

"Watch what you're doing, Gwladys. We'll break the innards of the clock at this rate."

On the opposite side of the road, a couple who had returned home triumphant with a settle, put it down outside their front door and sat watching the parade.

"Well done, Sara! I see you got your stuff back," Blodwen shouted. "What a night! Have you ever seen anything like it?"

"Hello, Mrs Coleman! I got my leather boots back from Phelps. I only paid for them last week," cried a deacon from Bethel.

"Hallelujah, Mr Jinkins!"

Mrs Coleman's attention was deflected by the sight of a mattress floating down the street, apparently of its own volition. "Who is under there?"

"Eira Jones, Zion. My brother is at the back. We are taking Gran's bed back home," came a voice piping through the horsehair.

Mrs Coleman was ecstatic. "God Save the King!" she cried.

By dawn the following morning the town was silent and peaceful. Uncannily so. The march on Cardiff had been postponed so that the men could get some sleep before setting out again.

*

Chapter 9

Early the following morning, Jimmy and Trevor were busy in the yard of the hostelry getting the sow out of the pigsty and into a cart. It was a noisy business, what with the squealing and grunting from the pig and roars from Trevor, who could get quite angry when thwarted.

"I don't think you should be going abroad today, son," said Mrs Evans, as she poured out tea. "Not after all the trouble there's been."

"The Waun fair passed off peacefully, Mother. I'm told Merthyr is quiet," Will said, buttering a piece of toast.

Eliza looked up from the hearth where she was poaching some eggs. "Mrs Jones told me that men were still roaming the streets; she heard that hundreds from Monmouthshire are on the way to see if they can join in."

Will frowned. He wished men would be more circumspect when they talked in front of women. He hadn't told Eliza about the plan for a march on Cardiff. "Well, the sow hasn't heard about the trouble and she can't wait, not if we are to have piglets for the winter. Anyway, I shall be on the Cefn road."

It was a dry, crisp morning. The horse's hooves and the rattling cartwheels were the only sounds breaking the silence as Will went on his way. At one stage he looked down over the sprawling mass of Merthyr. A stranger would not have guessed that anarchy was threatening there, nor that the town was in uproar under the mackerel sky that hung over it. A blackbird was singing somewhere in the hedgerow.

As he approached the bridge at the beginning of Cefn, Will was startled to see men and youths running around the corner. He pulled the horse up to ask them the reason for their haste, but they ran past as if he didn't exist. As he was about to start up again, two soldiers on horseback trotted round the corner, looking neither right nor left as they went by. Will jerked the reins and went cautiously forward.

When he reached the village, he was surprised to find it crowded. Everyone seemed to be out on their doorsteps or leaning out of windows. They were looking North, staring in silence at a troop of soldiers, wearing kilts and carrying muskets, marching four abreast and getting nearer. Will jumped down and joined a group of men standing on the roadside. There was no need to ask where the troops were going. He heard a child asking its mother why the soldiers were wearing skirts.

The boots crunched on the dusty road; the Highlanders were tall men who stared straight ahead, some perspiring after the long march over the mountain.

As they came closer, Will decided to count them. "8, 12, 16, 20, 24, 28....."

"Oooh! What a lot of knobbly knees!" a woman shouted.

"Why don't you turn round and go home?"

The expressions on the soldiers' faces didn't alter; they behaved as though they were deaf. Will thought they might be considering the tasks that could await them at their journey's end.

"30, 34, 38, 42, 46.."

A woman leant out of a window and yelled: "Why don't you go home and put your trousers on?"

A man standing near Will raised his voice. "It's dangerous where you're heading, ladies! There are men down there."

"50, 54, 58, 62.".

The marching feet passed by; the sound of their boots faded but the dust thrown up lingered after they disappeared round the corner.

"There were 80 of them," Will said, speaking to no one in particular.

"Aye! Argyll and Sutherland Highlanders," said an old man, as he shook his head. "From the barracks at Brecon."

On his way home, Will stopped to ask a passer-by for news.

"Militia have arrived from Cardiff and Swansea; there are tents in the grounds of Penydarren House. Soldiers are patrolling the town."

He turned for Dowlais with a sinking heart.

The next morning he went to Merthyr after breakfast, to get news from the Colemans, carrying a loaf of bread and a ham-bone, on Eliza's orders. The town was strangely deserted; front doors were shut, which was odd. He found his mother-in-law on her own, making Welsh cakes.

"They are for old Mrs Rees's funeral," she explained. "She's in a better world now, I hope. You heard all about it, I suppose."

"I should think the whole of Glamorgan has heard about it. What a terrible thing to have happened! Small wonder people took to the streets."

"Huw and Gwilym got home about three o'clock. They are fast asleep upstairs now. I think I'll leave them till dinner time; they are fair worn out."

"No wonder," Will said quietly. "By the way, Eliza sent this for you."

He put the bag with the bread and ham-bone on the table as the sound of running feet outside reached his ears. Seconds later a young friend of Huw's ran in.

"Good morning, Mrs Coleman," he panted, eyeing Will suspiciously. "Is Huw about?"

"Hello, Danny! This is my son-in-law, the landlord of the inn at Cwm Rhyd-y-Bedd," she explained. "Huw is asleep in bed. What do you want?"

"I've got some news for him; can I go upstairs and see him?" he asked, changing his cap from one hand to the other nervously.

"What news?"

"They want as many men as possible there, in case, like," he mumbled.

"Who does? Where? In case of what?"

Danny frowned and scratched his head. "In High Street. I dunno why, but Huw will want to know."

"Tch! I don't know what the world is coming to, I really don't. You'd better go up and tell him, I suppose," she said wearily. "How is Eliza, Will?" she asked as she started to cut out the dough with a cup.

"Very well. She thinks the babby will be here before long," he said eagerly.

Further conversation was impossible after the first banging, shouting and cursing that came from the room over their heads. Gwilym appeared at the kitchen door, having jumped down the stairs three at a time.

"Where's my shirt, Mam? I need my boots too. Hello, Will."

"Here's your shirt," replied his mother, pulling it down from the ceiling-rack. "Your boots are where they always are, at the bottom of the stairs. You are still half asleep, boy!"

Huw and Alwyn appeared; Huw with tousled hair, fastening his belt around his waist. "We got to go out again, Mam. Now!" he said.

"When will you be back?"

"That depends," her husband said. "We don't know what's going on yet."

Will sat helplessly on the settle as Gwilym went out to the yard and put his head in a bucket of water, rubbing his hair with a towel when he returned. "That's better! I'm awake now!"

"You'll have something to eat before you go," Mrs Coleman said indignantly.

"No time," Huw snapped as he ran out.

"Come on, Gwilym, we got to hurry, boy," his father said.

Gwilym followed the others, pulling his head through his shirt as he went out to the street.

"There's no sense in it," Mrs Coleman said. "People can't go on without proper sleep night after night and without anything to eat."

"They must be so tired."

"Well, you and I can have a cup of tea, at any rate. I'm glad to see that you've got more sense than to get mixed up in all this business."

"I can understand their grievances, Mam. They are quite right to press for Reform," he said in a low voice, feeling uncomfortable. As an innkeeper, he didn't share the hardship of the workers, even though the rent he had to pay had gone up by a third in the last year. Equally, he wasn't a target of resentment like the wealthy traders. Still, he felt uneasy being on the side-lines like the women.

After a while, he left and walked in the direction of the High Street. Even had he not heard the conversation at the Colemans, his ears could have directed him to the centre of the town. The sound of chanting and general uproar reached him, growing in intensity as he approached the surrounding streets. He was alarmed before he arrived, but wasn't prepared for the sight he met when he got to the square. He hadn't seen so many people gathered together before. He stood on tip-toe at the back of the crowd to make out what was happening at the front, before edging his way along the houses opposite the Castle inn where Guest and Crawshay were standing at an upstairs window. Bruce's head was just visible at the front door, where he seemed to be reading something from a parchment. What he was saying it was impossible to tell, as his words were drowned by the chanting of the jubilant workers standing in front of him.

"CHEESE WITH OUR BREAD! CHEESE WITH OUR BREAD!"

They shouted in unison, their eyes bright with fervour. Many had their elbows held in front of them in order to breathe, so tightly packed was the square. When the first volley of shots rang out, Will ducked instinctively; a pane of glass in the window of the house behind him shattered, scattering splinters on the crowd, who stampeded in panic. He was lucky not to be trampled on, such was the pandemonium that followed. As he ran he was aware of cries and shouts behind him, but he didn't turn round or stop running until he reached the Colemans' house, staying outside for a few seconds to get his breath back before going in. He shut and bolted the door behind him.

"What on earth is going on?" Mrs Coleman asked as she came into the passage.

"Trouble - deep trouble," panted Will, as he put his hands on his knees and lowered his head.

"Come and sit down. Where have you been?"

"Militia fired on a crowd of people in the square. I didn't see what happened exactly....I was at the back. I ran."

"Where are the others?"

Will shrugged his shoulders and slumped on the settle while his mother-in-law bombarded him with questions which he couldn't answer. A few minutes later they heard banging on the door.

"Stay here!" Will whispered. "I've been here all morning, remember."

He ran to the parlour and looked out. Gwilym was standing outside with one arm around his father's neck. When Will opened the door he saw that Gwilym's foot was soaked in blood.

"Thank God you're alive," Will said quietly as the two men came in - Gwilym hopping on one foot. When he had bolted the door once more, Will joined them in the kitchen.

Mrs Coleman was kneeling on the floor, undoing Gwilym's boot laces.

"Where's Huw?" Will asked.

"I saw him going off with a group of Cyfarthfa men," his father said. "He was all right."

"How did this happen?"

"I fell over a musket that was lying on the ground - I don't think it's as bad as it looks."

Alwyn Coleman looked at Will and shook his head as his wife went to get a bowl of water. His face was ashen. "Danny Cheeseman is dead; a lot of soldiers are dead too," he whispered. "There was a pile of bodies at the door of the Castle inn. Don't tell Blodwen."

"What will happen now?" Will whispered.

"Revenge!" Gwilym shouted. "Ouch! Mam, be careful!" he yelled as his mother pressed a rag on his foot.

Suddenly they stopped talking and exchanged glances as they heard footsteps running down the street. Will and Alwyn walked to the parlour window but could see nothing, although they heard strident voices shouting.

"Run! Leave him! It's no good, we'll be caught."

The footsteps died away.

"Stay here; I'll go and look," Will said, going to the door and drawing back the bolt as quietly as he could. When he had lifted the latch, he held the door ajar for a few seconds while he listened for further sounds. Slowly, he put his head out and glanced up and down before his eyes came to rest on a man who was spread-eagled, face down and motionless, outside the next-door house. A dark wetness trickled in rivulets through the surrounding dust.

"Quick! Help me to pick him up."

Will and Alwyn Coleman half-carried, half-dragged the man into the passage.

"Look at that blood!" screamed Mrs Coleman, as they turned the man over, revealing a gaping wound in his stomach. She stumbled back into the kitchen while Will and Alwyn watched him die.

"What's going on out there?" Gwilym shouted, as his mother rocked to and fro with her face in her apron.

"Let's carry him to the yard," Will said quietly. "I'll get a bucket of water to clean up the step."

They put the body by the wall outside the back door, where Alwyn stayed looking at the marbled face before getting a sack. Will knelt at the front door, mopping up blood and throwing water on the pavement, his eyes constantly looking up and down the deserted street.

"Who is he, Dada?" Gwilym called gently.

Alwyn Coleman shook his head. "I never saw him before, but by his clothes I would say he was a collier."

Will left at tea-time, walking through quiet alleys where people were standing at their front doors, talking in subdued voices and staring at passers-by. More than one asked him if he had seen so and so - a son, father, husband or brother who hadn't come home. Will asked in turn if they had seen Huw Coleman, only to be met with a shake of the head.

When he reached the yard of the hostelry, Jimmy was leaning over the pigsty emptying a bucket of swill. In the kitchen, Eliza was sitting miserably at the table while her mother-in-law rubbed her back.

His mother smiled. "Yes, the babby has started. Jimmy has taken Mary up to Eluned's and on his way back he told Mrs Llewellyn to come."

Eliza sighed. "I'd forgotten this feeling! It's just as well that women forget, otherwise we'd never have more than one."

"There, there. Get up and walk about again," Will's mother said. "I'll make you a cup of dandelion tea. That'll help."

Eliza got up slowly and walked to the mantelshelf which she held while she groaned.

"I think you'd better get Mrs Jones to help you in the Saloon tonight, Will, and ask me before you tell any travellers that there's supper," Mrs Evans said as she took a cup and saucer from the dresser.

"I don't think we'll have many travellers tonight, Mother. There was some trouble in Merthyr this morning, people will be staying at home. It's nothing for you to worry about, dear," he said quickly as Eliza looked up. "Gwilym cut his foot, but not badly."

"What sort of trouble?" Eliza asked as she walked over to the dresser with her hands at her back.

Will sighed. "Militia fired shots over the heads of a crowd in the square. It's all quiet now, though."

Mrs Evans eyed her daughter-in-law. "I think it's time to go upstairs, Eliza fach. I'll bring the tea up to you. There's cold chicken and ham for you in the larder, Will."

Will went to the outside larder to get the meat.

Jimmy came in a few minutes later. "Is there anything you want me to do, Mr Evans?"

"Er..you've fed the animals?"

"Yes, Sir."

Will looked at the ceiling. "You can go next door and ask Mrs Jones if she can come and help out tonight, Tell her..um, tell her that my wife has stomach ache and isn't feeling very good."

The message resulted in Mrs Jones, Mrs Llewellyn, the mid-wife, and a friend, Mrs Bevan arriving five minutes later.

"We hear your wife's time has come," Mrs Jones said excitedly. "We're all here to help."

"She's in the back bedroom," Will said wearily, as he sliced a loaf of bread.

He was glad when the women had gone upstairs. After eating some food he went into the Saloon where a few men sat in silence. One had just returned from Merthyr.

"The militia are all inside Penydarren House now. There aren't any in the streets as far as I could see. My sister said that her son had gone down to Pont-y-ty-pridd to get on a barge going to Cardiff. Lots have gone there; they think the best thing to do is to get out of the place."

"Have you got any news of Huw Coleman?"

The man shook his head. "Mrs Harries, Carmel is going daft because she can't find out what's happened to her husband."

By eight o'clock the Saloon was empty save for two men drinking quietly in one corner. Trevor sat at the counter playing tiddlywinks. Jimmy sat by the kitchen fire stroking the cat.

"Would you like a lesson, Jimmy?" Will asked. It was as good a way of passing the time as any and he felt he had to do something. "How far have you got?"

"Mrs Evans was going to teach me words with a TH in them," the lad said eagerly as he went to the dresser for the quill and ink.

"Right. Let me see. 'I think that the cat is there, though the dog was there this morning'," he wrote. "How about that? Can you read it?" he asked, putting the paper in front of Jimmy.

As the boy put his finger under each word and tried to read, Will looked at the stairs and ran his fingers through his hair. No travellers turned up, for which he was grateful. After a while he put the kettle on for Trevor's supper and carved some more meat. The minutes seemed like hours. While Trevor came out for his meal Will sat in the Saloon, with his head in his hands. He returned to the kitchen suddenly when he heard a woman's voice, but it was only Mrs Jones asking for old newspapers and scissors. He checked Jimmy's letters and wrote a few more words. He was about to light the lamps when there was a noise in the yard. A second later Huw ran in through the door.

"Huw! God, you look terrible! Come by the fire. Let me get you a brandy."

Huw was unshaven and bleary-eyed. He slumped into the rocking-chair and moaned.

"I'm tired, mun."

"Where have you been?"

Huw looked at Jimmy. "Here and there. I came to get news of the family."

"Jimmy lad, I think that had better be all for tonight. It's time you went to bed anyway. Off you go," he said, as he filled the kettle and hung it over the fire.

As soon as Jimmy left, Huw asked for news of his father and Gwilym.

"Gwilym fell over a musket and hurt his foot but he's all right. Your father is well. I was there with your mother when they came home. They are worrying about you though," Will said, putting the brandy in Huw's hand. "What will happen now?"

Huw swallowed a mouthful and breathed deeply. "This is good," he said, draining the glass and looking at his brother-in-law. "Ten thousand men are on the way over from Monmouthshire," he whispered triumphantly.

"Ten thousand? But more troops will be sent now."

"We have right on our side. Besides, the road to Cefn is blocked and we routed a band of militia from Swansea; they've run back home by now, I shouldn't wonder."

"Who is we?" Will asked.

"Hundreds of us; you should see how many have joined in from

Hirwaun and Aberdare and the towns up that valley. You heard about last night, did you?" he asked with a grin.

"Yes. It must have been an incredible sight."

"We're going to do that march on Cardiff one day, but we've got to deal with these bloody troops first. I'm going back to Penydarren House now; we've got the militia penned in there."

"You can't go on without proper sleep, lad. Stay here tonight; we have plenty of spare beds."

"There's too much to be done. The others are just as tired as me. I only came for news of Gwilym and Dada and for you to tell them I'm fine."

Will rolled his eyes. "But you're too tired to think. There will be things to do tomorrow and someone will need a clear head. If you don't sleep now, you'll be no good to anyone."

Huw stared at Will and blinked.

"You're right, I suppose. I feel like sleeping for a week."

"When did you eat last?"

Huw frowned. "I dunno. Last night, was it?"

"Oh! This is ridiculous," Will said, getting up. "We've got plenty of food. I'll get you some straight away."

"Where's Eliza?" Huw asked, realising for the first time that she was absent.

"Well might you ask. She is upstairs, having the babby. She's got half-a-dozen women with her; why they need so many, I don't know. Here, eat these pickles with the ham and bread and butter. You shall have some apple-tart and cream afterwards."

Huw sat at the table and ate mechanically as Will filled the teapot.

"I'm glad of your company tonight, I can tell you, with my Eliza up there in so much pain."

They sat for a while in silence until Huw spoke suddenly. "Have you any iron bars or bits of stout wood, like? You know....anything that could come in useful to a man."

"What good would those be against muskets?"

Huw shrugged his shoulders.

"You could have some chain maybe, but....I wouldn't like to lose any hammers." Will's voice drifted away. "When you've had a night's sleep we'll look around the yard. When do you expect the Monmouthshire men? Where will you meet them?"

Huw spoke nonchalantly. "They should be here by first light; they're coming over Dowlais Top."

Will leapt to his feet, looking wildly around. "Dowlais Top? You mean there could be fighting on our doorstep tomorrow!"

Huw gazed into the distance. "This is only the beginning," he continued calmly.

Will was worried. "Are you sure you can win, lad? What if you lose? Have you thought of that?"

"My friend Danny Cheeseman is dead; Thomas Jones had his arm hacked to pieces; one man had his ear sliced clean off; they killed a boy of thirteen and an old woman who lived opposite the Castle was shot through the head. Do you want me to go on? I could tell you plenty more."

Will saw that argument was useless. They sat drinking their tea and staring into space. At one point Huw's head fell on to his chest and he woke with a start.

"Why don't you go and sleep in the guest room," Will said gently. "I'll sleep here on the settle tonight. Go on! I'll call you at five, if you like. You'll be near Dowlais Top, fit and ready to meet the men from Monmouthshire."

Huw stretched his arms out as he got up. "What a day! You will be sure to wake me up if I stay?"

Will nodded. "I think I should get Jimmy and Trevor inside for the night, too. There are five beds in the guest room."

"Good idea!" said Huw as he went up the stairs.

Will crossed the yard to the stable and called out softly: "Jimmy! Jimmy lad! Are you asleep?"

A startled Jimmy crawled to the edge of the loft.

"It's all right, but I want you and Trevor to come inside and sleep in the guest room tonight. There's going to be a meeting in the yard first thing in the morning."

Will knew he wasn't making sense, but Jimmy didn't question the situation. He nudged Trevor, who started making a lot of noise, but eventually climbed down the ladder, glaring at Will and putting his head on one side. Will smiled and patted him on the back as he pointed to the house.

"Take Trevor up and show him a bed; he'll understand then," Will told Jimmy.

After they had gone inside, Will walked to the gate. It was a soft summer night with few clouds about. He tried to imagine the men climbing through the darkness from Brynmawr, Nantyglo and Ebbw Vale, guided by the lights that lit up the skies over Dowlais Top. Then he looked at the steady orange glow of the lamps in the bedroom where Eliza was lying. He had never felt so helpless.

Will didn't know how long he had been asleep, but he heard the chimes at three o'clock. When he punched the cushion under his head before settling down again, he was vaguely aware that the animals were restless. Two minutes later, his eyes were wide open. The yard gate had been opened. He swung his legs down to the floor and sat upright; the sound of footsteps reached him as he stood up and walked to the door. He was looking back at the hearth as he lifted the latch, so that the voice that thundered in his ears made his knees buckle. An army officer, dressed in a scarlet jacket and blue pantaloons, with a low-brimmed hat on his head, was standing not a yard away. On each side of him stood soldiers with muskets at the ready.

"How many people are in this house?"

Will leant against the wall, colour draining from his face as he closed his eyes and swallowed.

"Just my family and staff and some women upstairs who are helping my wife; she is having a babby." His voice had come in short stabs as he watched the yard filling with soldiers.

"Search!" ordered the officer, stepping aside to let his men in. Before Will knew what was happening, soldiers were everywhere.

He thumped the wall with his fist when he heard women screaming; Jimmy and Huw ran down the stairs with their breeches in their hands. He put an arm out to Jimmy, who was shivering with fright.

"It's all right, Jimmy. You won't be harmed," he said quietly. "Put your breeches on."

Trevor lumbered slowly down the stairs, followed by a soldier.

"Who is left up there, Sergeant?"

"Only four women together in one room, Sir."

"Question these men, then send them to an upstairs room and put a guard on the door. Corporal, clear the largest room on this floor for a casualty station," the officer snapped before walking out to the Saloon.

"Right," said the sergeant, looking at Will. "Who are you?"

"I'm Will Evans, the landlord. This is Jimmy James, the Boots. That's Trevor, the manservant. We don't know his surname because he's deaf and dumb."

The soldier looked at Huw. "I work as an ostler at the Duke of Bridgewater Inn," he said calmly, answering questions that hadn't been asked, in order to alert Will. "I'll be leaving at daybreak to get back to work."

"No one leaves this inn. Now get upstairs! If anyone causes trouble he will be shot."

The officer returned as they were going up. "This inn is commandeered," he said to Will quietly. "You will be recompensed for any damage and costs. In the meantime, I hold you responsible for the good behaviour of all civilians under this roof, Sir," he added politely.

As the door shut behind them in the guest room, Huw threw himself on one of the beds and cursed.

Will sighed. "Jimmy lad, lie down and try and get some sleep. I think we should all do the same," he said as he put a finger on the edge of the curtain and held it back an inch.

A group of officers were talking in a corner of the yard, one of them swinging an arm as if deploying men over a wide area.

He turned to Huw. "Come and look. Those are not Highlanders or Glamorgan militia. Could they be the Swansea militia?" He stood aside for Huw to look out.

"They came back. Aw! I shouldn't have stayed here. I'll never get away now."

"That's a fact and you'll have to get used to it," Will said, as he sat

74

wearily on one of the beds. "We have all got to try and sleep; tomorrow could be a lot worse."

Whether the others slept or not Will didn't know, but he found it impossible. When the cockerel started crowing, he crept to the window again. The rim of the sky was reeking red and gold, seeping into an aquamarine glow which faded into the darkness on either side. Militia were lined up in three rows, each man holding a musket pointing at Dowlais Top.

He tip-toed to the door and lifted the latch, surprised to find no one outside. He went downstairs where two officers were drinking tea.

"May I get some breakfast?" he asked.

"Yes, but take it upstairs."

"Are we allowed out for a pee?"

"One at a time, for your own safety."

Will looked around when he went to the yard. Not only were troops facing Dowlais Top, but a cordon faced Merthyr in the other direction. All were motionless and alert. Soldiers standing guard around the inn followed him with their eyes as he went to the outside larder for food before returning to the kitchen.

"The animals will need feeding later," he told the officers as he sliced a loaf of bread. "The women will want to go out, too."

One of the officers sighed. "You may do anything within reason, Mr Evans. It's a difficult situation for all of us."

A piercing scream from Eliza was followed soon afterwards by the wailing of a baby.

"God be praised!"

The officers grinned. "Go and see your wife."

Will ran upstairs two steps at a time and knocked gently on the bedroom door. It opened slightly to allow his mother to put her nose round.

"She's a little girl," Mrs Evans said proudly. "Now go away, boy, you can't come in for a while yet, but bring us some hot water."

Will and the others spent an anxious morning. When the midwife and her attendants came downstairs, they were escorted out through the front door. Huw fed the animals, moving slowly, taking in as much as possible. The only persons who were relaxed and happy were Eliza and her daughter. When Will was finally allowed in to see them, he paused on the threshold of the bedroom feeling overwhelmed, until a smile from his wife brought him to his senses.

"Come and see her, Will *bach*. She's beautiful! Look, isn't she lovely?"

Will looked at his daughter in amazement. He thought she resembled an angry lobster, but her tiny flailing fists touched his heart.

"Who do you think she looks like?" Eliza asked.

Will stood speechless.

"Aw! Go on! She's just like you!"

"Like me? Are you sure?"

She rocked the baby in her arms. "Well, Miss Bethan Coleman Evans, say 'Hello' to your father."

Will knelt on the floor. "Eliza! Thank God you are both alive. I've been so worried."

"We have a beautiful daughter, Will. I'm so happy."

Eliza let her head fall back against the pillow. "I could sleep for a week, but I just want to hold her and look at her. Do you know, my mind was wandering all over the place during the night. Once I even imagined that soldiers were in the room, would you credit it! How have you been managing downstairs? Are there any travellers?"

Will cleared his throat. "Yes, quite a few, but everything is under control."

"Look at her little fingernails. And those eyelashes. She's going to grow into a beauty."

A week later Huw Coleman disembarked from a ship that had taken him from Newport. It was a misty morning in Liverpool, where he stood dejectedly on the quayside staring at the seagulls that swooped and squawked above the docks, smelling the unfamiliar tang of seaweed, already feeling alien in a foreign land. In his pocket he had money that Eliza had given him to pay for a ticket that would take him across the Atlantic to another life, which he didn't want, and the letter she had written for him to send back before he sailed. The fact that his fate was better than that of his friends who had been arrested and languished in prison was little comfort.

A few hours later he approached the gangplank of a ship bound for Boston, feeling no excitement or apprehension about the voyage. Suddenly he was startled by voices shouting.

"Huw Coleman! Hello, boyo! Where have you been? What took you so long?"

Half-a-dozen Cyfarthfa men were waving and grinning from the top deck of the vessel. Huw blinked furiously to clear his eyes as he ran up to join them.

Chapter 10

"There it is, in the hollow, the hostelry that they told us about this morning," cried the taller of the two men, as they paused on the brow of the mountain.

"I'm glad to see it; we have walked enough for one day," his companion said. "I'm ready for a tankard of ale."

The travellers made their way down through the dust and clinkers towards the lime-washed inn at Cwm Rhyd-y-Bedd, stopping by the small stream which was blackened by coal dust, its eddies choked with potato peelings and other matter which didn't encourage close inspection.

"This is a God-forsaken place, Edwin," said one of them as he looked at the septic sky.

"To be sure! Although we had been warned, it's an odious sight."

"What an ugly scene! What a stench! I wouldn't have believed it unless I had seen it with my own eyes. So much for the Iron Capital of Great Britain!"

The tall one held a handkerchief to his nose. "Let's not tarry in this impure air."

They picked their way carefully across the stream and walked into the courtyard where straggling geraniums lingered in the half-barrels by the front door. The tall man stooped as he entered.

"Good day to you, gentlemen!" Eliza said cheerfully, as the clock struck the hour.

"Good day to you, Ma'am! Have you some good Welsh ale for thirsty travellers?"

"Indeed we have. Have you travelled far?"

"We left an inn at Abergavenny at sunrise and would welcome a night's lodgings."

They were shown upstairs by Jimmy, who cleaned their boots and brushed their top-coats. When they came back downstairs, their ale awaited them on a low table in the inglenook by the fire where Eliza was putting on more logs.

"Can you tell us the meaning of the name of this district, Ma'am?"

Eliza smiled. "Cwm means a valley, Rhyd means a ford and Bedd is a grave. They say that Ifor Bach is buried near here, though none can say where. He was a Welsh chieftain, although he was a tiny little man. He lived at Morlais Castle and he stormed Cardiff Castle once. That's all I know, but my husband could tell you more, no doubt."

The men listened intently. "I'll wager the ground was covered with trees in Ifor's day," said the shorter of the two, wanting to hear more.

"Maybe, but I've not known it any different. Did you know that the railway line from Moscow to St Petersburg is being made right here in Dowlais?" she asked.

"Yes, indeed. We came to see the greatest iron works in the world. We have been told that at night the place is like Dante's Inferno."

Eliza didn't know what they were talking about. "Will you be wanting supper, gentlemen? We can offer fowl with Glamorgan sausages or steaming potatoes and afterwards we have trifle and cream and Caerphilly cheese, if you wish."

"Glamorgan sausages? Are they special?"

"Indeed! They are made with leeks, potatoes and breadcrumbs bound with eggs. I can recommend them."

"They sound capital, Ma'am. We look forward to our supper."

The Saloon was crowded. Will, Trevor and Jimmy had their hands full trying to keep pace with the thirst of the miners and colliers, who jostled for attention. Some were singing noisily in one corner; others were arguing, their voices raised in excitement, as everyone awaited the arrival of Dr William Price, who was going to address a meeting of local Chartists.

"Two suppers!" Eliza called out when she returned to the kitchen. "We must hurry. Does the fowl need basting, Mother? Mary, get the dishes ready on a tray. Bethan, clear your things from the table."

Eliza had learned how to organise the family in a hurry, sending them off in all directions while she did half-a-dozen things at once, using both hands and a foot, if need be.

In the eight years that had passed since Bethan was born, Merthyr had continued to grow. Thirty thousand people now lived cheek-by-jowl, without any drains. It was small wonder that cholera arrived three years after Huw left, claiming the lives of fifteen hundred, including two sons that Will and Eliza had had, as well as one of Eluned's babies.

The shadow of a gallows still haunted the country, reminding people of an innocent bystander who had been hanged in Cardiff following the rising. Mention of the name Dic Penderyn was enough to make Eliza's heart beat faster, moved by anger and pity; Huw had been far more involved and certainly just as guilty as those who had been deported. As if to ensure that no one forgot the retribution meeted out, a barracks now overlooked Merthyr higher up the mountain, facing Dowlais Top.

People had become used to the sight of soldiers in the town and twenty-year-old Myfanwy was walking out with one of them. She had been promoted to the post of assistant nursery maid in Dowlais House which was presided over by Josiah Guest's new wife, not much older than Myfanwy herself. Lady Charlotte, an earl's daughter, took an interest not only in the iron works and the locality but in the language and culture of Wales, her adopted country.

Mair visited the hostelry as often as she could, regarding it as her home after her parents died. She hopped from job to job as a domestic servant while flitting from suitor to suitor. The latest news Eliza had was that she was being courted by the son of Williams, the pipe-maker in Merthyr.

Mary was a serious little girl with long red-brown hair tied behind her ears with ribbon. Her half-sister Bethan, an irresponsible flibbertygibbet, was the prettier and could sing like a lark. The two didn't always get on well, but arguments and scenes could generally be settled by Jimmy, now a lanky youth of eighteen whom both girls liked. He knew every aspect of the hostelry and earned a weekly wage, enabling Will to lead a more leisurely, indulgent life.

While Eliza and her mother-in-law busied themselves that wet September evening, hardly able to hear each other speaking above the uproar in the Saloon, Gwilym appeared in the kitchen doorway, his fingers pressed against his ears and his face contorted in amazement at the din. Old Mrs Evans grinned at him, rolling her eyes as she did so.

"Good evening, Mrs Evans, Ma'am," he shouted, taking his cap off and shaking it outside before advancing to the hearth.

"Hello, Gwilym. How are your parents?" the old lady asked as she filled the kettle.

"Very well, thank you," he answered, bending towards her. "They've had another letter from Huw," he said, handing it to Eliza who took it eagerly.

"Read it out loud!" he shouted. "It came two days ago and we've been waiting till now to hear what it says."

"He's had a son at last! Aw! There's lovely for him. They are going to call him Alwyn. Here Mary, you read it out for everybody while I get on with things."

Huw had married a Swedish girl whose family had settled in Connecticut previously. They had four daughters. He used to dictate his letter to his wife, Karin, who added family gossip. The last letter had described their wooden house not far from the place where Huw worked for a clockmaker of Welsh descent. He admitted that going to America was the best thing he ever did and kept urging Gwilym to go out and join him.

Mary stood in the middle of the room, raising her voice and reading slowly. When she hesitated, Eliza prompted her as she bent over the fire to make gravy, but before the letter had ended William Price arrived in the yard, descending from a small carriage drawn by four goats. He towered in the doorway as he removed his soaking wet fox-skin hat and shook it carelessly over the kitchen floor.

"Good evening all! How are you this long time?" he boomed.

The girls liked him, being mesmerised by his strange white tunic and light-green scalloped trousers, excited by the effect his visits had on all around him.

Gwilym bowed. "Good evening, Doctor. It's good of you to honour us with your presence. The men are looking forward to hearing what you have to say."

"Well, I can't stay long because I am joining the Guests for dinner and have to be there by a quarter to eight. I can speak for about ten minutes or so. Have they all arrived?"

"Yes. The Meeting Room is full."

Mrs Evans took the doctor's headgear and hung it on the hook behind the door. "You will have a glass of parsnip wine before you go, Doctor?"

"With pleasure, Ma'am."

"Doctor, you are in a hurry I know," Eliza said. "But can I ask you about two matters? I've finished that inflammation ointment that I bought from you, can I buy some more, if you please?"

"Certainly, but I'm afraid I have none on me tonight. I can send you some."

Eliza took her purse from a drawer in the dresser. "Half-a-crown, is it?"

"Correct, Ma'am. What was the other matter?"

"Well, you remember the young commercial traveller from Bristol who had those nasty boils when he was staying here - you put ointment on them and left the bill with him."

"Ah! Yes. His neck was most inflamed, I seem to recall. He improved shortly I hope."

"Yes, he did and was grateful, but he thought that you must have made some mistake when writing your account - it says the charge was five shillings and he assumed that you meant to write one shilling - that's what he gave me when he left. The bill is here," Eliza said, as she put it on the table.

Dr Price took a deep breath and looked at his fingernails before speaking. He picked the bill up and perused it disdainfully.

Will's mother put the parsnip wine in front of him. "Thank you kindly," he said, as his expression softened. He took the glass and swallowed it in one gulp. "I did make a mistake; the patient was quite right to draw it to my attention. Have you a quill and ink? I shall amend it straight away."

Eliza hadn't seen him look so angry before. He sat down at the table and waited in silence as she brought a small tray from the dresser with the ink, sand and quill, and placed it in front of him. After a moment's consideration he took up the quill and altered the bill.

Gwilym appeared in the doorway. "We are all ready, Doctor Price. You are expected now."

"I shall be there without delay," the doctor said, looking up at Eliza sternly. "When will the gentleman be returning?"

"He should be here next week. Shall I give you the correct money now, Doctor?"

"No, no. I can wait. Goodbye, children. Thank you, dear," he said to

Mary, as she handed him his hat. "Good night, Ma'am. Your wine was excellent," he said to old Mrs Evans with a bow. "Good night, Mrs Evans," he murmured to Eliza as he followed Gwilym out.

"Aw! Thank goodness! I thought I had offended him," Eliza said, picking up the bill. "No! Never!" she gasped, as she stared at it.

"What's the matter?" her mother-in-law asked.

"He's made it more expensive! Instead of five shillings he's put ten shillings!"

"Ten shillings for putting ointment on a few boils?"

"Look at it. I remember him saying that he made this stuff himself and that it was expensive but this is too much. Aw! I'm vexed with him for this. The poor young man will be most upset." She snatched a rag to open the oven door. "I heard that William Price could be the very Devil on occasions, but this is the first time I've experienced it myself."

Dr Price didn't return to the kitchen after the meeting, but left through the Commercial Room, startling the travellers who were standing outside looking at the fulminating sky.

"What an extraordinary man!" whispered the tall traveller.

"What an extraordinary place!" his companion said. "We shall have a lot to relate when we get home."

They watched in silence as the doctor drove his goat-cart around the corner and meandered up the hill towards Dowlais House.

Gwilym had been exhilarated by the meeting, reminding Eliza of Huw's enthusiasm at the same age. "We're going to draw up a petition to hand to the Prime Minister! We want as many signatures as we can get. Will you sign, Eliza? Will and Jimmy have."

"I doubt it. What would I be putting my name to?" she answered absently.

"To say you support the Charter, of course."

"Aw! That! I have signed to say that we don't want one of those Workhouses built here, but I don't see what the Charter has got to do with me."

"Come on, the Charter affects us all. We want the vote for everyone over the age of twenty-one and Members of Parliament to be paid. Now you got to agree that is a good thing."

Eliza grinned. "You mean I could have a vote?"

"Don't be daft, Eliza," her brother said.

"Gwilym *bach*, I remember Huw risking his life so that Merthyr could have a Member of Parliament who would solve all our problems. What has happened? We have a barracks and soldiers in the town. What has the Member of Parliament achieved? Nothing. The only time he has opened his mouth in Westminster has been to ask the Speaker if the windows could be opened."

"But don't you see, that's why we want Members of Parliament to be paid, so that an ordinary working man can be elected. Aw! Mrs Evans, you will sign, won't you?" Gwilym pleaded, putting the large piece of paper on the table in front of her.

"I'm not so sure, young man. We don't want any more trouble in these parts. Look what happened to Lewis Lewis - his poor mother tells me he's boiling in the sun in Queensland, living on mutton and dampers. It takes a year to get a letter from him."

"But this is different! This movement is going on all over the country, not just here in Merthyr and no one is going to fight anybody."

Mrs Evans narrowed her eyes. "To my way of thinking we don't need to write our names on anything now that we have a Queen in charge of us. She will do for Great Britain what Lady Charlotte does round here."

"What can Queen Victoria do for Dowlais? She doesn't know anything about the place!"

"Just you wait. Lady Charlotte will have told her about us, I'll wager. The Queen is godmother to young Ifor Guest, you know."

Gwilym wondered what it was about women that made them so stupid and stubborn. He went to the Saloon after a few minutes to ask Will if he would persuade the women to sign.

"Eliza and my mother are forceful women, with minds of their own lad," Will said with a rueful smile. "In any case, I don't want to upset Eliza just now, she is in a delicate state of health again."

"I see. When....er....when?" Gwilym asked, looking embarrassed.

"Next March. It's worrying for all of us, you never know what the outcome will be; when this happens Eliza is reminded of the others that died when they were babbies. Suppose you leave the page here. I'll see how many names I can get for you. Everyone I meet is for the Charter."

"Good idea! Do you think you could sell some blue ribbons as well, like the one I am wearing?"

"Leave me a boxful. I'll try, you may be sure of that. How was Dr Price?"

"Tremendous. He's the leader of the Newbridge branch now. He's travelling far and wide to stir up support. He said that Lady Charlotte was behind the workers and she's trying to persuade her husband to see the righteousness of their cause."

"I wish it well, so long as there is no violence like the last time," Will said, giving his brother-in-law a meaningful stare.

"Aw! Here comes Trevor. Let's get him to sign," Gwilym said eagerly, tapping the paper and nodding his head. He picked up the quill and dipped it in the ink, which was always kept on the counter.

Trevor crossed his hands in the air and walked over to the fireplace, where he sat down.

Will grinned. "He thinks you want him to do some work and he won't lift a finger when it's his rest day," he said, smiling at Trevor and raising his eyebrows.

Trevor moved his hand slowly up and up, put a finger to his eye and pointed to the floor.

"He's climbed a mountain and looked down at a valley," Will explained. "He enjoys his long walks. Someone saw him near the lake at

Talybont last year. He likes to go to the inn at Cefn, too. Leave him alone now. He's tired and we are busy. I'll ask him tomorrow morning."

"He would enjoy the marches that we're going to make soon. Dr Price want us to go all over the place, joining up with other branches, carrying banners from town to town."

"Be careful, Gwilym," Will said. "Remember Dic Penderyn!"

The rain continued without respite for another week. North-east winds battered the tiny hostelry, sending flurries of litter across the yard; doors slammed, lumps of soot crashed down the chimneys, and the stream became a torrent, clearing one lot of debris only to replace it with more muck. Trevor insisted on going for another ramble on his rest day, returning home soaked, but quite unconcerned. He went to bed early, leaving Jimmy to put his clothes through the mangle in the out-house before giving them to Eliza to hang on the ceiling rack above the kitchen stove.

Few travellers visited the inn and the numbers of regular customers dwindled; the family welcomed the opportunity of taking life at a more leisurely pace until the weather improved. Will sat by the kitchen fire in the evenings, reading the newspaper. Trevor and Jimmy played shove-halfpenny in the Saloon while the girls enjoyed the full attention of their grandmother.

On one particular evening, Mrs Evans and Bethan started arguing about the merits of the forthcoming railway that was being built from Merthyr to Cardiff.

"I recall that three score years ago, Tom Evan ap Rhys foretold that a headless horse would be seen running down the vale of the Taff. Little did I think that I would live to see the day when his words became true!" the old lady said, with a scowl.

"Grandma! How can a horse run without a head?"

"Iron waggons with human beings are going to run at twenty miles an hour without a horse's head in sight. What do you say to that?"

Bethan looked at the ceiling. "The waggons are pulled by a steam engine on wheels."

"Where does the steam come from, pray?"

"There's a big coal fire inside the engine."

Mrs Evans was not impressed. "An open fire in a big oven - rushing along at twenty miles an hour? It will set hedges alight; cows will stampede and their milk will curdle! Horses will bolt. There will be pandemonium."

Bethan groaned. "The fire in the oven can't escape. It's there to boil water that will give off steam. Now do you understand?"

"Boiling water! Flying through the air at twenty miles an hour! If you ask me, the world is getting too big for its boots. It's time someone reminded Crawshay who laid the foundations of the world. You'll never get me to sit in a railway waggon, I'll tell you that much. The good Lord gave us legs; if he'd wanted us to move at twenty miles an hour he'd have given us wheels on our feet and we'd have steam coming out of our ears."

Mary took the argument over, speaking gently, concerned that her grandmother should understand. "They've had railway waggons for passengers for many years in England, Grandma. It's the fashionable way to travel now."

"So I've heard. And on the first journey ever made, the railway train ran over a Member of Parliament. I'll wait to hear what the deacons from Soar have to say after they have travelled to Cardiff - if they ever get back, that is."

The argument was interrupted as the door opened and Myfanwy came in.

"Myfanwy! What a surprise!" Eliza cried, lifting her hands from the pastry bowl. "Take those wet things off and come by the fire."

"I've had tea with Eluned and I thought I'd come down here to see how you were all getting on."

"Why aren't you working?"

Myfanwy shook her shawl and hung it behind the door. She had grown into a beauty, with luminous eyes and long dark eyelashes. "I don't know, but something is afoot to be sure. Last night Lady Charlotte ordered the babies' things to be packed and taken downstairs and before I knew what was happening, three nurses and all the children and another nursery maid left the house. I had to clean the place this morning and then the housekeeper said I could have two days off. I don't have to go back until Friday."

Eliza stared through the window. "That's strange. Have the children gone anywhere without Lady Charlotte before?"

"No. She takes them with her when she goes to Dorset or to their summer home in Sully, but they don't go there in the winter. Anyway, I don't care where they are - I have two days to myself."

"Well, you must stay and have some broth with us. Do they feed you well in Dowlais House?" Mrs Evans asked.

"I should have thought you would be meeting your soldier friend," Bethan said.

Myfanwy blushed. "You impudent child! Well, I won't be able to meet him for a while." She looked at Eliza. "The soldiers are confined to barracks for some reason. Isn't it a shame, when I have so little chance to get away."

Eliza frowned as she rubbed her fingers free of bits of pastry. When she had washed her hands, she left Myfanwy talking to the others and went into the Saloon, which was unusually empty.

"Will, something is going on hereabouts. Lady Charlotte has sent her children away from Dowlais and the troops are confined to barracks, so Myfanwy says. She's in the kitchen. What do you think can be happening?"

Will blinked before casting his eyes round the customers. Most were elderly, except for John Jenkins who had a club foot, and Morris

Edwards who had a bad chest. The able-bodied men were absent.

"What her ladyship is up to is hardly something to worry your head about. Why not ask Myfanwy to stay here tonight; we have no travellers and she can sleep in the guest room."

Will's calmness distracted Eliza from her morbid thoughts, and the chatter around the table at supper dispelled her anxieties. Mary and Bethan wanted to hear about the five children that Myfanwy saw every day, but she was circumspect in her replies, giving only vague answers to their questions. She declined to stay the night, however, in case Eluned might think that some misfortune had befallen her.

The family went to bed as usual, unaware that hundreds of men from surrounding towns and villages were walking through the night, heading for Risca where they would link up with columns from the North prior to marching through Newport and from there to Monmouth.

From every valley and mountain-side they streamed. And Gwilym was with them.

Chapter 11

Gwilym told his mother that he was going to a meeting in Dowlais and warned her that if the rain persisted, he would stay the night at the hostelry. He set off in high spirits, not in the least perturbed by the weather. He was jubilant when the Merthyr group joined two hundred men at Treharris. They squelched on until they arrived at Hengoed where they were due to link up with the column from Newbridge, headed by Dr Price, but there was no sign of it. Tempers began to get frayed as they hung about getting soaked to the skin.

Some thought that they should go on without delay, in case the Doctor's men had gone on ahead - they were late as it was. Others argued that a few Newbridge men would have remained behind to alert them if that were so. The result was that some stayed and some went on. By the time the vanguard reached Crosskeys three hours later, they were a cold, anxious rabble. A few more joined as they passed through various villages, but when they arrived at Risca it was clear that plans were going awry. Not only was there no sign of the Newbridge men, but the columns from Blackwood were nowhere to be seen.

As Gwilym sat in despair on the window-sill of a small cottage, rain running down his face and neck, he listened to the arguments raging around him.

"What's the point of going on now, mun? It's better to abandon the plan and find out what's gone wrong."

"And let the Newport men down?"

"If we get to Newport, there won't be much we can do on our own and we might get the Newport men in trouble. They surely won't go on without us."

Gwilym couldn't decide on the best course of action. His feet were numb and the group was dwindling before his eyes as two or three at a time scrambled back through the mud along the road they had taken. He couldn't see any good coming if he stayed, so without a word, he walked away on his own with his head low. He reached the hostelry in a sorry state at six o'clock the next morning.

"Whatever is the matter?" Eliza cried. She was kneeling in front of the kitchen grate, lighting the fire, her hair streaming down the back of the shawl she had flung over her nightgown.

Gwilym was too miserable and tired to answer. He stood in a pool of muddy water which spread slowly over the kitchen floor.

"Stay where you are. I'll get the tub for you to have a hot bath while I light the fire in the Guest Room. You can put your wet clothes in this bucket." She went to the foot of the stairs. "Will, get up and come and help Gwilym. Will, do you hear me?"

She hung the biggest of the kettles over the fire before grabbing a pile of papers and a box of matches. Once upstairs, she pulled the quilt off Will. "Get downstairs quick. We need boiling water."

Dr Price had sent word to the Newbridge men telling them that the march would have to be postponed because of the weather, adding that the other columns would be sure to see the futility of setting out in such atrocious conditions. He was worried however, knowing how many hotheads existed; his own future could be threatened this time if trouble broke out, as he had made no secret of his involvement in the workers' cause. He brooded at home, standing at a rain-swept window, listening to the howling of the wind.

Suddenly he came to life. He had to flee the country - that was the only option if he were not to face deportation. Goodness knows he had enough enemies to testify against him, whether their words were true or false. He went to find his woman, the faithful Meg, with whom he had shared his life for the previous six years. As soon as she saw his face, she realised that something ominous was about to happen.

He took her hand and led her to the settle in their kitchen. "Meg, my beloved, I could be in mortal danger if there is trouble in Newport. I would be the first person the authorities would look for. I have to leave you, dearest; I have to leave my home and my country without delay."

Meg sat quietly with her head bowed, betraying little emotion. She had always known that one day William would leave her - that had been understood from the beginning. Either of them could leave without any recrimination or ill-will, having rich memories of the years spent together, and remaining friends.

"This house and everything in it is yours until I return. I know that you will care for the children, but you mustn't feel that you have to wait for me; you know that you are as free as the air and the flowers in the field."

William stood up, still holding her hand.

She smiled sadly. "When will you be leaving?"

"Today, as soon as I can. It won't be easy because if someone has already betrayed the Chartists, troops could be searching for me already. I must be disguised, maybe as an old woman - yes, that's it. I know a tunnel under the Duke of Bridgewater inn that leads to the canal. We can get a barge to Cardiff and then find the first ship that leaves to go anywhere. You shall pretend to be my granddaughter and do all the talking, because I shall be totally deaf. Now clothes.....what can I wear?"

At dusk, a bent old lady in a mop-cap walked slowly along the foggy quayside at Cardiff, carrying a large bag. Her long hair hung down over the shawl that was draped over a black satin gown. She leaned on the arm of a young woman who held up an umbrella to protect them from the elements.

"Good evening, ladies!" cried the policeman who stood at the bottom of the gangplank leading up to a small steam ship. "What a terrible night for you to be travelling abroad."

"To be sure, officer," answered the younger of the women. "My grandmother has to board this ship to get to Spain, where her son is at death's door. Is there anyone who could help her to a cabin, Sir?"

"I shall escort her myself, Ma'am. It would be an honour."

"I'm afraid the lady cannot converse with you, because she's totally deaf, but I'm sure she would be grateful for your help."

Meg waited anxiously while William was helped up on to the deck. It was a ludicrous way to end the years of loving and laughing that she had treasured, and to part in such frightening circumstances was beyond bearing, but she stood waiting calmly until the policeman reappeared on the deck. The women that William singled out for his affections were not made of ordinary clay.

"Your grandmother has a most comfortable cabin; you needn't be anxious on her behalf."

"Thank you kindly, Sir," Meg said with a curtsy, before turning her back and walking slowly away.

When the ship arrived at Milford Haven, en route for Cherbourg, Dr Price disembarked for a few hours, calling for half a pint of ale at a coaching inn where he left some letters and a small parcel, after which he walked cheerfully back to the ship and stood on deck to watch the lights of Wales receding in the darkness. A few weeks later, he found a small apartment in Paris and formed an attachment with an attractive young widow who was not without means of her own, remaining happily with her for the next seven years, forgetting the Charter, the ironmasters, the druids and his debts.

The Newport men had waited for hours for the others, but only a handful appeared to join them. It was not until nine o'clock in the morning that they approached the centre of the town and headed for the Westgate Inn where a detachment of militia waited for the order to fire. Gwilym was asleep in the Guest Room in Cwm Rhyd-y-Bedd when twenty-two Chartists died and hundreds were arrested.

"Lady Charlotte knew about the march - she must have," Eliza said, when the news reached them. "That's why she sent the children away. Perhaps she feared there would be an attack on Dowlais House; I remember my mother telling me that the house was besieged once, long ago when I was a child. The soldiers weren't only in the barracks, some were billeted in the stables of Dowlais House, so Myfanwy has learnt. How did Lady Charlotte know? Who told her?"

She was talking to Gwilym in the parlour at the hostelry.

"I wouldn't be surprised if Dr Price was the culprit," he said bitterly. "He promised to lead us and then he let us down. He said we would be helping future generations, but when it came to a fight, he wasn't there. He doesn't care if others suffer as long as he's safe."

"Your Charter is right and I believe what is right will win in the end, whatever happens. You mustn't lose heart, Gwilym. I'll sign your petition," she said, clutching at any straw in an attempt to console her young brother.

"What good will that do now?"

"Will tells me that they've got nearly ten thousand signatures here in Merthyr. Josiah Guest can't ignore that. You mustn't give up, especially now. You owe it to the men who were killed."

The sound of a cart entering the yard caught her attention and she went to investigate. The carter was jumping down as she opened the door.

"Good afternoon to you, Ma'am. If you are Mrs Will Evans, I have a parcel for you."

"A parcel?"

"From Milford Haven."

"Where's that?" Eliza asked.

"In West Wales. Do you know anyone there?"

Eliza shook her head. "Thank you, anyway."

She returned to the kitchen where, by this time, most of the family had gathered. They watched in silence as she cut the string with a knife and undid the wrapping paper. Inside was a tin box containing a dark, glutinous substance. Eliza looked at Will and raised her eyebrows.

"There's a piece of paper here!" Gwilym pointed out. "What does it say?"

"There's something on the other side!" Jimmy cried.

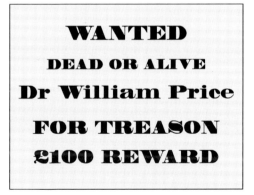

WANTED

DEAD OR ALIVE

Dr William Price

FOR TREASON

£100 REWARD

INFLAMMATION OINTMENT
1/4lb. Rosin 1/4lb. Beeswax
1 pint Olive Oil
2oz. Burgundy Pitch (enclosed)
Stir together over a gentle heat.
When cool apply to inflamed limbs.
Wm. Price

"I paid Dr Price for more ointment; he said he would send me some," Eliza whispered. She put her nose near the contents of the tin. "This must be the Burgundy pitch."

"Posted from West Wales," Gwilym snapped. "So that's where he is."

"Not for long. Milford Haven is a port. Price will have left the country by now," Will said, shaking his head. "The audacity of the man! He must have torn this notice from some door."

Eliza shook her head. "He's an extraordinary man. One minute kind and the next......."

"Treacherous," Gwilym shouted. "I'm glad he's left Wales and I hope he never comes back."

Will's mother sighed. "Well, at least that young traveller from Bristol won't have to pay ten shillings for having his boils cured. I'm pleased about that."

Eliza made the first batch of ointment as soon as she had bought the rest of the ingredients. The kitchen became infused with a sweet, cloying aroma, a mixture of spices and pine-needles. Mrs Evans was disappointed that no one needed treatment, but Eliza felt that the texture was not the same as the ointment that Dr Price had used, so she made some more a few weeks later.

"I wish I knew how long I should let it simmer; the last lot was too thin."

It was a cold February afternoon. The water in the barrels had been frozen that morning and the sky had a portentous lilac hue.

"Why did the Queen choose to get married at this time of year?" asked Mrs Evans. "A wedding is much nicer in the spring or summer."

"She didn't consult me, mother *fach*," Eliza murmured. "I don't suppose she minds what the weather is like really."

"Will that foreign prince be called King now?"

"I wonder."

Mrs Evans took an avid interest in the young queen. "Will she have to do what her husband tells her, do you think?"

Eliza didn't bother to reply, knowing that her mother-in-law could continue the conversation by herself, regardless of any answers. She stirred the ointment listlessly, thinking about the news Eluned had given her the previous evening.

"Dai will be out of work soon, now that they've finished the railway; he's seriously thinking of looking for a job in Cardiff. They've built docks there and they need lots of men to load the ships and the pay is good."

"Cardiff! I've never been there but they say it's a nice little place, only - 'Luned, you mean you might leave Dowlais?"

Eluned sighed. "Yes. Dai wants us to live in a town where the air is fit to breathe; the sea air will be healthy."

"Aw! This is a shock. I can't imagine not having you here, but I understand. Dai's quite right."

"Well, it won't be for a while yet; he's going there on Sunday to look for a place to live."

The sound of running feet and children's voices were heard as Eliza held the spoon over the cauldron to check the consistency of the ointment.

Mary ran in, unusually excited. "Mammy! Lady Charlotte wants another nursemaid, well not a proper one, but a girl who wants to learn to be a proper one, and she asked Mr Morris if he knew of a Christian girl who was twelve years old and industrious, sober, strong, neat and conscientious and Mr Morris asked me to ask you if he could give my name to Lady Charlotte. You will say 'yes', won't you? You wouldn't say 'no', Grandma, you would let me go, wouldn't you, and Dada will say 'yes', I am sure. Aw! Mammy! Just think of it."

Eliza dropped the spoon into the cauldron and put a hand on her stomach. "When did this happen?"

"This afternoon. Lady Charlotte was in the school last Monday asking us questions."

"What did she ask?" Mrs Evans asked eagerly.

"Aw! Just things like what presents did the Wise Men bring the baby Jesus and what was our favourite verse from the Bible. I told her the one I recited in chapel last Sunday."

"What was it?"

"You know - 'There is one greater than me who will bring beauty for ashes.' Lady Charlotte said she liked that one too."

Eliza took the cauldron off the hook and put it on one side of the stove. She wiped her hands in her apron and sat down in the rocking-chair. "Well, Dada and I will have to think about this. It will be hard work, you know. When does Lady Charlotte want the nursemaid to start?"

"Next week!"

Eliza stared at Luke Thomas's child as if she hadn't seen her for a long time. "Oooh! I'm not sure. You must give me time to think."

"Aw! Please, Mammy. Please!"

"Mary, not another word until I have talked to Dada. This needs a lot of thought."

Will came in from the yard. "What does?"

Eliza gave him a swift glance. "Mary has asked if we'll let her teacher recommend her for a job as an assistant nursemaid in Dowlais House."

"Mary? Our little Mary going out to work? Well I never. What do you think, Mary?"

"Aw! I'd like it; it would be wonderful. Myfanwy is there and she says it's good. I could come home often, it's only up the hill. I could wave from the window at you all. You'll let me, Dada, please!"

Will looked at Eliza, who avoided his eyes. "I'll talk to your mother about it later."

Mrs Evans, who had been absorbed by the drama, gave Mary a knowing wink.

"Has Trevor come back?" Will asked.

"He hasn't been in here," Eliza replied. "Bethan, it's your turn to lay the table for tea."

Will frowned.

An hour later it started to snow. By nine o'clock the air was filled with swirling flakes making it impossible to see anything outside. Will and Jimmy hung about downstairs long after the others had gone to bed. Already a good four inches or so covered the yard and still Trevor hadn't returned from his ramble.

"We could take lanterns and go to the top of the hill, calling for him," Jimmy suggested.

"He could be miles away. Maybe he is at the inn at Cefn; they will have persuaded him to stay the night," Will said, trying to be cheerful.

"But he could have fallen somewhere and be lying out there in the snow," Jimmy said.

When Will saw the stricken look on Jimmy's face he reached for a lantern. "You take this one. I'll light the small one from the Saloon."

They walked around the hostelry and up the hillside towards the Cefn road. Flares from the furnace chimneys flashed silently over the glistening snow and lit up the flakes as they fell.

"Trevor! Trevor? Are you there?" Jimmy called instinctively, before he groaned, "Aw! He won't hear! What can we do?"

"Nothing I fear," Will answered gently. "We can only hope that he'll be back when the roads are clear. He will have found shelter somewhere, you can be sure. Come on, boy. We can't do any more tonight. Would you like to sleep inside?"

"No thank you, Mr Evans. Trevor might come back and go straight to the loft. I'd rather be there."

"As you wish. Try not to worry," said Will, who was more than a little anxious himself.

Trevor didn't return the next day nor the day after. The east winds strengthened, causing banks of snow to build up around the inn. The clinkers on the hillside hissed and steamed, adding to the graphic display in the sky. Indoors, not only the family were miserable; customers talked in low voices and there was no singing.

Eliza was doubly concerned. All had been arranged for Mary to start work at Dowlais House on Monday. Mrs Evans had given her a Bible, Jimmy bought her a new comb, Eliza parted with her Paisley shawl and Will gave her a box of lace-trimmed handkerchiefs. Eliza knew that she should feel pleased that Mary was going to be doing interesting work, in a respectable house, for a considerate employer who lived within sight of the hostelry. It couldn't be more suitable, she kept telling herself, but she remembered what she had been like at the same age, so innocent, so ignorant, so vulnerable, so silly. When it came to that point, Eliza reminded herself that Mary was far more sensible and mature. It was just that....letting go of Luke Thomas's daughter was like shutting a door on part of her own life. When she told Will how she felt, he was rational and logical, which was no help at all.

By Sunday afternoon a thaw had begun to set in. Lumps of snow still lined the edges of the roads, but the slush in the middle added to the squalor and difficulties of getting about. After tea, Eliza and Mary left the hostelry where the family remained on the doorstep, waving until they were out of sight. Mary was excited but her mother couldn't hide her anxieties.

"Now remember, you are somebody. You can hold your head high. Your father was a gentleman, don't forget that. Lady Charlotte is lucky to find somebody like you."

Mary listened with embarrassment. "Mam, I'm not going to the other side of the world."

"I know, dear, but you're leaving home and that makes me sad. I can't help it."

Eliza's eyes were brimming by the time they reached the servants' entrance.

"Mam! There's no call for crying. Don't let me say goodbye like this."

Eliza blinked and snatched her handkerchief from her pocket. "You're right," she said, straightening her back. "I'm pleased that you're going to work here and very proud, too. Go on! Away with you! Come and see us as soon as you can. God bless!"

Mary gave her mother a kiss and walked through the wrought-iron gates. Eliza watched as a door at the side of the house opened and then shut behind her daughter, leaving the step empty. After a few seconds, she walked slowly back to the inn, turning round now and then to stare at the imposing mansion that Josiah Guest had built.

By the time she reached home her eyes were red and raw.

"Eliza! For mercy's sake! Don't be so daft!" Will cried. "Anyone would think we'd thrown Mary into a lion's den!"

Eliza looked at him reproachfully. "Maybe we have, for all we know," she wailed.

"Now sit down and have a sip of brandy, dear," Will's mother said. "You'll feel better then."

"Mother, men have no idea, have they! No idea at all," she sniffed.

An hour later, as Eliza was lifting the big kettle she paused suddenly and put it down, steadying herself with a hand on the mantelpiece. The others didn't seem to have noticed.

"Mother, I think it's time that Jimmy took Bethan to stay with Eluned for a few days."

Mrs Evans's jaw dropped. "But, it's too soon! Heavens!"

Eliza didn't move.

Will came to life. "Bethan, you're going to stay with Auntie 'Luned, get your shawl."

"Now? Nobody told me! Why?"

Will didn't answer the question. "I'll come with you as well; your mother and grandma want to be on their own for a while."

In two minutes the kitchen was empty.

"Aw! Another one! Mercy!" Eliza cried, putting her hands on both sides of the bannisters.

By the time Will and Jimmy returned, the baby had been born. "She's a tiny little mite, Will. Not much bigger than a snowflake. Shall we call her Eira?"

"I can't believe it! She wasn't supposed to be here until March! What a surprise!"

"One daughter leaves home and another one arrives! You must admit I'm clever."

"You are, dearest," Will said, as he kissed Eliza's forehead. "I have a present for you."

"A present?" He hadn't done that when the others were born.

Will went to his wardrobe and brought out a small silver tray which held three crystal bottles; one was filled with ink, another with sand while the third contained a wick. In a tiny niche was a stick of red sealing wax. It was indeed a pretty gift.

Eliza stared at it. "Will! Whatever has come over you? It's beautiful! That must have cost a lot."

"No more than you deserve, my love. It won't be long now before we'll be able to post a letter for a penny, so I knew you would appreciate this."

"Indeed I will!" Eliza said, trying to think which of her relatives could read or write. She looked at her husband - dear, impulsive, generous Will. Whatever would he do next, she asked herself.

Eluned brought Bethan over the following evening to see her new sister. "Eliza! How are you? Aw! Just look at her. She's lovely! What do you think of her, Bethan?"

Bethan scrutinised her sister. "She's bald."

"So were you at her age!" Eliza said. "Do you like her name?"

Bethan nodded, but became bored after a while and went downstairs.

"Eira is a lovely name," Eluned said. "She didn't waste her time getting here, did she?"

"Look what Will gave me yesterday," Eliza said, pointing to the silver inkstand. "Isn't it pretty? You never know what he will do next. Tch! I'll wager he bought it with my money."

"There's beautiful!" Eluned exclaimed.

"Yes, and useless too, not that I'd tell him that. He means well, bless him. Now, what did Dai think of Cardiff?"

"Ah! He liked the docks and could have got a job there and then, but when he went to look for somewhere to live! The streets around the docks were as bad as Merthyr. Half-a-dozen families sharing one lavatory. He said he'd rather live in an awful place where we had friends than in an awful place where we wouldn't know anybody."

"So, you are staying! I can't pretend to be sorry," Eliza said.

The sound of singing reached them. It was a sad dirge, in a minor key, beautifully harmonised. "Someone must have died," Eliza said. "I wish they wouldn't do that, I don't see what good it does."

Eluned sighed. "It makes them feel better, I suppose, and they are paying their respects in the only way they know. The harmony is beautiful."

Will was glad that Eliza was upstairs when the news came. Two men came into the Saloon early, looking solemn. "It's bad news, Mr Evans. Poor Trevor."

Will put a hand on Jimmy's shoulder. "Where is he?"

"They found him in one of the ditches round Morlais Castle. He must have stumbled in through the deep snow."

Nothing was said for a minute.

"Is he badly hurt?" Jimmy asked.

The men looked at each other before one of them shook his head.

"Would you like to go and feed the animals, Jimmy lad?" Will asked gently.

Jimmy nodded and walked away.

"Trevor and Jimmy were like brothers. Poor old Trevor. This is sad news for us. He was part of our family," Will said.

"Everybody will miss Trevor, Mr Evans. This place won't be the same without him."

Will put his head in his hands. "I know, I know."

Chapter 12

Eira survived more than one fever until she was two years of age, so that it was a cruel blow when she succumbed to small-pox shortly afterwards. They had been more worried about little Owen, who was a year younger. When Eira died, Eliza was heart-broken and Will seemed to turn in on himself. The only person who understood was Eluned, who knew what that grief was like.

"If I hadn't gone as a wet-nurse to Lady Charlotte's baby when my last one was still-born, I think I might have died," she said. "All that waiting and hoping, all that pain and then....nothing. At least, I was able to hold her little mite in my arms and suckle him. Myfanwy tells me he's a fine lad now."

"Lady Charlotte's children have all lived. Why should my child have to die?"

Eluned sighed. "Eliza *fach*, you know there are no answers to that question."

Eliza thumped her breasts. "Well, I've only got a stone inside here now! My two little boys and now my little girl. I know it happens to all of us, but ......you feel so cheated. Aw! Where is the loving God, 'Luned? Tell me!"

"You have a fine son and two daughters who need you, Eliza, and Will loved Eira too, remember. He's looking melancholy these days. He shares your grief and worries about you, no doubt."

Will was indeed going about in a dejected state of mind, which was unlike him. "What shall we eat for our Christmas dinner, Will?" Eliza asked one December morning, trying to wake him out of his lethargy.

"Oh! You decide, I really don't mind," he murmured, not lifting his eyes from the *Merthyr Guardian* which he had been holding in front of his face for the previous two hours.

Eliza threw down the cloth that she had been dusting with and shouted at him. "Now Will, I'm getting sick and tired of you moping about the place, not bothering to talk to any of us. I know it isn't easy, God knows I do, but we must try. We can help each other. Is anything worrying you, dear?"

"Oh, leave me alone; I have a lot on my mind."

"But I care about you. Are you feeling ill or in pain?"

"Please don't fret on my account. I'm concerned because that new mare has gone lame twice now. I shall have to sell it and that means a lot of money wasted."

Eliza wasn't satisfied. "That is a botheration, to be sure, but it isn't the end of the world, surely to goodness. We can get over a thing like that. We are not poor people, between us. Use some of my money, if it will help. There's no cause to make everybody miserable."

Will threw down the paper and went out to the yard, slamming the door behind him.

They had a pigeon pie on Christmas Day, followed by mince-pies. In the evening they enjoyed the plum porridge that Mrs Evans made. When they had cleared the dishes, Jimmy produced his Jew's harp and Bethan sang some songs; her voice was such that she had been chosen as a soloist in the Sunday School anniversary the previous summer.

Mary couldn't get away until Boxing Day, but Eliza kept some of the previous day's meal for her. She arrived not long after Myfanwy and Mair, and was wearing a blue ribbon that Lady Charlotte had given her that morning.

The new "Boots", who had been with the family since Trevor died, was called Charlie. He had been a door-boy in a coalmine until a law was passed forbidding children under the age of ten to work underground. His mother had died when he was born, and he had been brought up by an aunt in Georgetown. Charlie had settled in well, endearing himself with his impish sense of humour. He was a tiny scrap with copper-coloured hair and a face plastered with freckles. Jimmy had taken Trevor's place and was responsible for training Charlie, which wasn't always easy. If Charlie was feeling skittish, he would call Jimmy 'Jimmy, my lad", or 'Sir', which sometimes resulted in Jimmy rolling up the newspaper to give the impudent boy some hearty thwacks. If he felt hard done by, Charlie would unburden himself to young Owen, sitting by the perambulator and telling the baby what he thought about the trials of life. He had cried for days when Eira died.

When Eliza called for Eluned one Saturday afternoon for their weekly visit to the cemetery, she found her cousin in high spirits.

"Dai has been offered a job in Pont-y-ty-pridd! Working for a grocer," Eluned cried when Eliza walked in. "The answer lay on our very doorstep!"

"Whoa! Tell me a bit at a time!"

Eluned laughed. "You know my lodger, Mrs Griffiths - well, her cousin is taking over a grocer's shop there and wants an assistant. Dai has been to see the shop and likes the people. They want him to start next week. I can hardly believe it."

"It's much better than Cardiff - I can come and see you on the train and get back the same day and Will seems to be going there every Saturday lately, so we won't lose touch. I'm happy for you, 'Luned."

"It's a beautiful place, Dai says. All green and quiet and it has a wide, clean river."

"I know," Eliza said wistfully. "I shall always remember walking along the bridle-path on our honeymoon. I wish Will would take me with him sometimes when he goes to market but he says we can't both be away from the hostelry at the same time."

"Dai told me that he saw him there last Saturday but they didn't have a chance to talk."

"Not last Saturday - Will went to Abergavenny market. It must have been the week before. He is looking for another mare; I hope he finds one today, perhaps it will cheer him up. He's been in a dismal turn of mind all this week again. I wish I could help him, but he seems to have stopped confiding in me these days."

"I thought he wasn't himself when I was with you on Tuesday," Eluned said quietly.

"He's concerned about the money he's lost on the mare, but that's silly. We've got enough between the two of us. I'm the one who worries when he spends too much or is over-generous. He never cares when he loses a wager on a bare-knuckle fight or in a cock-fight. I've asked his mother about him, but she just goes quiet and tells me not to worry because he will cheer up one day."

They walked slowly towards the cemetery gates, where they fell silent. The children's graves were at the top of the hill, in a far corner where there were few headstones. They paused by the small mounds of earth where Eluned's four children were buried and then Eliza went further along to a bigger plot that Will had bought and where Eliza herself wanted to be buried one day. She picked up a few weeds and sighed as she recalled the argument that she and Will had had about putting up a gravestone. He considered her morbid, which had vexed her; she had decided to pay for the stone herself but even that made him angry.

When she made her way back along the row, Eluned stood waiting for her. "Eliza, there is something that has to be said. I cannot hold my tongue any longer, but it grieves me to be the one to bring you misery."

Eliza stared at her cousin. "Whatever is wrong?"

"Dai says I should tell you before someone else does. It is so unfair that people are gossiping and you don't know," Eluned said, wringing her hands.

"'Luned! For mercy's sake, what are you talking about?"

"I know what's making your Will anxious and morose," Eluned whispered, looking away down the hill.

"Well? Tell me!"

Eluned swallowed. "He's been gambling for a long time now, at the New Inn. He was there last Saturday, Eliza, whatever he told you. He plays cards with some other men. He's probably lost a lot of money."

"Gambling? Gambling?" Eliza cried, looking helplessly around. "How can you be sure?"

"Pont-y-ty-pridd is a small place. When Dai heard he didn't believe it but he made it his business to find out. Then, he saw Will on Saturday - the inn is opposite the grocer's shop. I wish it weren't so, Eliza, but you must know."

Eliza straightened her back and took a deep breath. Her eyes darted wildly over the rows of headstones clustered round the church before she stared into the distance, seeing nothing.

"Come back home with me, Eliza; I'll make a pot of tea and you can stay awhile to get over the shock," Eluned said gently, as she put a hand on her cousin's shoulder.

Eliza walked forward, stumbling now and then, and stopping every few yards when a fresh thought struck her. "He can't afford a gravestone for our children, yet he can go gambling every week! It doesn't bear thinking about. How could he do this to me, 'Luned?"

"Perhaps I was wrong to tell you; he might have won some money back and then perhaps everything would be all right. He would be his old cheerful self again and you need never have known and been upset," she argued, trying to convince herself.

"Balderdash!" snapped Eliza with a contemptuous wave of her hand. She was beside herself with anger and her cousin's prattling, at that moment, was unbearable. She needed to be able to absorb the shock in silence.

Eluned persisted in pointing out the positive side of the situation. "Well, now that you know, you can talk to him about it, Eliza. I'm sure Will wants to tell you, but is afraid to."

Eliza groaned. "I need time to take it in; it's no good just confronting him; I must calm down." She stopped suddenly. "His mother knows; she has known all along!" she cried, as her face hardened. "How long has this been going on?" she shouted as she neared the last row of graves. "How much has he lost?" she added in a whisper, as a funeral cortége approached the entrance gates.

When they reached Ivor Street, Eluned busied herself making a pot of tea while Eliza sat by the kitchen fire staring at the poker, thankful that her cousin wasn't talking. She pondered the situation, quietly and deliberately.

"Will has been miserable for a very long time, so he has been losing money for a very long time. Yet sometimes he has been recklessly generous - do you remember the silver inkstand he gave me when Eira was born. Perhaps he was gambling as long ago as that, but then he was winning. Of course! I can see a pattern."

"Here you are," Eluned said, holding out a cup of tea. "This will make you feel better."

Eliza took a sip. "I shouldn't say this, but Will is a fool! He's not a wicked man, but he can be stupid and weak. This gambling has made the whole family miserable and we were happy! Working hard but happy!"

"Will isn't an ogre, Eliza. When things are going well he's the friendliest, most cheerful person on earth, and he has been good to you."

Eliza groaned. "I know. I mustn't forget that. This needs careful handling. He has a terrible temper when roused and these days the least thing...." her voice trailed away.

Eluned looked at the floor. "I feel bad about leaving Dowlais just now, at the very time when you are in need of a friend to talk to, but I couldn't go without telling you, could I?"

"I had forgotten about that for the moment," Eliza said, draining her cup. "In ten days' time. It will be strange without you, it will be awful, but I mustn't be selfish." She stood up and smoothed her skirt. "Life has been hard for you these last few years and now it will be better. I mustn't begrudge you that."

"It's not far away," Eluned said. "We'll see each other often and we'll talk about this misery in the future as if it were only a little thing. We've both been through worse, haven't we?"

Eliza nodded. "I'm glad it was you who told me, anyway. I'll say nothing at home. I need a night's rest and then, in the morning, we shall see," She sighed. "We shall see."

On the threshold of the inn she paused and drew herself up, pulling her shawl tightly around her before walking into the kitchen.

"Hello! You're late today. The kettle has been boiling its head off," her mother-in-law said.

"I don't need tea, Mother, thank you. I went back to Eluned's and had some there. I'll go up and put my hat and shawl away."

In her bedroom, she threw the shawl on the bed and opened the top drawer of the dresser, feeling underneath a layer of handkerchiefs for the black velvet box that Luke Thomas had given her. Her heart beat faster as she opened it. It was empty. She swung round and sat on the bed, realising that things couldn't be much worse. After a few minutes, she replaced the box, put her hat in the big coffer and hung the shawl on the hook behind the door. As she walked downstairs, she told herself to act as if nothing had happened, and no one seemed to notice that she was subdued for the rest of the evening.

She went through her duties in a trance and, as it happened, the inn was busy, for which she was grateful. Will, she realised, was acting in the same way and she asked herself why she had let the situation persist for so long. As usual, she went to bed after the dishes had been washed and put away. Will spent another half an hour or so, checking the animals and waiting for Jimmy to stack the chairs. When she heard his heavy footsteps on the stairs she turned on her side and pretended to be asleep.

The next morning, after completing the shopping, Eliza made her way to Messrs Wilkins' bank where she considered the situation ruefully as she sat waiting to be ushered into the manager's office. Will, like every other bridegroom, had promised to endow her with all his worldly goods - the bride had no need to give any such undertaking.

The manager, Mr Owen, looked distinctly uncomfortable as he rose to greet her in his office. It was a long time since Eliza had seen him, having no need to collect her income in person. Will looked after their finances, giving her cash weekly and not stinting with it. It was a practice she had accepted since they were first married, when all that she possessed became his anyway.

"The weather has turned much colder, hasn't it, Mrs Evans?" Mr Owen said nervously.

"It has indeed, Mr Owen," Eliza said, facing him haughtily. "I want to know the state of my finances, if you please. When I last enquired I had accrued £210; this sum will have risen considerably by now, and I wish to draw £100."

"Er, um, well.....," replied Mr Owen, clearing his throat. "It's like this, you see...."

Eliza felt sorry for him; it was hardly his fault. "Let me help you. There's no money left in my account, is there? Of course, I should refer to it as *our* account and my husband has had some heavy expenses lately."

Mr Owen lifted his eyes momentarily from the heavy oak table that separated them. "This isn't easy for me, Mrs Evans. I can't discuss your husband's financial affairs with you, I'm afraid, but yes, you are correct when you surmise that the account is not in credit, er....um....in fact the payments from the Court estate will be taken by the bank for the next few months."

Eliza sat back and nodded. "To repay debts."

Mr Owen lifted his hands in the air.

"There is just one more question - regarding the money bequeathed to me for life, how long will it be before I will be able to obtain some for myself?"

Mr Owen perused the leather-bound tome in front of him, chewing his lips as he made the calculation. "Six months," he said, almost inaudibly.

As Eliza walked home, she worked out that Will owed the bank £180. Her anger grew with each step, so that by the time she reached the inn she had decided on a monumental confrontation. Such a plan had occurred to her as she had tried to sleep the previous night, but she had rejected it, being fearful of Will's wrath. Now, whipped up by fury, she saw it as a justifiable response to his reckless behaviour, but she had to wait until the next afternoon.

It was easy for her to leave the hostelry after breakfast the following morning - she visited her parents every fourth Saturday, spending most of the day with them, doing their washing and cleaning and returning home by dusk. It didn't surprise her when Will announced that he was going to Pont-y-ty-pridd, in fact, she was relieved to hear it.

"Will you be able to manage, Mother?" she asked. "There's broth for your dinner and I'll roast a chicken when I get back."

"We've always managed before, haven't we?" her mother-in-law answered. "Go you!"

Will set off an hour or so later. Bethan opened the gate for him as usual and watched him cantering up the hill. He made his way along the familiar route, acknowledging the greetings of acquaintances only briefly as he passed. Surely, he told himself, his luck must change today - this run of bad luck couldn't go on for ever. He had experienced bad fortune before, but it hadn't lasted this long. He had tried doubling and trebling the stakes in an attempt to recoup his losses - he checked himself - Eliza's losses, that was the galling part; he had had to dig deep into her money and if that was not won back, she might find out.

The three men gathered in the small gaming room behind the parlour at the New Inn, exchanging cursory nods. They talked little on some occasions and this was one of them. Will's losses had become embarrassing and tension was running high. Bowen Morris, Newbridge, Griffiths of Taff's Well and Will had known each other since they were youths; they had aged and prospered together. Outside the inn, none of them referred to their Saturday afternoon pastime. Had Griffiths's wife protested, she would have received a cuff over the ear for her pains. Morris, a wealthy widower, lived with his ailing daughter who had a limp. His comfort came from the turn of the cards and his lovely Lucy - a nubile wench from Newcastle who plied her trade from a dingy house in Ynysybwl. "Juicy Lucy" was the lodestar in his otherwise dreary existence.

Will shuffled the cards with trembling hands. Morris cut in silence. Their eyes followed the fall of each card on the green baize. Griffiths passed his tongue swiftly around his lips before wiping the palms of his hands with a crimson handkerchief. Two hours later, Will was five pounds poorer and fear gripped his entrails. Griffiths was dealing another round and it was Will's turn to mop his brow. Bowen Morris was the first to look up; Griffiths paused and followed his gaze. Will was the last to realise that the door had opened quietly and that someone else was in the room. Eliza was standing quietly on the threshold. How long she had been there they didn't know but, as soon as her eyes met Will's, she turned and left without a word, not attempting to close the door behind her.

Eliza had timed her exit to coincide with the departure of the Merthyr train. As she sat in the Ladies' Waiting Room she clasped her hands tightly to control her trembling. The look of fear and shame that she saw in Will's eyes for that fleeting second had moved her more than she realised; pity replaced her anger until she told herself that there had been no other way. She knew that Will would resent her action and she resolved to accept that for a while but then they would talk quietly and sensibly and sort out the problem. Her first priority was to retrieve the brooch from the pawnbroker. There would be no question of self-righteousness on her part, nor would she reproach Will. What she had done this afternoon was punishment enough.

It was getting dark when she reached the hostelry. "Is everything all right here?" she asked cheerfully as she bent down to coo at Owen.

"It has been quite quiet really," said Mrs Evans. "How did you find your parents?"

"Just about the same," Eliza replied, as she picked Owen up and held him over her head. "Mam's legs are still bad, but they have some good lodgers there now and they are very helpful."

By seven o'clock they were busy. Eliza began to worry about Will, who was always back in time to take charge of the Saloon, especially on a Saturday evening. He wouldn't expect Jimmy to cope with the rowdy crowd at his age. She was irritated by Bethan's chattering and general unhelpfulness and her mother-in-law's anxious questions.

"Where can he be? Do you think he has met with some misfortune? What can have happened?"

It crossed Eliza's mind that Will might not come back at all - but, surely not. Mrs Evans stood at the door, peering through the rain that had begun to fall.

"Maybe the horse has gone lame again," Eliza ventured with a wry smile. "Still, there will be plenty of people about to help him. Don't worry, Mother, he'll be here soon and in a foul turn of mind, no doubt. Come back in, you are getting wet."

A moment later Eliza thought she heard a horse's hooves clattering beyond the gate. She picked up the lantern from the dresser and, grabbing her shawl, went out. "Stay inside, Mother; it's too wet," she called as she shut the door behind her.

Will was trying to steady the mare, although he didn't seem too steady himself. He was cursing and swaying, going round and round in circles as he did so. When Eliza walked towards him, she realised that he was very, very drunk - something unusual for him.

"Ah, ha!" he cried. "My devoted little wife, ish it?" He gave a loud belch. "Ish it indeed she who vowed to love, honour and obey me?" He scowled. "You shamed me this afternoon, Eliza. In front of good friends. That was unforgivable. Do you hear me?"

His voice rose to a frenzy. "Whoa there, you idiot!" he shouted as the mare reared. He slipped in the saddle, but managed to right himself before breaking into a fit of giggling.

"Tee hee! Whoops!" he cried, as the mare turned full circle. "When I get down, my pious little woman, I am going to teach you a lesson that you will never forget. I'll show you who is master in this house."

Another belch turned to a groan. Eliza seemed to be made of stone.

"Open the gate, you despicable creature! Perhaps you would rather see me jump over it."

He tittered again and took the mare backwards, as if he intended to do just that.

Eliza came to her senses and undid the iron loop. Her back was turned as Will fell. She heard the heavy thud, followed by silence, broken only by the sound of the mare's hooves as it ran round the yard. Will was lying motionless, his face whiter than she had ever seen it; raindrops fell unheeded on to his lifeless eyes.

"Will! Will?" Eliza whispered in horror as she sank to the ground.
She cupped her hands over her mouth before sinking back onto her heels. "Oh, God! What have I done?"

Chapter 13

The hostelry remained closed the next day, much to the consternation of those who patronised it. A large notice was nailed to the front door:

WE REGRET THAT OWING TO BEREAVEMENT
THIS ESTABLISHMENT WILL BE CLOSED
UNTIL NEXT WEEK

Eliza sat in her widow's weeds by the kitchen fire, oblivious of her surroundings most of the time. She hardly spoke, feeling that an unseen hand was gripping her throat, making it difficult to talk; when she had to reply to anyone, her voice was hoarse, little above a whisper. Will's eldest brother, Geraint, had taken old Mrs Evans back to his home and whatever needed doing around the inn was carried out by Eluned. Jimmy and Charlie looked after the animals and the only time that Eliza stirred herself into action was when baby Owen cried.

Will was buried in his father's grave in St. John's churchyard in Cardiff. Bethan went to school as usual and Eluned sat with Eliza after sending Charlie out to do the shopping; he was carrying a note with him asking for payment to be made from Mrs Eliza Evans's account.

Eluned tried to make Eliza aware of all the things that needed to be done, of decisions that had to be made. "Titus will be coming back here with Will's brother. They will have a meal in Cardiff, no doubt, but we need to think about some supper for them. They are staying the night in the guest room."

Eliza nodded and sighed, showing no sign of concern, her eyes returning to look at the flames flickering in the hearth. After a while she turned to her cousin. "I killed him," she said in a hoarse whisper. "It was my fault."

"What are you talking about! You are still too shocked to think sensibly. Let me make you a cup of tea," Eluned said. "You know, if only you had a good cry you'd feel better."

Eliza's gaze returned to the hearth while she ruminated in a world of her own. Nothing that Eluned could do or say made any difference until the men arrived at about four o'clock. Geraint, Titus and a red-eyed Jimmy came in through the yard. It was when Titus took her hands in his that her tears began to flow.

Geraint looked at Eluned. "We want to have a talk with Eliza. Perhaps we could sit in the parlour. Could you bring a glass of warm brandy for her. Jimmy, would you bring us a large pot of tea."

The two men sat on either side of Eliza, who made an effort to stifle her sobs. "I am sorry to embarrass you by crying like this," she said, wiping her nose. "I remember you were there, Titus, when.......when I wore these clothes before. You were so good to me then and here you are again."

He smiled. "Geraint and I are both here to help you now. You have much to be grateful to Geraint for. He has been working hard for you in the past three days, you know."

Eliza looked at her brother-in-law quizzically.

Geraint cleared his throat, not knowing how to begin. "Eliza, I am aware, and...you, I expect, know that...er, Will, God rest his soul, lived life to the full; he was endowed with many wonderful qualities; he would throw himself life and soul into everything he did, sometimes not always wisely, I fear. Did you know that he was in somewhat of a financial quandary of late?"

He looked at Eliza keenly, not wanting to cast a slur on her husband, but anxious to assure her of the steps he had taken to put matters right.

Eliza realised the difficulty he was in. "It's all right, Geraint," she said in a whisper, "I know that Will had been gambling; he had lost a lot of money." She looked at Titus. "He owed the bank £180."

Geraint was relieved. "Well, that situation no longer exists, my dear. My brothers and I have paid that much and more into your account. Should you receive any demands for outstanding debts, please refer them to me. You have no more to worry about on that score."

"That is indeed kind," Eliza said quietly.

"Just one more matter to clear up," Geraint said as he pulled Will's gold watch and Eliza's brooch from his pocket. "A week ago Will came to me to borrow money. He told me the whole sorry story and gave me his pawn tickets."

At that point, Jimmy appeared, carrying a large tray which Titus took from him.

"Thank you, Jimmy. Here, Eliza, drink some some of this brandy. It will ease your throat."

When Jimmy had left, Titus took up the conversation while Geraint poured the tea. "That reminds me of the next matter that we need to discuss - Jimmy."

Eliza frowned. "Jimmy?"

"Yes. A vacancy has occurred for an ostler at the coaching inn at Brecon. I thought it would be a good opening for the lad. Between us we could provide excellent references. Do you think he would like that?"

Eliza sat upright. "I don't understand. What do you mean? Why should he want to leave?"

The men exchanged glances. For a moment neither of them spoke.

"The new tenants have two grown sons; one of them will be employed as the barman," Geraint said softly.

Eliza opened her mouth as if to speak, but said nothing as her eyes darted round the room. She put the glass of brandy on the table as she looked at Titus with her head slightly to one side.

"My dear Eliza, you couldn't possibly run this hostelry on your own just with a twenty-year-old boy. Had you not thought about that?" he said as gently as he could.

"I haven't thought about the future at all, only about Will's death. I hadn't realised.........I didn't think.....you mean.....the hostelry is no longer my home?"

"You have your other home, remember," Titus said. "Eluned is leaving on Friday to join her husband, which will work out admirably for you. I suggest that Jimmy stays on for a week to show the new people how things work. Charlie will stay on as the "Boots", of course."

Eliza swallowed. "I've lost my husband and his dear mother, I didn't realise that I would lose my home as well - and now, Jimmy. My whole world has gone!"

The men were at a loss. Geraint wrung his hands. They were thankful when Eluned came in to say that the attorney had arrived.

Mr Middleton was a short, plump, middle-aged man with receding hair. He bowed when Geraint introduced him. "Mrs Evans, it is indeed sad that we meet under such grievous circumstances. May I offer you my sincere condolences, Ma'am."

Eliza inclined her head. Eluned intervened. "Shall I bring the gentlemen some sherry, Eliza?"

"That would be capital," Titus said, drawing up another chair.

Mr Middleton cleared his throat. "This is a very simple will; it consists of only one sentence - 'I bequeath all that I own to my dear wife, Eliza,'" he said, withdrawing a vellum document from his case and handing it to her.

Eliza took it and looked at Titus, who anticipated the question she was about to ask. "Will rented the hostelry and the furniture," he said, "but the animals, whatever is in stock, personal possessions and all that you brought with you when you came here would be included in the bequest. We can make an inventory and offer whatever you wish to the next tenants. I would ensure that you received a fair price."

Eliza sat impassively as Eluned returned with a tray containing the sherry which she offered to the men. Before leaving, she bent down to whisper in her cousin's ear.

"The chicken is doing nicely, and I have prepared all the vegetables. Do you think we could eat at about half-past-six?"

Eluned was determined that Eliza should have to make as many decisions as possible, or at least concur with her suggestions.

That evening, after they had eaten, Titus and Geraint listed the items in each room, after which Eliza went to bed early, leaving the men to talk to Jimmy. She bent over Owen's cot, tucking the quilt around him before turning quickly away and moving to the window. Lady Charlotte was with the children at her home in Dorset and the nursery wing at the top of Dowlais House was in darkness. Curtains were drawn in the room where Mary slept when she was there. Eliza's eyes wandered up above the crimson and yellow smoke billowing out from the chimneys of the ironworks. It was a clear, cold night. One star seemed brighter than the others, pulsating and throbbing high in the darkness.

"Dearest Will, forgive me!" she gulped.

Three days later, she left the hostelry. Jimmy and Charlie loaded her furniture onto the cart. The new landlord, Mr Davies, carried out several boxes and a hamper of food. Bethan held the ginger cat tightly in her arms, determined that it wouldn't be left behind. After the usual pleasantries, Mrs Davies waved goodbye and Jimmy led the horse forward. Charlie and Bethan sat with the luggage while a grim-faced Eliza walked behind, pushing baby Owen in the perambulator.

The neighbours were standing on their doorsteps just as they had been sixteen years previously, but this time it was impossible to avoid them. Mrs Richards actually walked down the road to meet the forlorn procession.

"Aw! Mrs Evans *fach*, widowed again! There's sad. Come back here to live! I was telling Mrs Morgan, as soon as I heard the news, that you would be back. Now, how can we help?" she cried, as she craned her neck to see what was in the cart.

Eliza's heart sank. "It's all right, the children will help me. We'll manage."

"I'll go and see if the fire is still alight," Mrs Richards announced firmly, opening the door to Number 7 and disappearing inside.

Jimmy fixed a nose-bag on the horse before helping Bethan down.

"I'll take the sampler," Eliza said. "Charlie, will you bring the boxes in?"

"You need to get some sticks to catch this fire before it goes out. Where did your cousin keep them?" Mrs Richards called from the kitchen.

Eliza didn't reply. She was standing in the parlour, which seemed much smaller than she remembered, staring at the nail above the mantleshelf where the sampler used to hang.

Charlie interrupted her thoughts. "Where shall we put the boxes, Mrs Evans?"

"Aw! That one can come in here, the hamper goes into the kitchen. I'd like the trunk upstairs in the front bedroom."

She went back outside. "You remember where the clock stands, Jimmy, don't you? The desk goes in the parlour."

Mrs Richards shouted. "I've found the sticks; your cousin was pretty untidy here, wasn't she? The back kitchen is in a proper muddle."

Eliza took a deep breath.

"Now what can I do next?" Mrs Richards asked, her eyes sparkling with excitement. "The hamper! I can unpack this. That'll help, won't it?"

"Really, I can manage. There's no need for you to do anything."

Mrs Richards flung the lid of the hamper open and started putting the contents out on the table. "If we can't help our fellow-mortals in time of need it would be a sorry world. We must do the Christian thing at all times, that's what I say."

Eliza walked to the foot of the stairs. "Bethan, what are you doing?" she called.

"I'm unpacking things in my bedroom, with the cat."

Eliza went to the door. "Jimmy, after you have brought everything in, would you and Charlie go to the well for water. The trolley is in the back yard. I'm going upstairs to unpack."

Mrs Richards was left alone in the kitchen where she remained for the rest of the morning, oblivious of the fact that Eliza rarely answered any of her questions. Bethan sat in a corner, holding the cat and glaring at the intrusive neighbour.

When the water cans were brought back nothing remained for Jimmy and Charlie to do. As they turned to go back to the hostelry, Charlie was pouting.

Eliza put an arm round his shoulder. "Come on, Charlie. We'll see you tomorrow in Sunday School and you can run down here, if Mrs Davies agrees, whenever you are free. Cheer up! Let me see you smile."

"Charlie, we've got a lot to do in the hostelry, remember?" Jimmy told him.

"Off you go!" Eliza said curtly, not sure that she could control herself much longer.

Jimmy smiled. "I'll come back next Friday to stay the night before going to Brecon."

"Yes, we can have a long talk then," Eliza said, reaching for her handkerchief.

She watched them walk away but turned suddenly and went inside to the kitchen, where she laid two places for a meal.

"What are you going to have to eat?" Mrs Richards enquired.

"Cold mutton."

"And that lovely tart afterwards."

"Yes. Wash your hands, Bethan."

"Aw! Well, then," Mrs Richards said, getting up from her chair, "I suppose I'd better be going - unless you'd like me to stay and keep you company."

"I'll see you again, another time. Thank you for your help, Mrs Richards."

When she and Bethan were left alone, Eliza closed her eyes and put her fists to her forehead.

In the afternoon, Eliza took Bethan and the baby to the cobbler to ask him to call at the hostelry to measure Jimmy for a new pair of boots. No sooner had they returned than Mrs Richards walked in.

"Hello! How are you now, my dear? I thought I ought to call because I know what it's like to be a widow all on your own. Took me a good two years to get over my Daniel, it did. Terrible it was. You have been out; I called earlier, but the door was locked. Did you go far?"

Eliza shook her head and went to the back kitchen.

"You'll find it strange after the hostelry, won't you? What are you going to do with yourself? You won't have to take in lodgers with your wealth."

Eliza gritted her teeth.

"I'm glad your cousin's lodgers have gone; that Mrs Griffiths wasn't an easy woman to get on with. Thought she was better than the rest of us. Aw! She was a rude woman and ugly! Have you ever seen an uglier woman? These Welsh cakes look nice; did you make them?"

"Help yourself," Eliza said.

"Aw! There's lovely. I'll bring you some of my egg custard tomorrow. Tell me, who laid out your husband? Was it Mrs Jones Caersalem? I laid out my Daniel myself. Scrubbed him all over and dressed him in his Sunday clothes and put his best hat on, so he would be fit to meet his Maker. Mrs Morgan said she'd never seen a smarter corpse."

Eliza and Bethan endured Mrs Richards for another hour, glad when she had to leave to get a meal for her lodgers. Eliza found things to do, but the house seemed small and dreary. She kept reminding herself how much she had liked it once, how grateful she should be that she had a home at all. Many other widows found themselves in the workhouse.

After putting Owen to bed, she and Bethan sat down to supper in silence. It wasn't long before tears rolled down Bethan's cheeks.

"I don't like it here. I want Jimmy and Charlie and Dada and grandma," she sobbed.

"I know, dear. So do I, but we must try hard to live by ourselves. Shall we ask your friend Helen Brown to come to tea after Sunday School tomorrow?"

Bethan let out a wail and ran from the room.

It was a long, desperate week. Eliza did all she could to pick up the threads of her former life. She cooked and baked, went to singing practice, the prayer meeting and the cemetery. Gwilym called one evening and rather than lifting the gloom only added to it.

"I've been to the hostelry. It's quite different somehow. The new people are all right but......" He didn't finish the sentence.

"Did you see Jimmy and Charlie?"

"Yes. Jimmy was busy so I didn't have a chance to talk. Charlie just shrugged his shoulders when I asked him how he was."

Eliza sighed.

"It was strange to have to walk in through the front door instead of going into the kitchen." He sniffed. "How are you feeling?"

Eliza pursed her lips. "Just like Charlie."

The week wore on and not a day passed without Mrs Richards walking in, repeating the same stories each time. When she was not gossiping about the neighbours, she was running down her daughters-in-law.

"How are you feeling today, Mrs Evans *fach*? Aw! Don't tell me, I know what it's like. What you need is good friends to help you. When you have company, you can forget for a while. I don't mind how much time I spend here, because I know it will take your mind off other things."

Whenever Eliza went out, Mrs Richards would appear on her doorstep to ask where she was going. If Mrs Richards happened to miss her on the way out, she would come in and ask where she had been and what took so long. By the end of the first week, Eliza was at screaming point.

Jimmy arrived shortly after breakfast on Friday, carrying his new boots in one hand and a sack containing the rest of his belongings in the other.

"I must find you a suitcase. You can't arrive in Brecon like this. Do the boots fit?" Eliza asked. "Bethan didn't want to go to school today because she knew you were coming."

"The boots are grand. Thank you very much, Mrs Evans."

"How did you leave poor Charlie?"

Jimmy shook his head. "He cried. He asked me to find him a place in the coaching inn at Brecon."

"When I saw him in Sunday School, he asked me if I needed a butler. Indeed, I've been giving it serious thought these last few days!"

They had scarcely sat down in the kitchen when Mrs Richards's voice reached their ears.

"Do you know how many times ....Aw! Good morning!"

"Mrs Richards, this is Jimmy James; Jimmy, this is Mrs Richards," Eliza said, as Jimmy stood up.

"How do you do, Ma'am," he said with a bow.

"Er....well enough," answered Mrs Richards, looking at Eliza for an explanation of the young man's presence.

"Jimmy and I have only got one day together before he leaves Dowlais," Eliza said. "I might not see him again for a long time. We have a lot to talk about."

"Aw! I see. Shall I make a pot of tea?" she said, advancing towards the hearth.

"That won't be necessary, thank you all the same. We've had breakfast."

Eliza waited for her neighbour's next impulse. Jimmy stood awkwardly, looking at his feet.

"That's a nice pair of boots, young man. Cost a pretty penny, I dare say."

Jimmy blushed. Eliza glared at her neighbour who had seated herself at the table. "There's no need for me to keep you, Mrs Richards. I want to be alone with Jimmy," she said quietly, wondering how rude she had to be to get through to her neighbour.

"Don't take any notice of me, I won't be in your way."

"Jimmy, let's go upstairs. I've got some things to give you," Eliza said, walking out of the room.

Eliza was surprised when Mrs Richards didn't follow them. They heard her leave sometime later as they looked through Will's wardrobe for clothes that might fit Jimmy.

That evening when Bethan came home from school, Jimmy went with her to the well and on the way back bought sprats for their supper which, mercifully, Mrs Richards didn't interrupt. When they had finished Eliza spoke quietly.

"Jimmy, there is something else that I want you to have - Will's gold watch. He'd be glad to think it was yours now."

"Mr Evans's watch? His gold watch?"

Eliza took it from a drawer in the dresser and handed it to him. He held it in both hands, looking at it and then looking back to Eliza.

"I can hardly believe it. Aw! You are uncommon kind to me, Mrs Evans."

"You have always been uncommon kind to us, Jimmy. I'm happy to think that the watch belongs to you now. It's by way of saying 'Thank you' for your friendship and the help you have given us over the years."

"What are you giving me?" Bethan asked

"You're not leaving home yet."

"Can I have your brooch when I leave?"

"That was given to me by Mary's father, it should go to her. Let me see - would you like the silver inkstand, it's valuable."

Bethan scowled. "I want the brooch."

"How about the figurine in the parlour?"

"I want the brooch."

"The grandfather clock with the chimes would look nice in the home that you will have one day."

"I want the brooch."

"Well, this isn't the sort of conversation I want in this house when it's Jimmy's last night at home. If you are not careful, my girl, you'll get nothing."

The next morning, Eliza was up early to dress Owen and get Jimmy a hearty breakfast.

"I wonder what you'll think of the Brecon Beacons - all covered with grass and heather; not a building in sight. No smoke, no dirt, nothing but fresh air and the empty sky," she said when she put a plate of bacon, sausages and eggs in front of him.

"I'm excited about the journey."

"Do you know the thing I found most peculiar in Brecon?" she asked, looking into space.

Jimmy shook his head.

"The silence. It's so quiet. You hear footsteps. It will take a while to get used to that."

Jimmy pulled the watch out of his pocket. "We ought to leave in ten minutes."

"I'll see to Owen; we'll do the washing-up when we come back.

Bethan, are you nearly ready?"

Even the trudge down to Merthyr was an adventure for Jimmy, who hadn't ever left Dowlais. Every now and then he put his suitcase down and looked at his watch.

"Now, I've put writing-paper and stamps in your case. I'll be upset if you don't write to us. The spelling doesn't matter so long as I hear from you," Eliza said.

"I will, Mrs Evans. Of course, I will."

"When Titus meets you, ask him which chapel he goes to, so you can go to the same one and keep in touch with him."

"I can see the coaching inn!" Jimmy cried, as he took out his watch again. "We're in good time."

"When you have dinner with Titus and his family today, remember not to talk with your mouth full and whatever else, don't blow your nose until the meal is over," Eliza told him, realising that it was a bit late to remind him about manners, which had caused her such torment in Brecon.

They walked into the yard where the coach was waiting. Ostlers were checking the harness and adjusting straps; baggage was being hoisted on to the roof and made secure. Passengers stood in small groups talking quietly.

"I'll get the ticket. Look after Owen, Bethan," Eliza said.

Five minutes later Jimmy clambered up behind the driver while Eliza pushed the pram round to stand near him.

"This is much better than being inside!" Jimmy whispered, his eyes like saucers. "I'll be able to see everything!"

"Hold on tight when it goes downhill," Eliza warned him. "The horses can slip." She suddenly wanted to say so much, but all that came out was: "Hold your head up, Jimmy Twice. I'm proud of you! You are somebody!"

He blushed and hung his head as the coach wobbled and then moved forward. Eliza and Bethan walked slowly after it and watched it disappear in the distance, not saying anything as they made their way to the Coleman household, where Eliza's mother was sitting by the fire.

"Hello, Mam. I've brought you some cold ham and a few other things."

"That'll be a help. So, how are you both?" Mrs Coleman asked, staring at Eliza's widow's weeds. "How's the baby?"

"He's all right, so far. Where's Dada?"

"Gone to the well. The boy that usually helps us died of the smallpox two days ago, and we haven't found another one yet. So, you're a widow again. The Lord giveth and the Lord taketh away. What are you going to do with yourself now, then?"

Eliza sat down. "I don't know. Can Bethan do any shopping for you?"

"Yes. Did you bring any bread with you?"

"I haven't baked any since.....since I left the inn. I haven't got a stick oven, and any bread that I made at home wouldn't taste like the bread

I used to make," Eliza said in a low voice.

"In that case we'll have to buy some for our dinner. I need other things too, sugar, eggs and a bag of salt. We are getting low on tea, too. Can you remember all that, Bethan fach? My purse is in the right-hand drawer, over by there."

"That's all right, Mam. I've got the money," Eliza said, getting up and feeling in the pram for a sovereign. "Bring all the change back, Bethan."

They were left alone.

"How is Mary and Myfanwy?"

"They've gone with Lady Charlotte to Dorset. They won't be back for six weeks. There's just the three of us now that Jimmy has left," Eliza said.

"Well, you've got your health and strength. Not like me. You've got money as well. There's lots who would change places with you. Look at poor old Mrs Basset, Tabernacle - lost her husband on the Tuesday, a son on Wednesday, and now they do say that she've got the smallpox as well."

Eliza was glad to have the washing to do; it was better than conversation with her mother.

It was after sunset when they returned to Ivor Street. The fire had gone out and the kitchen was cold and gloomy. That night in bed, Eliza let her tears flow unhindered as she remembered how Will used to put his arms around her. With him there, she felt she could cope with anything life threw at her; without him there was no solace, only endurance and loneliness. The thought appalled her.

In Soar chapel the next morning, the Minister didn't spare his congregation. He spoke about Samaria, describing it as a blot on the fair land of Canaan.

"It was a hot-bed of paganism, heresy and everything that was putrid, vile and rotten." The faithful listened with no great interest until he thumped his fist on the maroon velvet cushion in front of him, sending up a cloud of dust as he leaned towards them with a confidential air. "My friends, Dowlais is the Samaria of Wales!" He paused, gazing out of the window at length. "Samaria was the Dowlais of Canaan!" he shouted triumphantly, looking around to assess the effect of his oratory.

Eliza smiled as he went on to talk about that other city of pure gold, whose streets were like translucent glass and whose walls were made of jasper.

"It has wide rivers of clear water and green hills; its trees grow tall and its children prosper."

He went into the hwyl, his falsetto voice rising higher and higher as he sang, rather than said, the words. By the time he came back down to earth, Eliza's eyes were fixed on a crack in the floorboards, her mind far away as she reflected on the imagery he conjured up.

Another city, but here on earth. Why not? Far away from the stench, the crowds, the open sewers, the disease, the painful memories and Mrs

Richards. She could rent a house with a stick oven in the back yard and a front room with big windows where she could sell bread and rice pudding; Bethan could help behind the counter. They would see people all day long. She stumbled to her feet when she realised that the congregation was singing the final hymn and walked home afterwards with a spring in her step.

"Bethan, how would you like it if we moved away and lived in a nice town somewhere else? I could open a shop and sell cakes and bread and you could help," Eliza said when they sat down to a meal.

Bethan's jaw dropped. "You mean we could move away from Dowlais? Aw! Mam! That would be wonderful!"

Eliza smiled. "A small town with a wide clean river and green mountains with trees all round."

"Where's there a place like that?"

"Pontypridd, where Auntie Eluned lives."

"Pontypridd - that's a funny name. What's it mean?"

"Nothing any more but people haven't time to say its proper name. Pont-y-ty-pridd is too long to say when you are in a hurry."

"When can we go?"

"Not for a while. I'll have to write lots of letters and go to stay with Eluned. It won't be easy to find a house with a stick oven. But we can think about it, can't we? Don't tell anyone yet though. Let's keep it secret. Mary must be the first to know and she won't be back till the end of July."

It took much longer than Eliza thought. It was not for another two years that they were able to leave Ivor Street for the last time, and it was too late for little Owen who died of cholera. Eliza endured her grief alone this time, although early on the day of the funeral, Titus came to the house and later stood by her side as the small coffin was lowered into the ground.

Before leaving Dowlais she saw to it that a headstone was placed over the grave:

HERE LIE THE CHILDREN

of

WILL and ELIZA EVANS

of this parish

THOMAS

IVOR

EIRA

OWEN

Suffer little children to

come unto me

In 1843, when Eliza was thirty-three years old, she left Ivor Street for the last time, heading for a bread shop in Taff Street, Pontypridd. Eluned had sent news that the previous owner was getting too old to carry on the business and it took only a few weeks to arrange for Eliza to take it over.

"Are you sure you are doing the right thing, Mrs Evans?" Mrs Richards asked. "What if you don't find good neighbours like you got here?

"I'll have to take that risk, Mrs Richards."

"Well, I should think twice about it, if I was you. You could be making a big mistake."

On a bright spring morning in April Eliza shut the door of Number 7 and put an arm round Bethan's shoulder. "Come on, we are off on a great adventure. I wonder what the future has in store for us."

Chapter 14

At four o'clock on week-day mornings Eliza was in the yard behind her shop, lighting the stick oven so that fresh loaves could be on the shelves behind the counter by seven o'clock. While Bethan dealt with customers, Eliza baked cakes and rice puddings. At nine o'clock every evening, except Saturdays, having put the dough for the next day in large earthenware vats on either side of the hearth, she went to bed, tired but contented.

Bethan was paid three shillings a week and all found for selling the wares. At fifteen, her voice was attracting attention in the town; she could not only sing like an angel but was developing into a beauty. Eliza felt that those two gifts bestowed on such a fragile character didn't bode well. Will Evans's daughter had inherited her father's good looks and could charm the birds from the trees when she felt so inclined.

Mary wrote regularly to her mother. She was enjoying life in Lady Charlotte's various households. Eliza had no qualms about her, although her heart missed a beat when she received a letter in which her seventeen-year-old mentioned 'a most handsome sea captain' whom she had met recently while wheeling the children in St. James's Park. The venue and lack of introduction caused Eliza some concern.

Eluned called frequently. She and Dai had settled happily in Pontypridd and now had two small sons, both of whom seemed to be thriving. Their house was crammed full of lodgers, mostly colliers, as trade had picked up and the navies of the world were being supplied with Welsh steam coal. In spite of a busy life, Eluned found time to serve customers in the bread shop each Monday morning, while Bethan did the washing.

Myfanwy had married the soldier whom she met in Dowlais, and followed him around his postings in England. Whenever he was moved to another town, she used to return to Wales with her small daughter until he could find somewhere for them to live. On those occasions, she stayed with Eliza, an arrangement which pleased everybody.

Myfanwy's sister, Mair, once came for six weeks, after her husband was crushed to death by an underground truck. Her marriage hadn't been a happy one - she had often been beaten black and blue, so she didn't grieve when fate set her free. Eliza offered her free board and lodging in return for acting as a general factotum while she looked for work as a housekeeper in the district.

Eliza was well organised as far as the household was concerned. Every morning, two young boys used to collect the cart before going to the well for water. They were given a halfpenny each when they returned, as well as a slice of rice pudding which served as their mid-day meal at school. In the evenings, a different pair arrived, and were rewarded with a halfpenny and a Welsh cake each.

Sammy the lamplighter often called for a cup of tea before most people were out of bed in the mornings and kept Eliza up to date with news and gossip, so that, even if she hardly ever left the shop, she was well aware of events in the town. In the evenings, Sammy became the Pied Piper of Pontypridd, as a cluster of children followed him, watching while he wielded the long pole with a hook at the end of it. They waited while he opened a window in each lamp to pull a small ring and envelope them in light.

One morning in 1846 Sammy arrived in a state of great excitement. "You will never guess who's come back!" he cried.

Eliza grinned as she poured him a cup of tea. "Well now, let me think," she said, sitting at the table opposite him. "Come back? Who has gone away?" she asked herself.

"Someone everybody knows!" Sammy said.

Eliza blinked. "You don't mean....never!" she said as her eyes widened. "Not Dr Price!"

"The very same! I thought you'd enjoy having that bit of news. He's got a house in Llantrisant."

"Well, well, well!"

"Already he's up to his old tricks. I saw Stephen Mortimer last night; he is in a devil of a state, I can tell you."

"Why?"

"Stephen saw Dr Price standing outside his furniture shop last Tuesday, looking at a chest of drawers, so he goes up to him and says: 'That's a fine piece of furniture, Doctor.' Price agrees with him. 'Shall I have it sent up to your house?' Stephen asks. 'If you wish,' says Price. So, Stephen takes it up there. When he saw Dr Price on Thursday he says 'Will you be keeping that chest of drawers, Doctor?' 'Yes,' says Price, 'Will you pay me now or shall I send you the bill?' asks poor Stephen. 'Pay you? Pay you?' snarls Price. 'I didn't ask to buy it, you gave it to me and you are not having it back.'"

Eliza closed her eyes. "Poor Mr. Mortimer. He will never get his money, I fear."

"Silly old fool! He might have known. When my brother made some gates for the doctor, going back some years I am now, he took them to the doctor's house and knocked on the front door. 'Well, put the gates up, man!' the doctor ordered. 'After you have paid for them,' my brother said. That's the only way to deal with Price."

Eliza smiled. "Well, life is certainly going to be colourful from now on."

"I must go," Sammy said. "Thanks for the tea. I'll let you know if I hear anything else."

That same morning, Eliza had just put some yeast cakes in the oven when Bethan appeared at the kitchen door, giggling and gesticulating as she pointed to the shop. Eliza wiped her hands and went to see for herself. Her face lit up when she saw Dr Price in his green breeches, white tunic and fox-skin cap.

"I haven't much time, Ma'am," he said impatiently. "I need to know if and when you can provide me with two small loaves, fresh from the oven. They needn't be bigger than the human ear."

"Dr Price!" she cried. "It's nice to see you again. Have you come back for good?"

He frowned. "When will you be able to bake these loaves?"

"You don't recognise me - Eliza Evans from Cwm Rhyd-y-Bedd. You sent me the recipe for your ointment when you left Wales."

Dr Price gaped at her. "Upon my soul!" he exclaimed. "What are you doing here?"

"This is my home now. I left the hostelry when my husband died. It seems a long time ago."

"Let me see.......you had brothers who supported the Charter, I seem to recall. How are they?"

"Both living happily in America - in Connecticut. Tell me, Doctor, I finished the Burgundy Pitch you gave me a long time ago and I've tried everywhere to buy some more but no apothecary seems to stock it in these parts."

Dr Price smiled smugly. "I am not surprised. It can only be found in Alsace, as far as I am aware. I brought a large amount back with me. Now, you will appreciate that I no longer supply Burgundy Pitch, nor the recipe, but I can sell you some of the ointment that I have made up, if you wish," he said, raising his bushy eyebrows.

"I'd be delighted. It's a wonderful cure for inflammation."

"The fresh bread?" he said in a soft voice.

"Yes, of course. I'll have your loaves here at eight o'clock tomorrow morning."

"No bigger than a human ear, remember."

"I'll see to it," Eliza said.

"Good day to you, Mrs Evans," the doctor said, lifting his fox-skin cap an inch.

Bethan had listened behind the kitchen door. "Well! What do you think of that! What about the £100 reward, dead or alive?" she asked.

"Aw! I should think that will be forgotten now. That was years ago. Everything has changed since the bad old days. I really can't get over it, though."

"I'm glad he's back. I always liked him," Bethan said.

"People either love him or hate him, it seems. I wouldn't like to be his enemy, of that I am sure!"

Bethan gave Dr Price his loaves the following morning, charging him a penny. He deposited a small tin of ointment on the counter and told her it would cost a shilling. Upon receiving the money he wrapped the bread in a linen handkerchief and left.

Sammy enlightened Eliza a few days later. "I've got some news but you're not going to believe it."

"Try telling me."

"You know Miss Siân Lewis?" he said.

Eliza frowned.

"You know - they call her Miss *Siân Can Punt* because she wears that dress coverered with silk patches to hide her gold sovereigns."

"Oh! Yes. I haven't seen the dress but Bethan has told me about it. What about her?"

"Well, she's got a parlour maid called Rhoda who has worked there for years, came as an orphan from the workhouse when she was eight. Bit slow like, Rhoda is, but she's nice-natured."

"Get on with it, Sammy."

"Well, Rhoda has been complaining for weeks about sensations in her head, like worms wriggling about. The doctors couldn't find any cause for such an odd affliction and so couldn't cure it. Poor old Rhoda began running around the house with her head in her hands, screaming at the top of her voice. When Miss Siân heard that Dr Price had come back, she consulted him and he came to the house with two fresh loaves which he held against Rhoda's ears. After about five minutes, he took the bread away and showed it to Miss Siân, who fainted on the spot. The bread was swarming with black beetles."

"I believe you," Eliza said. "I sold the doctor the loaves."

"Well, he'll be back for more. The treatment has to be repeated once a week for a month."

Bethan told her mother more about Rhoda. "She's in the same class as me in Sunday School. You should hear some of the stories about Miss Siân! Do you know, Rhoda is only allowed to put one teaspoonful of tea leaves a week in the teapot? On Sunday mornings. Every other day she must put a pinchful more but the pot is only emptied on Saturday night!"

"Ych-y-fi! It must taste awful! No wonder she's so rich if she's that mean."

When Bethan was seventeen years old she sang Mozart's Hallelujah at the chapel anniversary and even Eliza was impressed. She had heard Bethan practising at home with no accompaniment but, with the sweet tones of the organ, the effect in the high-roofed building was magnificent. The two of them became separated outside the chapel, and it was some time before Eliza was free to return to the bread shop. As she came round the corner of Taff Street, she saw Bethan leaning against the door, talking to a tall youth. Only as she neared them did they become aware of her. The youth removed his cap and bowed.

"Good day to you, Ma'am. I have taken the liberty of escorting your daughter home."

"Good day. I think you should introduce us, Bethan," Eliza said, not taking her eyes off the man, who was vaguely familiar. Then she realised that she had seen him more than once in the shop.

"This is David Williams, Mam. He's a......what is it you do?" Bethan asked him

"I'm an anchor smith, in the chain works," he said, looking at Eliza.

"Thank you for walking Bethan home," Eliza said, feeling at a loss. It seemed extraordinary that her daughters were old enough to attract the attentions of the opposite sex and she didn't know how to cope with the situation. With a nod of her head she opened the door to the shop and held it ajar for Bethan to follow.

"How did you enjoy Hallelujah?" Bethan asked once they were inside.

"It was wonderful. I hadn't realised it was such a nice melody until I heard it sung with the organ. Now, tell me about that young man."

"Him? He comes in here most days to collect bread on his way home from work - you must have seen him. He's from Pumpsaint in Carmarthenshire where his father is the village blacksmith. He taught himself to read and write and he's very learned, always buying pamphlets and borrowing books. I don't know half the things he talks about. He ought to be a teacher by my reckoning, not working with his hands. He helped to make the anchor for the S.S. Great Britain. That's all I know about him," said Bethan, who didn't seem very concerned. "I'm hungry after that singing. Let's eat."

Eliza called to see Eluned on her way home from Sunday School. It was a still, dank day but mild. Bethan had gone out to tea with friends, so it was a chance for the cousins to have a chat on their own.

"Where's Dai?" Eliza asked.

"Taken the boys to see Iorwerth Morgan's racing pigeons. They'll be back before long I expect. The kettle has boiled, come by the fire."

"Bethan sang Mozart's Hallelujah this morning and it was really beautiful, I must say. People were all over her afterwards."

"There's nice."

"When I got home I found her with a young man on the doorstep. That's both the girls starting to attract followers. I had another letter from Mary about her sea-captain yesterday; he's sailing down to South America soon and she's upset because it will be six months before she sees him again. It makes me feel old for the first time."

Eluned smiled. "You'll be a grandmother in no time at this rate. Here, have a Welsh cake."

"Grandchildren will be lovely - it's the sons-in-law that I wonder about."

"Get away with you. Worrying about problems before they happen. Let me tell you about a real vexation. It's Mair; she didn't like the housekeeping job in Treforest. I don't know what you are going to think but I must tell you. She was here on Friday and....." Eluned pulled a handkerchief from her sleeve and wiped her nose.

"What is it, 'Luned, fach ?"

Eluned wrung her hands. "She said she'd left that place and gone somewhere else, in Llantrisant."

"Who do we know there, except Dr Price?"

Eluned shook her head. "I don't know how she could do such a thing. She's the silliest girl! I get so aggravated with her. What are people going to think?"

"She isn't working for Dr Price, for heaven's sake! What's the problem?"

"That's just it - she is!"

"I don't believe it!" Eliza said, putting her cup down.

"She told me as bold as brass. She says he's the kindest man she's ever known. I haven't told Dai yet. He'll be shocked."

"But.....who else is in the house?" Eliza asked in a whisper. "What happened to the woman he used to live with?"

"She married. Went to live down Swansea way. No one else is in the house," Eluned answered, averting her eyes.

A long silence followed. Eliza started to speak more than once, but then sat back and looked at the floor.

"I know what you're thinking, Eliza, and it's what I've been thinking as well. Our Mair, my little sister, is his woman now and she knows no shame. What will people say? The children will get teased, the lodgers will talk and I don't see how I can go to chapel again. She doesn't seem to realise what she is doing to the family. She doesn't care. She says she's happier than she's ever been! How could she do this?" Eluned said, with mounting anger.

Eliza sighed. "Aw! 'Luned, I understand how you feel but let's think about this calmly. It's difficult to take in, but we mustn't be hasty." She sat back in her chair and looked into the distance. "You know, I've always liked Mair. She's had a rotten life so far. If this is what she wants, if she has thought about it seriously, she may well be happy - for some years at least. We mustn't begrudge her that, 'Luned. We must stand by her. What good would it do if we had nothing more to do with her?"

Eluned didn't move.

Eliza continued. "I don't approve of this situation, not at all, but what friends will she have if we desert her? I think that people are more important than principles. Come on, you were kind to me when I was in trouble and people were talking about me; we must be kind to Mair."

Eluned stared at the floor.

Eliza waited for her response but none came. "'Luned, she will always be welcome in my home. I'll tell the girls that Mair and Dr Price are married; I'll think of them as married. Try doing the same!"

Eluned put her head on one side before speaking again. "Do you really think it will be all right? I've heard that William Price has been kind to the women he's lived with, and Mair could certainly find more happiness than she did with that awful husband of hers," she said tentatively.

"William Price couldn't have been kinder to me when I'd done wrong. He gave me Luke's address; he assured me that Luke would help me. It would be wicked of me to judge him or Mair. 'Let him that is without sin cast the first stone'. Mair has never been so happy? Well, God bless her and good luck to her, and if and when the doctor throws her out after seven years, she can come and live with me." Eliza put a hand on Eluned's arm. "You know, I'm quite excited about this, now that I've got over the shock."

"Have some more tea. You're doing me the power of good, Eliza."

Eliza realised that nothing would prevent gossip but knew that it wouldn't be repeated in the presence of the family for fear of the doctor's wrath - something to be avoided at all costs. In any case, the circle in which they moved was made up of the doctor's admirers, who were accustomed to his eccentricities.

William Price's relationship with Eliza took on a deeper significance in the years that followed; there was no question of paying for the ointment, which was supplied on a regular basis. He often drew the goat-cart up outside the bread shop to deposit his beloved Mair, returning to pick her up at the end of his rounds.

At first, Eluned was uneasy in his presence but both she and Dai, who had exploded with anger when he first heard the news, became fervent admirers after William pulled their youngest son through a bad bout of whooping cough. The family saw another side to the doctor's character and what they saw they liked.

Returning to Wales was not without its hazards for Dr Price, whose creditors pursued him. He was hounded by Lady Llanover, the largest land-owner in the district, who demanded rent for the years he had been away.

"That woman is a confounded nuisance!" he told Mair. "She has no right to claim that she owns the land for miles around when everyone knows that this part of the world belonged to the Druids centuries before she was born."

"She's a powerful woman. Will she make trouble for you?"

"I dare say she will try. I shall fight her in the courts but we ought to have some contingency plans in case she pre-empts the situation. What would you do if I were arrested and thrown into gaol to await trial, my pet?"

"What could I do, William?"

"Exactly! If the bailiffs or the police approach our house, we must drive them away. We need to gain time."

"How?"

He smiled. "I was given a present when I was in France - a magnificent, valuable gift. Let me show it to you."

He produced a mahogany box from the sideboard and opened the lid, revealing a pair of duelling pistols and accoutrements lying in crimson velvet pouches. The polished handles of the guns were inlaid with delicately carved ivory.

Mair gasped. "You can't challenge Lady Llanover to a duel!"

"I don't intend to, my little goose."

"You're not going to shoot her!"

"Not that either, much as I should like to. I am going to give you lessons in markmanship - not that you will aim at any specific target, just the reverse in fact. You shall learn to fire these guns without harming anyone."

"William, I knew that life with you would never be dull but this could prove too much for me."

"Come on! You will look magnificent with a pair of pistols in your hands. Here, let me see you with them."

Two weeks later, half-a-dozen policemen and two bailiffs approached the house, striding resolutely towards the front door.

"Not just yet, dear," William whispered. "Give them a few more seconds."

When the first man was six feet away, the door opened to reveal Mair with a pistol in each hand, pointing at the intruder. Before anyone could react, she fired the guns into the ground on either side of her, with her eyes tightly closed.

William watched the ensuing rout from a nearby window. "Well done! I knew you could do it," he cried, as he drew her inside and slammed the door.

Before he could take her in his arms she slumped to the floor, unconscious. When she came to her senses he was sitting on the floor beside her.

She frowned. "What happened?"

"You fainted, that's all. Not an uncommon occurrence for ladies in your delicate state of health," he answered with a smile.

A blush suffused her cheeks. "Since you know so much, perhaps you will be good enough to tell me when the happy event is to be expected, Sir."

William looked into the distance. "A few months before I appear before magistrates in the Crown Court, I should think."

In fact their daughter, Rhiannon, was three months old when William first stood in the dock. He refused to take the oath as he wasn't a Christian. When he was asked to affirm that he would tell the truth, the whole truth and nothing but the truth, he objected on the grounds that the entire case was rooted in falsehood. To prove his point he deposited 750 documents in front of the judge, whereupon the court adjourned for two months.

"I wish you could have heard him," Mair told Eliza in the kitchen behind the shop where they were having a cup of tea, "His understanding of law, his contempt for the judges, his knowledge of the history of Wales, his courage and skill! What a man! There he was, conducting his own defence and making the prosecuting counsel look stupid. In fact, I thought at one point that Lady Llanover's barrister was going to burst into tears. William says they will never be able to convict him."

Eliza smiled. "They say he once sued a bailiff for tenpence but the man paid up before the case was heard in court."

The clanging of a bell signalled that the shop door had opened. "Just a minute while I see to a customer," Eliza said.

When she returned to the kitchen she was grinning. "That was one of Bethan's admirers, hoping to see her. He looked very sheepish when I appeared. He asked for two Welsh cakes! Bethan flirts with so many young men."

"What about the one from the chain works that we met here the other day?"

"David Williams? He is the nicest of them all, I think. He's steady and serious; he'd make a good husband, but Bethan finds him dull."

"Never!" Mair said. "William thought he was very interesting. He was amazed that the boy was so well read."

"Well, the chain works are sending him up to Staffordshire soon; goodness knows when he'll be back, it all depends how long the job lasts. He's fed up about it. I'm hoping Bethan will miss him."

By the time David Williams returned to Pontypridd, three years later, Mary had married her sea-captain. After her wedding in London, she sailed with him to New South Wales, not returning for twelve months. Eliza received letters from many ports of call during the voyage and kept them in a large tin box, taking them out now and then to re-read them, studying every dot and comma and peering at the postmarks.

David Williams called in the bread shop as soon as he came back, only to learn that Bethan was walking out with a young man called Brian, who had a good tenor voice; they sang duets in different chapels and churches and had won prizes in local eisteddfodau.

Eliza didn't approve of Brian Phillips who couldn't read or write, was constantly borrowing money, didn't attend any chapel and whose father was in prison for theft.

David continued to walk Bethan home from chapel on Sundays; she treated him politely but nothing he could do or say made any difference. Eliza, however, invited him to supper quite often, and made a point of doing so if she knew that William might call. The two men exchanged books on some occasions and had animated discussions about modern authors and the theories that were expounded.

When Brian Phillips arrived to take Bethan out for the evening, their giggling and silly behaviour irritated Eliza, who considered it unseemly. Whether Brian didn't notice the cool reception that he received from Bethan's mother, whether he didn't care or was just brazen she didn't know, but she was always relieved when they left.

One evening, Brian took Bethan to a local beer-house which his father frequented. It reminded her of the Saloon in the hostelry on a rowdy Saturday night. In no time the pair were persuaded to sing one of their duets and the rafters rang with applause. After two encores, they were given drinks, despite Bethan's protests, and an hour later she was more than a little drunk, although she didn't realise it. While Brian's father stayed on, Brian persuaded her that it was time for them to leave and in an alley near the smithy she was in no state to resist his advances. Frightened and ashamed, she stumbled away, leaving Brian calling after her in vain. When she reached home, she sat hunched at the kitchen table, rocking back and fore.

Early next morning, the cracking of the twigs in the yard and the shadows cast by the flames flickering in the darkness woke her up. She groaned as she turned her face into the pillow, remembering what had happened the previous night.

"Didn't you sleep well?" her mother asked when they sat down to breakfast.

"No."

Bethan remained subdued and grizzly for the rest of the day and that evening announced that she wouldn't be going out with 'that Brian Phillips' any more.

"I see," Eliza said, although she didn't. "Well, I can't say I'm surprised. I hoped you would come to your senses one day. There are much better fish in the sea."

David Williams came into his own. While Eliza was pleased that Brian Phillips was no longer around, she was perplexed by Bethan's sudden change of heart. Despite his intelligence, David was gullible and guileless. He didn't seem to realise that his overwhelming feelings weren't reciprocated; that his beloved was nowhere near as happy and carefree as she had been when in the company of his rival. It didn't occur to him to question Bethan's motives - he was a supremely happy man and lost no time in asking Eliza if he could marry her daughter.

"Are you sure that she loves you, David?" Eliza asked. "I have no doubt that you love her and that you would make a good husband, but only a short while ago Bethan was besotted with Brian Phillips. This might sound odd, but it's your interests I have at heart. I think it would be wiser to wait for some months maybe, until we are sure of Bethan's true feelings."

Eliza spoke to Bethan the next day to no avail.

"I do love David! He wants us to be married as soon as possible because he's being sent up to Sunderland in a few weeks and wants me with him."

A month later they were married.

"Whatever is the matter with you, Eliza?" Eluned asked. "Anyone would think that Bethan had married Brian Phillips. You've always said David Williams would make a good husband, so why are you so miserable?"

"She doesn't love him, that's why. I suppose that I must just hope and pray that they'll both find some happiness, but it won't be like me and

Will, or you and Dai or Mair and William. I'm afraid Bethan has made a big mistake and it's too late to do anything about it. She's so impulsive, so headstrong and foolish. Poor David!" Eliza raised her hands in the air. "He's good and trusting and.....vulnerable. I'm afraid. I'm afraid."

David wrote regularly to his mother-in-law. He seemed to find the work and the surroundings interesting. The few letters that Bethan sent gave no indication of her feelings and Eliza could deduce little about her state of mind. It was a relief when they returned to Pontypridd in the summer of 1854. They wanted to live in the bread shop and Eliza was happy to have them.

It was only when they returned that David told Eliza that Bethan had had three miscarriages, which had left her depressed. He felt that it would do her good to be occupied behind the counter and he said that he would worry less about her, knowing that Eliza would be at hand to cheer her up, should the need arise.

Chapter 15

Even though there were eight steam-hammers in the Brown Lenox chain works, the strength of skilled, strong men was needed to forge the anchors and chains of the ships that were now being built. An anchor smith earned more in a day than a collier could earn in a week, and for far fewer hours. Mr Lenox was a considerate employer who knew how demanding the work was; he gave the men an hour's rest at mid-day but, even so, David Williams was exhausted by the time he finished work at four o'clock. On the way home he often called at the Public Lending Library for books before striding eagerly towards the bread shop, savouring a night by the fire, when he could open the first page of some new author and lose himself in a world far away from the foundry. He had tried reading out loud to Bethan, to share his pleasure and excitement; it saddened him that she showed so little interest.

His mother-in-law, on the other hand, liked to hear him describing the characters from Charles Dickens's novels, and was interested in the theories propounded by Mr Disraeli and Robert Owen. Sometimes, while she was kneading the dough before going to bed, she asked him to read a poem by Wordsworth or Keats; she particularly liked the sayings of Marcus Aurelius.

William Price respected the knowledge and vision of the self-taught young man, who enjoyed an argument; they rarely agreed on anything and had nothing in common except intelligence and a desire to put the world to rights. Sometimes, when the others had gone to bed, they would sit in the lamplight, surrounded by the aroma of warm yeast, and talk away like mandarins.

"I'm reading Jeremy Bentham's works at the moment," David said, one summer evening. "He writes so simply that it's easy to grasp his philosophy and it makes sense. It's just common sense!"

"Is sense so common though?" William asked drily. "Every man should count as one and none as more than one. That is a truism, but where does it lead us?"

"The greatest good for the greatest number is also a truism; since there are far more workers than employers, the employer shouldn't count himself as more important than any one of the others!"

William sighed. "I agree, but where would the workers be without the employer - that is what Crawshay would point out."

"Not if we formed a society like the one Robert Owen has in Lanarkshire, or if the world were organised as Marx suggests - to each according to his needs, from each according to his ability. I like those principles. He calls his theory Communism."

"Jesus of Nazareth would not have approved," William murmured softly, raising his eyebrows. "He said 'Blessed are the poor'; presumably He accepted the wealthy."

David's shoulders fell. Their arguments often faltered when one of them turned to religion. William smiled and rose to his feet. "I must be getting back to Mair. Good Heavens! Look at the time."

"I'll have an answer for that when we see each other next."

Eliza appreciated the world of letters and culture that her son-in-law had introduced to the house, while David considered that he had a mother-in-law many would envy. Both of them were pleased when Bethan finally presented him with a son, Idris Coleman Williams, born on Christmas Day 1854. David's pride was a joy to see, and Bethan, for a while, seemed contented.

The bread shop flourished. Eliza was now selling pickled herrings, which were ready for collection by breakfast time. The smell of fresh bread mingled with that of herbs and spices which Sammy claimed he could detect at the end of the street. She particularly liked making wedding-cakes to order, spending a good deal of care on the icing and decorations. The evening before the marriage, the cake would be placed on a table in the shop window with a card that David had written, giving the names of the bride and bridegroom. This usually resulted in small groups of people gathering outside to admire the finished work.

In addition to the edible goods available, a shelf which David had put up held Bacon's maps of the world and copies of Mr Pitman's Shorthand Writing books, which were much talked about. He also sold candles of varying sizes, thereby increasing his income and enabling him to buy reference books.

When Idris was a year old, Myfanwy wrote to Eluned, wanting to return to Pontypridd while her husband went off with his regiment to the Crimea. After consulting Eliza, whose household was now comfortably full, she talked the problem over with Mair, who welcomed the prospect of taking in her sister and children as paying guests.

"It would help me," she said. "William is still being hounded by Lady Llanover for rent. I'm very worried, to tell you the truth. You know what he's like. He refuses to charge poor people, but business men and preachers won't call for him unless every other doctor fails, so we live on air these days."

"He's too good to some people - why won't he charge them just a small amount, or let them pay a little every week, like the other doctors?" Eluned asked.

Mair shook her head. "It's no good talking to him about it. He can be very stubborn."

Myfanwy and her children took over three rooms at the top of William's house and, as far as possible, lived as a separate family. During their stay they were witnesses and participants in yet another of William's escapades, which none of them enjoyed and which brought heartbreak to Mair. He could not avoid being brought before the magistrates in Cardiff yet again. The start of the case was delayed for a whole day when William objected to each of the jurors as their names were called. During his cross-examination he frequently consulted his attorney, the 'learned Countess of Glamorgan' (his pet name for Rhiannon) who sat in Mair's lap on the front bench. He would cross the court room and bend his head to her ear, leaping up after a pause to pronounce her opinion. When he was found guilty, 'learned counsel' requested leave to appeal, whereupon he was allowed to leave the court.

That evening, after the children had gone to bed, he sat with Mair by the fire in their sitting-room, discussing plans for an escape, should the necessity arise. When Mair protested, William asked her if she would rather see him in gaol; when he received the answer, the conversation proceeded. Every possible contingency was reviewed and the need to involve Myfanwy was agreed.

After they decided that nothing had been left to chance, when Mair had accepted that they might have to part at any moment, William went to a small cupboard and produced a bottle of champagne.

"Crawshay gave me this. I can think of no better time for opening it." He poured out two glasses and handed her one. "To you, my beloved," he said, looking into her eyes. "And to our children! I must thank you for all the happiness that you have given me. The years with you have given me as great a contentment as I have ever known. I can't ask you to wait for me, that wouldn't be fair, but it would be wonderful to find you again one day."

William stroked her cheeks, which were wet with tears. "Come!" he whispered, as he took her hand and led her upstairs.

William didn't appear in Cardiff on the day of his appeal, thereby placing himself in contempt of court. A warrant was issued for his arrest. Knowing that it would be useless for one solitary constable to carry out the task of apprehending him, a posse approached his home early one morning. Myfanwy spotted them from her bedroom and gave the alarm as she ran down to bolt the back door and close the shutters on the windows.

"Children! Get your shawls and put your boots on. We're going out straight away," she shouted.

Two constables went round to the rear of the house and another clambered on to the roof. The bravest of them knocked on the front door, which opened slowly after a prolonged interval,

"Good morning, Ma'am. I wish to speak to the doctor without delay."

"Why, if it isn't Constable Jenkins. How are you this long time?" Mair asked cordially.

Constable Jenkins cleared his throat. "I'm here on serious business. I have a warrant for the arrest of Dr Price."

"Hah! About time too! You know, it's funny you should call today, just as I'm leaving him. I've had enough. He's impossible to live with. My cousin and I are getting out of the house. You're welcome to it and to him," Mair snapped.

The constable looked back at the rest of the force for a second.

"Come on, Myfanwy. Bring the children out," Mair said calmly.

"I take it the doctor is in the house?" the policeman said.

"Yes, but be careful. He's got a loaded pistol with him. I think he's in the attic."

Myfanwy took the children outside. "Constable, do you think your men could lift this trunk on to the cart?" she asked, pointing to a wicker hamper in the hall.

The constable called the men forward. "Help the ladies," he ordered.

"It's got all my belongings and a valuable clock that I'm not leaving behind," Mair explained. "Be careful with it; I'd hate the innards to be damaged."

When the trunk was lifted on to the hand-cart, Mair took the handles and began pushing it down the path, followed by Myfanwy and the children.

"We're not staying - it's too dangerous. I don't want to be here when the trouble starts, constable," Myfanwy called over her shoulder. "You understand, don't you?"

He raised his hat. "Of course, Ma'am. This is no place for ladies," he said. He ordered three more men to climb on to the roof and called the rest to follow him indoors.

The women and children proceeded down to the main road, where Mair lowered the cart as soon as they were out of sight of the house. William flung the lid of the hamper open and climbed out with a groan.

"I must fly, my beloved!" he cried, as he sped away down a small path. "Go to Eliza - she will take care of you all!"

The children stood staring after him while Mair put a hand on her heart.

"Come on! We mustn't linger!" Myfanwy said.

Rhiannon started to cry. "Where are we going?"

"To Auntie Eliza's shop."

A letter arrived from William two months later, addressed to Mair, care of the bread shop. Once again he was in Paris, sounding his usual carefree self, but complaining about the drains. He said that he was sharing a house with the poet Heine, sent his warmest regards to everyone and asked for letters, expressing no concern about the financial straits in which he had left his family.

Eliza showed Mair how to make William's inflammation ointment, which they put in small cartons and sold for sixpence in the bread shop; David put up another shelf and printed a notice advertising the doctor's remedy. He also taught Mair how to make tallow candles which he then bought from her and sold for a small profit. The duelling pistols fetched a good price, which helped, but Mair had only a bare minimum to live on until she was able to let the large dining-room in the house to a local man who wanted to open a school. Her own children and Myfanwy's attended free of charge.

Thus they survived for four difficult years, during which time Myfanwy's husband died in hospital at Scutari and Mary's husband was drowned when his ship foundered with all hands during a storm off the Falkland Islands. On many a morning, alone in the darkness of the yard, waiting for the oven to reach the correct temperature, Eliza looked at the sky, searching for the star that shone more brightly than the rest, to find comfort and strength from its steadfast light.

But 1860 was a happy year, highlighted by three significant events.

William Price returned without warning, ringing his front door bell one April morning, and sweeping Mair into his arms. "Mair, my darling! Do you still love me? How are you this lovely spring day?"

That evening they clambered into the goat-cart and trotted off to see Eluned, calling at the bread shop on the way home. Before leaving, William removed every carton of ointment from the shelf, telling Eliza that she should have charged twice as much for it.

In July, Mary came to stay for three weeks, bringing her four-year-old daughter with her. Mary had married again, another ship's captain, and planned to sail with him to India. Eliza was delighted at the prospect of looking after little Cathy until her mother returned.

On a stormy night in September, Mair and Eliza were upstairs with Bethan, who was in labour once more. William sat by the kitchen fire, keeping David company, ready to be called if his services became necessary. On the floor between them lay a book: *The Origin of Species by Means of Natural Selection* by one Charles Darwin. A patient had given it to William in lieu of payment.

"Come, David, my boy, even if you disagree with every word, you really ought to read it - it's the book of the century! I found it fascinating."

"The man is a blasphemer. I'm not happy about the book being in the house!"

"But you can't condemn it without reading it. You are too intelligent to be taken in by nonsense written in the papers by ignorant bigots."

The sound of a child's cries reached their ears. David stood up. "God be praised!" he whispered. "I must go and see them. Forgive me, William."

When William was left alone he slid the book in between others on a shelf in the dresser.

It was four o'clock in the morning of September 10th, 1860, when Bethan produced her daughter - a sturdy little mite with a mass of jet-black hair. William and Mair arrived again that evening bringing a bottle of champagne with them.

"I was born on the same day, sixty years ago," William announced.

"We must celebrate."

The family stood around the table as he filled the glasses.

David proposed the toast. "To Elizabeth Coleman Williams!" He looked at William before adding: "A God-given daughter."

"To Elizabeth! Long life and happiness!"

Chapter 16

It was a damp autumn evening in 1868. Sammy was being followed by Eliza's two grandchildren as he made his way slowly along the street. Each of the small girls had a blue satin bow pinned on her shawl, indicating that she had signed a solemn pledge to forswear strong drink for the rest of her life. The ceremony had taken place at the Band of Hope, a club for children organised by Sardis chapel. Elizabeth Williams always enjoyed the proceedings and had taken the pledge five times, a fact which the preacher overlooked, considering that logic and accuracy were less important than the need to ram the message home.

Elizabeth and her cousin Cathy were fascinated at the way Sammy could make each lamp come to life, kindling silver rods of light that shimmered in the puddles on the road. They trod softly after him in silence, respecting his mastery over the elements. When they reached the corner where they had to leave him, they stood as still and forlorn as the leaves that littered the pavements and watched him disappear into the evening mist.

"Let's go to the smithy!" Elizabeth cried, speeding away towards Taff Street.

They arrived breathless at the open doorway and stared spellbound at Dai Davies as he tempered the red-hot shoes. It was even more spectacular than gas-lighting and a good deal warmer.

"Hello, Elizabeth! Hello, Cathy!" Dai murmured as he hit the glowing metal, sending golden sparks into the air. He was a fat young man, whose stomach leant gently over the leather belt which had a tenuous hold on his trousers. The blacksmith was one of the most respected people in the town, not because of his skill at work, but because he possessed a glorious bass voice. No one could sing "O Isis and Osiris" as he could. When Dai Davies stepped onto a platform, you would hear a rustle of expectation as the audience waited to hear the rich, sonorous notes that he could produce.

The children watched in awe as he placed half a dozen nails in his mouth before banging them into the horse's hoof. Their enthusiasm waned, however, when the smell became unbearable. Slowly they ambled home, Cathy's spirits sinking as she thought about having to return home to Portsmouth in two days' time.

"I wish I could stay in Pontypridd for ever," she said with a sigh. "I don't want to go home to my new father. I don't like him."

Elizabeth gave the matter thought. "I know," she said. "Let's ask if we could change places. I'd be glad to get away from the old shop and

134

having to make candles every night and clean my brother's boots."

"Oh! I love the smell of hot bread and herrings and the nutmeg in the rice pudding. It's fun to help behind the counter, too. I don't mind making candles, because then your father reads to us, lovely stories. I live in an ordinary house; it's not exciting like it is here. Anyway, I'm by myself there."

"When will you be coming back again?" her cousin asked, as she stopped outside the lighted shop window, loath to go inside where she had to bide her tongue.

"I don't know. I'll be leaving school soon and then I'll have to find work," she answered, kicking the pavement with the bottom of her boot.

"Why don't you find a job here?"

Cathy's eyes brightened. "I could work for Lady Charlotte in Dowlais House, like my Mam did. She enjoyed that."

"*Ych-y-fyi* ! Dowlais is a terrible place. Now, if I was to be a lady's maid, I'd go to Osborne House, far away on the Isle of Wight. I'd comb the Queen's hair and polish her boots and....um....cut her toe nails, and....fill her bathtub full of hot water. Then, after a bit, I'd marry a rich gentleman, like Grandma did, and have a house full of nice furniture."

The strident clanging of the brass bell echoed through the household as they went inside.

"Where have you been all this time?" Elizabeth's mother asked.

"Just walking home," Cathy said. "We knew we wouldn't have to go to the well because the barrels are full."

"There's still work for you both to do. Uncle William is coming tonight, and I want supper over and the place cleared before he gets here. Now, in you go and hurry up about it."

"Aw! That means Dada won't be able to read us *"Alice in Wonderland,"* Elizabeth cried.

"The world doesn't revolve around you, young lady. You know how much Dada enjoys talking with Uncle William, so that's that."

Elizabeth grimaced, casting her eyes upward as soon as her mother's back was turned, entering the kitchen in a state of exasperation.

"Hello, you two. Your tea is all ready for you. Did you enjoy the Band of Hope, Cathy?" their grandmother asked, as she put the kettle on the fire.

Eliza wore steel-rimmed spectacles now, and the front of her hair was beginning to turn grey.

Cathy pouted. "Yes. There isn't a Band of Hope in Portsmouth."

"Perhaps they've started one there now. It's been six months since you left, hasn't it?"

Eliza, too, would be sorry when Mary's daughter left. Cathy's presence in an otherwise tempestuous family exerted a restraining influence on the tensions not far beneath the surface. They all liked Cathy. For Eliza though, the child was special, being a reminder of a stage in her life that the rest knew little about. It worried her that Cathy resented the fact that her mother had re-married yet again and left for a voyage to New South Wales with her third husband, who was the first mate on a cargo ship. She gave the letters that her step-father sent her to her grandmother. "Keep them with your other letters," she said. "I don't want them."

Eliza had tried talking to her without success and finally decided that only time could heal the jealousy.

"What's for tea?" Elizabeth asked.

"Your favourite - kippers and brown bread and butter."

"Aw! Good!"

David Williams sat on the rocking-chair reading the local newspaper, which he lowered when the girls came in. He had grown an impressive beard and moustache which left only his eyes and forehead visible. "I've been waiting for you two for a long time," he said threateningly.

The girls smiled. They liked being teased by him.

"I've had to smell those kippers cooking since five o'clock. Grandma wouldn't let me start eating without you."

"Where's Idris?" Cathy asked.

"He's gone to fetch some medicine for Auntie Bethan," Eliza answered grimly, looking at David as she spoke. Their eyes met momentarily before both looked down at the floor. "He will be here soon, we might as well start."

She buttered the bread with annoyance, not bothering to look up or speak when Idris came in. He was a lanky boy, with light-brown hair which he combed straight back over his head. Since it kept falling over his eyes, he had a habit of flicking it back with his hand. At fourteen years of age he was intelligent, witty and not without guile. He had recently impressed boys at school by beating the local bully, thereby earning the title of Williams the Conqueror, which pleased him. It was David's greatest wish that his son should have a University education and to that end he had already started saving two shillings a week.

Elizabeth didn't know what caused her mother to be ill so frequently but was used to hearing about her bad back, her sore head and her legs. It was true that when she was pregnant, Bethan's legs had become painful, with the veins standing out and aching. She had had to rest then with her feet propped up on a cushion. Now, when Bethan had a headache, she used to sit in a corner with a brown paper bag pulled over her ears. Eliza, recognising the symptoms of boredom or the spleen and vapours, would stifle her anger, knowing that if she remonstrated, David would be told when he came home. Imperceptibly, a collusion had developed giving Bethan control over the family, whom she manipulated to gain her own ends.

One evening a few months later, as Elizabeth was coming home from school, hurrying to catch Sammy up, she stopped as she saw Idris emerging from the gin-shop, carrying a paper parcel. She waited for him to cross the road and confronted him when he reached the pavement.

"Whatever were you doing in there?" she asked in a horrified whisper.

"Hello, fat face!" he said, ignoring the question.

"You were in the gin-shop!"

"Tell me something I don't know," he said, as he sauntered slowly up the street.

"That's terrible. What if Dada found out?"

"What if Dada found out!" he mimicked in a babyish voice.

"You're drinking gin. You'll burn in hell-fire. Aw! How could you!" Elizabeth cried, as she wrung her hands.

"This is Mam's medicine, you dafty. I don't drink it - it tastes awful, but she gives me a penny every time I go and fetch it for her, so shut your gob."

"That's a dreadful thing to say. Mammy doesn't drink, she's chapel," Elizabeth said crossly as she hurried to keep up with her brother. "I'll tell her what you said, you wicked thing."

"I'd think about that if I was you. She'll give you a thick ear."

Elizabeth thought about it. "I'll tell Dada then."

"He knows," Idris said in a bored voice.

"You're telling lies. Dada wouldn't let her drink. We're not Tavern people."

"Ask grandma, then. She won't lie," Idris said with a shrug of the shoulders.

Elizabeth stood with her hands at her mouth, watching her brother walking into the shop. After a while, she ran after him and was in time to see him place the parcel on the floor behind the counter before he went through to the kitchen. She followed slowly, pale and frightened, staring at her mother, her father and her grandmother in turn.

"What's the matter with you?" Eliza asked with a grin.

Elizabeth looked at the floor and shook her head.

"Has the cat got your tongue?" her father asked.

She gulped and ran out into the yard.

Elizabeth hardly uttered a word for the rest of the evening, causing Eliza to put a hand on her forehead to check her temperature, which seemed normal. Elizabeth kept staring at her mother as the family ate supper, and watched her go into the shop afterwards to fetch the jug which she put on the floor near the wall on the other side of her armchair.

In Sardis chapel on Sunday, Elizabeth twisted her handkerchief into knots as she heard the minister describe his vision of hell. When her turn came to walk to the front with the other children to recite their verses, her courage almost failed her. She stood riveted before Mr Morris as though she had stage fright, but he was well used to this.

"Where is your verse, Elizabeth?" he asked benevolently.

"It's in my pocket."

A titter ran round the congregation as she realised that she had said the wrong thing. "And Paul said: 'Take a little wine for thy stomach's sake," she shouted, waiting for a thunderbolt from heaven to strike her dead when she heard the intake of breath from the deacons in the Big Seat. Mr Morris decided that discretion was the better part of valour. He raised his eyebrows expectantly and looked at the next child. "Now, Peter. Your verse."

After chapel, Elizabeth left with her friends but when they had gone off to their own homes, she found herself alone by the smithy. She couldn't stop thinking about her mother burning for ever in hell, and there was no one that she could tell. As her tears began to fall she went into the alleyway at the side and let her knees crumple beneath her. She stayed crying, her head against the wall, for a long time.

At six o'clock, Eliza and David were attending the evening service, while Idris was with an older boy chasing two girls from the pickle works. Elizabeth was alone with her mother. When Bethan decided to take a leisurely walk to the small hut at the far end of the yard, Elizabeth looked behind the chair where the jug still stood, three-quarters full of gin.

She waited until she heard the latch click on the door in the yard and then picked the jug up and carried it outside, tip-toeing to the wall that divided their yard from the one next-door. She discovered that she wasn't tall enough to pour the contents over the top, so she picked up the brick that her grandmother used to block the oven door. When she stood on that she was just able to tilt the jug so that the gin slopped out into the neighbour's property. Unfortunately, the brick wobbled as she stepped down, bringing her crashing back onto the cobbled floor with a cry of pain. Her mother couldn't believe her eyes when she emerged from her seclusion.

"Whatever....what have you....that's my medicine jug! Aw! You wicked child! It's empty!" Bethan cried, lifting her right hand behind her head and bringing it down across Elizabeth's ear.

The child tried to get up, covering her eyes with both hands to fend off the blows that rained down. She managed to get to her feet and turned to run back into the house but slipped and fell once more, her head landing on the kitchen step.

"Get out of my sight! Go to bed and stay there till tomorrow morning. You ....you...wicked, wicked child."

Elizabeth crawled upstairs and got into bed, too frightened to cry. What conversation took place in the kitchen when the rest of the family returned she could only surmise, but she put her faith in her grandmother, who would never hit her. When Eliza came into the bedroom at nine o'clock, Elizabeth pretended to be asleep.

"I've brought you something to eat, dear," her grandmother said gently.

Elizabeth didn't budge. She couldn't open her right eye anyway and her body was as bruised and aching as her spirits.

"Come on, sit up and eat this rice pudding," Eliza urged, as she leant over and lifted her grandchild up. She was shocked when she saw the state that Elizabeth was in, but merely said: "Here, you must be hungry."

Elizabeth couldn't hold the spoon because of the pain. Eventually Eliza sat on the bed, took the spoon and fed Elizabeth as if she were a small child. When the last mouthful had gone Elizabeth sank back and turned to the wall. Her grandmother said nothing, but went downstairs, instead of undressing and getting into bed, as she usually did.

The next morning, Elizabeth lay half-awake, not attempting to get up. When her mother came into the room, she didn't move.

"Elizabeth, come downstairs straight away if you want any breakfast," Bethan said, closing the door.

Elizabeth stayed where she was, not responding when her grandmother brought her a bowl of soup at mid-day. By the evening Eliza thought that she had a temperature. The next morning, William was sent for.

"I'm sure she's got a temperature; she won't eat. We're worried," Eliza told him as she led him upstairs. "She fell in the yard on Sunday and hit her head. Do you think she may have cracked her skull?"

William stood at the side of the bed for a while before turning Elizabeth's head gently in his hands. "Where is the pain, Elizabeth?" he asked, lifting her eyelids.

No answer came.

"She hasn't spoken since she fell," Eliza said.

William ran his fingers over the soles of her feet. "Why did she fall?"

"She was looking over the wall, standing on a brick when it wobbled, so Bethan told me."

"She fell on her right side yet her jaw hurts on the left. How do you expect me to make a diagnosis when you withhold all the facts, Eliza?" William said.

Eliza sighed.

"I am waiting."

"She had upset her mother. Bethan smacked her."

"Go on."

"Well, that's all."

"I am running out of patience. What has this to do with the neighbour's back yard?"

William dragged the truth out, and then stroked Elizabeth's forehead before putting an arm around Eliza's shoulder and taking her out of the room.

"There's little physically wrong with Elizabeth. Get two kittens, put one in each armpit and she will be fine tomorrow," he said in a low voice. "I wish I could help Bethan as easily."

Their eyes met, each understanding what was left unspoken.

"Maybe you could have a talk with David," Eliza whispered.

William sighed. "I have on many occasions, Eliza *fach*, but how can he help her? How can any of us help when tears are at the heart of things? Her chosen medicine consoles her for a little while at least. Be gentle with her."

The next morning, Sammy arrived with two kittens in a sack. "I've heard of the doctor's weird remedies, but this one beats the lot. How can two kittens cure a broken skull?"

"I don't know, but I'll try anything," Eliza said. "I've not known William's remedies to fail."

Eliza did as she was told. When she went into the room an hour later, Elizabeth's left eye was open and she was smiling at one of the kittens. By lunch time, she was talking: "Where's the other one?"

Eliza found a kitten under the bed and put it back where it belonged. "Would you like some broth?"

"That would be nice. Can I have some bread with it? I'm feeling hungry."

Elizabeth was still awake that night when her grandmother came to bed. She waited until Eliza had blown the candle out before speaking.

"Grandma, I've decided to become a Druid. I don't want to go to Sardis anymore. I'd rather go to the Rocking Stone with Uncle William on Sundays. Druids are nicer than chapel people."

Elizabeth recovered from her aches and pains fairly rapidly but the deeper hurt took longer. The gulf that developed between mother and daughter took years to heal. Trust and confidence had gone; they treated each other with a certain wariness as Elizabeth joined in the family collusion, knowing that when her mother retreated into a twilight world of her own, the medicine was at work again. She herself often withdrew into a dream world, staring at the wick that she twirled in jars of tallow every evening, thinking about her future, imagining the dress that she would wear on her wedding-day, picturing the sort of house that she would like to live in. Only one thing remained constant - there would be no drink in her home - ever.

Her feeling of isolation increased shortly after her ninth birthday, when her parents decided that she should leave school in order to help her mother with the housework.

"But I can't read or write properly yet!"

"I'll help you in the evenings," her father said.

Elizabeth looked at her grandmother but Eliza didn't lift her eyes from the dough that she was kneading.

"Is Idris going to leave school as well?"

"No. It's different for boys; he has to work hard and study to go to college."

"I'd like to go to college too."

"Women don't have to go to college. Besides I couldn't afford to educate two children."

Elizabeth already stayed at home on Mondays to help with the family's washing. Her legs were too short for her to bend right down to the bottom of the wash-tub without standing on a pile of books. They were dreary days and it wasn't easy to make up the lessons she had missed.

Elizabeth was desolate when she went to bed that night, seeing a future where she would remain at home for ever or, at best, get a job in the pickle works. She longed to get small-pox and die - perhaps then they would be sorry. She imagined her death-bed with her father and mother weeping and promising to send her to college if only she would live. The next day at school she wrote a poem that expressed her feelings:

O, black, unending darkness
Will you show no chink of light?
Let me please to get the small-pox
And die this very night!

She left school at the end of the week, despite the efforts her grandmother made to get her daughter and son-in-law to change their minds. Eliza knew that, left to himself, David would never have curtailed his daughter's education and she was angry that he should have given in to Bethan, who admittedly was expecting another child and suffering from swollen legs. Eliza had offered to pay for domestic help, but Bethan argued that there were days when she would be able to do a little work and she didn't want a stranger about the place. "David agrees with me," she told her mother.

Eliza and David guessed that the motive was fear of the family secret coming to light. William Price would remain silent; Eliza told no one, out of loyalty; Idris gained financially from the conspiracy; David put his head in the sand like an ostrich, pretending that no problem existed; Elizabeth was too ashamed to refer to the matter and consequently became the sacrificial lamb.

Elizabeth often stood forlornly behind the shop counter in the afternoons, staring into space, with her face cupped in her hands. At other times, she walked toe-to-heel around the shop on an imaginary line, pretending that it was a tight-rope. The child's boredom was matched by her grandmother's despair, especially after Bethan's baby was still-born.

One afternoon, Eliza went into the shop and put her arm around Elizabeth's shoulder. "I've had an idea," she whispered in conspiratorial fashion. "What would you think if I bought you a piano?"

"A piano?"

"If you can play the piano, who knows what it might lead to, apart from the pleasure it could give you for the rest of your life."

David was pleased when Eliza told him of her intentions and Bethan didn't object. A Bechstein with an ebony frame, brass candlesticks and ivory keys was installed a month later. Mrs Thompson, the organist at Sardis, agreed to give Elizabeth lessons twice a week. When the session finished, Mrs Thompson used to play a few melodies to encourage her pupil, crouching over the keys like a cat before flinging her arms high into the air and pouncing from one end of the keyboard to the other in grand style.

Elizabeth was ecstatic. "Play some more, Mrs Thompson! Play some more, please."

Progress was slow at first, with few pleasing sounds emerging. Scales were practised, endless scales, which even Eliza found trying. Arpeggios were more interesting and easier on the ears but after a year had passed the family was pleased when Elizabeth played simple hymns. She had a light touch and the piano itself was magnificent. The upper range of notes sounded like crystal, while the lower notes had a resonance and depth of tone that was a joy to hear. If Elizabeth could have had her way, she would have played the piano all day long.

Mrs Thompson sometimes stayed for a cup of tea afterwards and the more Eliza came to know her, the more she liked her; David was astonished when he found out that she had read *War and Peace*.

When Bethan was forty-four years old, her last child was born. One April night, Elizabeth woke in the early hours, aware that her father had come into the room and was whispering to her grandmother. That had happened before when her mother was about to give birth. The arrival of relatives late at night, low voices, strained looks, and groans from her mother's bedroom, were part of a ritual that Elizabeth feared could result in everyone being miserable again. She pulled the quilt over her head and tried to sleep.

By the time she went down to breakfast, the mid-wife had arrived and her father had left for work. Her grandmother was cooking bacon and eggs. Elizabeth cut a slice of bread, put it on the end of the toasting-fork and sat on the floor in front of the fire.

"I've asked Sammy to let Auntie Eluned know what's happening. He's going to get a message to Uncle William as well," Eliza said wearily. "You must tell customers there won't be any pickled herrings this morning."

Eluned arrived at nine o'clock to make the yeast cakes and currant loaves while Eliza went upstairs to be with Bethan. William called three times during the day but had gone to see another patient when David came home at four o'clock. When Elizabeth went to bed the baby had still not been born.

William came quietly down stairs at midnight and put a hand on David's shoulder. Bethan and her baby son had both died.

Chapter 17

David lost interest in his books and went to the cemetery every evening after tea, coming home to sit looking at the hearth, trying to come to terms with the situation. His misery rubbed off on Elizabeth who tip-toed around looking bewildered and frightened.

A week after the funeral, when Elizabeth had gone to the Band of Hope, Eliza sat down opposite her son-in-law who was slumped in the rocking-chair. "David *bach*, we must talk. I've been thinking. It might be as well for all of us if I gave up the shop."

He sat up. "I thought the shop meant everything to you."

"I'm sixty-five and would have to give up in a few years, anyway. There are important things to consider - like Elizabeth's future, for one thing. Now is as good a time as any to move to an ordinary house," she said gently.

"If that's what you feel, Mother, by all means," he said, without any emotion. He didn't seem to care one way or the other.

Eliza put her hand on his arm. "I'm thinking of all of us."

Eluned and Myfanwy scoured Pontypridd for a suitable house, eventually finding one in Feeder Row. It was on a slight incline, within easy reach of the town and nearer the chain works. Two months later, the bread shop in Taff Street was under new management. Eliza had no regrets. In fact, she welcomed the opportunity of living at a leisurely pace, but she kept David busy putting up shelves and installing cupboards. She knew that when he sat with a book in his hands, more often than not he wasn't reading it.

Idris was now an unenthusiastic pupil-teacher at his old school, bored with Pontypridd and longing for life in a big city, doing anything other than teaching. Elizabeth was more than pleased to leave her old home behind and appreciated her grandmother's company when they went for walks alongside the canal or sat near the Rocking Stone and the Druid's Circle where William conducted druidic ceremonies on Sundays. They went to tea with Eluned and Mair, and once they went by train to Cardiff to buy Elizabeth patterns for a skirt and blouse, which they cut out and made together.

The piano lessons continued, the cheerful presence of Mrs Thompson helping the family to get through those first difficult months. She was a widow, in her early forties - a short, dumpy woman with thin, greying hair tied haphazardly in a bun on top of her head, although a few stray pieces always seemed to be hanging around her ears. She couldn't be described as smart or good-looking but her bubbling nature and enthusiasm made her excellent company.

Gwen Thompson seemed more interested in other people than herself, repeating such phrases as "You don't say!" or "Well, I never did!" while clapping her hands or rolling her eyes, giving the impression that she found life an endless source of interest and amazement. She enjoyed teaching her diligent pupil but after the lesson, Eliza was impressed with the way Mrs Thompson related so well to David, discussing books that they had both read.

After many months, the family learned that her husband had been a teacher at Vaynor, that one son had emigrated to Patagonia and another was a pupil-teacher in Tregaron, her childhood home. She earned a living by giving piano lessons and by playing the organ at weddings and funerals. In addition, she had taken in a married couple who fended for themselves.

They all looked forward to her visits and to listening to the duets that she and Elizabeth played. Eliza and David realised that Elizabeth had inherited Bethan's voice when they heard her singing items from a song-book that Mrs Thompson lent her. Eventually, the teacher's visits often lasted longer than the requisite one hour but the pleasure was mutual.

As Eliza and David walked home from chapel one morning, they discussed Elizabeth's future. "I think she would make a good dressmaker," Eliza said. "She's patient and neat; you saw how well she made that skirt and blouse for herself."

"What a good idea!"

Eliza continued. "Do you think that between us we could arrange for her to be apprenticed to a dressmaker? We're paying less rent now and I still have my income from the Court estate and my house in Dowlais, remember."

"How long would it last?"

"In Miss Jones's Dressmaking Academy it can be up to two years or more, but it's less for gifted pupils, depending how they get on. It has a high reputation. Shall I make enquiries about the fees?"

David became excited. "Have you said anything to Elizabeth?"

"No, no. Of course not! You and I must know what's entailed financially first and in any case she might not share your enthusiasm."

Elizabeth could not have been more interested. "An apprenticeship? In Miss Jones's Academy? A dressmaker? Aw! That would be wonderful! I could work as a seamstress for famous people, in stately mansions, making beautiful gowns! Just think of it!"

David frowned. "And work long hours. Earning a living isn't all fun. Think seriously about it and we'll talk more about it later."

Elizabeth and Eliza were interviewed by Miss Jones a fortnight later. She agreed to accept Elizabeth, but explained that there was a long waiting-list which meant that no vacancy would be available until the following June.

When Eliza had nothing particular to do, she liked to settle down to write letters in the parlour, where she sat at her writing-desk, with the silver inkstand in front of her. She had answered Mary's last letter, which urged her to come and stay for a few weeks in Greenwich, and had written to Jimmy Twice in Brecon, where he was now the manager of the Castle Hotel and the father of five sons and a daughter.

Huw and Gwilym corresponded regularly, having learned to read and write at last. They both had large families and saw each other quite often. Gwilym had married the only daughter of a wealthy business man and inherited a factory on his father-in-law's death. When Eliza last heard from him, he was living in a large house outside Hartford.

One afternoon, after posting a letter, Eliza called to see Eluned, who was busy making a rabbit pie.

"It's strange to be the one sitting down, watching the other doing the work," she said from the rocking-chair by the fire. "It isn't easy to get accustomed to so much leisure. I don't think I shall ever get used to it."

"Get away with you! I'd give anything not to have to cook for lodgers day in and day out."

Eliza pursed her lips. "I don't like having time to think. It's quiet in Feeder Row and I find the days long sometimes."

"Very different from your days in the hostelry and the bread shop! You were often too tired to hold your head up."

"I know, but I was fulfilled. I'm restless nowadays. Mary has asked me to stay with her for a few weeks - I keep thinking about it. Huw and Gwilym have invited me to go out to America to see them, would you believe it! What an adventure that would be. Maybe I'll take them up on it one day, when David has found himself another wife."

Eluned was shocked. "Another wife? How can you say such a thing, Eliza! Why, it's hardly any time since poor Bethan died."

"Eleven months and three weeks," Eliza reminded her. "It doesn't alter the fact that David is lost and drifting. You wouldn't expect him to mourn for the rest of his life."

Eluned looked up. "I know you, Eliza. You are trying to tell me something."

Eliza looked at the ceiling. "Well," she said slowly. "You know the organist at Sardis?"

"Mrs Thompson, Elizabeth's piano teacher."

"That's right," Eliza said, stretching out her hand and studying her wedding-ring.

"Get on with it, for goodness sake!"

"It's nothing really, only..........." she looked into the distance, "David is never late coming home on the days that Gwen is there; they exchange books and, last Sunday......

"Eliza, you are driving me daft."

Eliza stared at her boots. "He walked her home from chapel." She stood up and went to the window, seeming to have become interested in the view of the yard outside. When she turned round she shrugged her shoulders. "That's all."

Eluned rubbed bits of pastry from her hands. "Is he....do you think......what sort of woman is this Gwen, as you call her now?"

Eliza smiled. "She is a particularly nice, warm, intelligent, caring, gifted, well-read, interesting person and Elizabeth is very fond of her."

"Put the kettle on," Eluned said, with a sniff.

Eliza made a pot of tea while Eluned finished the pie and cleared the table. "And another thing," Eliza said with a grin.

"What?" Eluned cried. "I can't stand much more."

"David wasn't the only one who came home late from chapel last Sunday. I had the dinner all cooked and had to lay the table myself - that's Elizabeth's job. When I went to the front door, I saw her ambling along the street with Morgan Richards. You know who I mean, his father is a time-keeper in the Maritime colliery."

"Is his mother that tall woman who wears a fox fur round her shoulders - always boasting about a son who works in the bank?"

"That's the one. Morgan is the youngest son, more like his father, a quiet, modest lad. He was staring at Elizabeth like a demented owl!"

Eluned laughed. "She's old enough at sixteen to attract admirers. Are you jealous?"

"I couldn't be more pleased. Perhaps, before long I'll be superfluous and then, who knows, anything could happen!"

Morgan Richards continued to walk Elizabeth home, not only from chapel but from Sunday School, the Band of Hope and singing practice. When Eliza heard that he had a sweet tenor voice she invited him to tea one Sunday and thought it would be nice if Gwen Thompson came as well so that the family could have a sing- song around the piano.

It was a successful occasion. Eliza sat in a corner of the parlour enjoying the music and observing the proceedings. For a few hours, those that she cared about most were happy and maybe, she told herself, the future held out hope; in the end, all would be well.

"All manner of things will be well," she thought.

Morgan Richards and a group of carol-singers tramped cheerfully through the snow on a cold, moonlit night in December, on their way to Feeder Row to pick up Elizabeth. She was to join them for their first visit of the week to a mansion a few miles away.

When they had left, David sat down for supper with Eliza. "Do you think we could ask Gwen Thompson here on Christmas Day?" he asked. "Her son is going to stay with his fiancée's people in Swansea, so she'll be on her own."

"Of course! She must come back here after the morning service and spend the day with us. Elizabeth will like that."

Silence followed.

"You like Gwen Thompson, don't you, David *bach*."

He looked up, somewhat embarrassed. "We have a lot in common."

"I was hoping there was more to it than that," Eliza said lightly.

He stared at her nonplussed. "Is it that obvious?" he whispered "I...er...well...."

Eliza put a hand on his arm. "Dear, dear David. Nothing would give me greater pleasure than to see you married again one day, and I can't think of anyone who would give you more happiness than Gwen Thompson. She's a fine woman."

"She is indeed but I thought that you........well, maybe...."

"That I'd be upset if you married again, is that it? Stuff and nonsense! I know it isn't fitting yet but, in another six months or so, if you love her and she accepts you, why ever not?" Eliza said, as she picked up his empty soup plate and carried it to the back kitchen.

"Mother, you are remarkable. I have known you for over twenty years and still you surprise me."

"How many sausages do you want?" Eliza called.

He became animated. "As a matter of fact, Gwen and I have talked about our feelings for each other."

Eliza put four sausages on his plate. "Well, that is good news. I'm glad and not only for your sakes; Elizabeth will be so pleased."

"I'm relieved that you brought the subject up; we have been wondering how you would react. Shall I tell her that we have spoken about this?"

"Of course, put her mind at rest. You ought to think about moving into another house, too. Gwen should start her new life in a home of her own. She shouldn't feel that she is moving into my house."

David's face fell. "You mean you wouldn't want to live with us?"

"Your sausages are getting cold. If you and Gwen really want that, then perhaps, eventually, after a little while, maybe....." Eliza was smiling.

"Mother, what is going on in that mind of yours?" David asked, cutting a sausage in half.

"Do you know, I've never had a holiday, not once. Actually, I never wanted one but now, after your wedding, I could go and stay with Mary and meet her husband and see my other grandchildren! I might even go and see Huw and Gwilym in America. Aw! Just to think about it makes me excited."

"And come back to us afterwards!"

"If that's what Gwen would like, but please, don't pressurise her. She and I will discuss it at the appropriate time, but we mustn't mention this to anybody yet, especially Elizabeth."

"I agree."

After the meal David reached for his pipe on the mantelpiece, looking thoughtful. As he filled it from his tobacco pouch he spoke quietly. "There's one thing I must say. Gwen and I didn't plan things this way, so soon after...after dear Bethan's death. God rest her soul! It just happened."

"I understand; you don't have to explain, David bach. I know how much you loved Bethan."

The ten carol-singers approached the home of Mr Hughes of Fairfield, keeping to the tracks that the carriages had made. Morgan Richards and his brother, Dewi, carried lanterns on the end of long poles as they led the way up the drive to the mansion, where lights from the windows flickered over the snow-covered laurel hedges in front of the balustrades.

Elizabeth could see guests moving about in the hall and sitting-rooms. "Look at that Christmas tree! Myfi," she said in a loud whisper.

"Did you ever!" cried Myfi Benion, bounding forward like a kangaroo.

As soon as they reached the wide steps, Dewi raised his lantern. "We'll stand by here," he said quietly. "Are you all ready?"

They huddled together in a small semi-circle, clearing their throats and arranging their feet. A dark figure in one of the hall windows cupped his hands against the glass, trying to see what was happening outside. Elizabeth stood next to Myfi, in front of the two contraltos; Morgan, the lead tenor, was next to Iestyn Jones, Rhydyfelin. 'Fat Onllwyn' was one of the baritones at the back; his voice had brought him fame since winning prizes at eisteddfodau in Swansea and Newport. The previous summer he had been the soloist when the South Wales Choral Union won first prize in a competition at the Crystal Palace. His brother Taliesin's voice wasn't yet as powerful but between them they made a major contribution to the timbre and resonance of the little choir.

Dewi raised his hands and signalled to Morgan, who had perfect pitch. They filled their lungs and a second later the music burst out:

"Here we come a-wassailing, a-wassailing..."

Every now and then Dewi would point at a singer whose voice needed emphasising, or spread his hands when a rallentando was needed. As she sang, Elizabeth watched the front doors open and glanced at Myfi with a smile. Long before the first carol, finished the basement windows had been lowered; kitchen maids, scullery maids, under-parlour maids, grooms and laundry women, perched precariously on chairs, craned their necks for a sight of the carol-singers. Guests walked out onto the terrace, the men with great-coats slung over their shoulders, the ladies with their long coats buttoned up, keeping their hands warm in muffs.

Staff piled more logs on the fire in the hall, sending golden sparks shimmering up the chimney. Edwards, the butler, appeared on the terrace carrying goblets of warm brandy on a salver and walked slowly among the audience.

After the first carol the choir sang 'Away in a manger' followed by 'It came upon a midnight clear'. As the recital progressed, the leading singers took turns to sing a verse or a line on their own. Elizabeth knew that they were doing well, which meant more than the dainty clapping and murmured approval from the terrace. She agreed with Morgan, that to be part of a choir and sing in harmony was more rewarding than listening to music, although that was one of the greatest pleasures in the world. They had decided to visit this house first because Mr Hughes had a reputation for being the most generous person in the neighbourhood, not that the financial reward was the reason for Elizabeth's participation - any money received would be handed over to her father as soon as she got home. She sang for her own enjoyment.

'While shepherds watched' was followed by 'Good King Wenceslas'. The singers rubbed their hands and stamped their feet between each item, smiling respectfully at their audience; Elizabeth stood on tip-toe to peer into the basement where the windows were filled with cheering spectators. Everyone was happy. The contrast between the lives of those on the terrace and those outside and below stairs was forgotten; the constraints and tedium of the ladies upstairs and the poverty and weariness of those in the basement were set aside in the celebration of Christmas. They all enjoyed the familiar rituals and melodies.

After the last carol, the housekeeper beckoned the choir inside, where Edwards stood with the salver once more, but this time it held ten gold sovereigns. Mr Hughes smiled proudly as he handed them to the singers who then proceeded to the back of the hall, where the green baize door was held open for them to go down to the world where they belonged. Elizabeth had to pull Myfi away from the sight of the tree which towered up to the ceiling. It was filled with paper dolls, sweet-meats, trinkets, silver bugles, tambourines, golden apples, elves and fairies, all glistening in the depth of the branches.

In no time the carollers were seated at a long table in front of the range in the main kitchen, accepting the compliments of the servants. The windows had been closed and began to steam up as roast turkey, cranberry sauce, and baked potatoes arrived in front of them. The men were given tankards of ale, the women glasses of elderberry wine, which Elizabeth didn't touch. Afterwards they had apple-tart and mince-pies.

"I told you, didn't I," Morgan whispered in Elizabeth's ear.

"But it's even more exciting than I imagined."

The experience was almost too much for Myfi who was unnerved by being waited upon. The boys, on the other hand, adopted an air of sophistication, acting as if this were just another meal such as they might have had in their own homes or lodgings, attacking the food with a ferocity that contrasted sharply with the restraint and gentleness with which they had sung 'Holy night' not ten minutes earlier. Fat Onllwyn's cheeks bulged without pause, his eyes fixed on the next portion of food to be consumed. "This is good, mun. Fit for a king, aye!"

When they could eat no more they got to their feet, reluctant to bring the festivities to a close, but the cook was bustling about, supervising the provision of a late-night supper for the upstairs guests. The singers left through a side door and made their way through a courtyard to a lane bordering the garden.

"Aw! I have enjoyed myself! That was the best night of my life!" Elizabeth told Morgan.

They laughed and pelted each other with snowballs along the two miles to Pontypridd, the group dwindling as one by one they took different roads home. Only four were left by the time they reached Feeder Row.

"Let's sing a carol for your family!" Morgan said. They had sung 'O, come, all ye faithful' at the bottom of the road when they set out. People had appeared at their doors to listen. Passers-by had stopped; a man who was buying holly from a basket-woman on the corner held out his hand to pay her but stayed motionless, as if made of stone, until the harmony finished. Eliza and David heard the singing and came to the front door where they stood, quiet and thoughtful, as if hearing the words for the first time:

> 'O, little town of Bethlehem,
> How still we see thee lie.
> The hopes and fears of all the years
> Are met in thee, this night.'

Eliza and Elizabeth enjoyed another shopping trip to Cardiff the following May, heading for David Morgan's, the big new store which displayed hundreds of ready-made gowns and hats of all shapes and sizes. They were going to buy Elizabeth a dress and bonnet for the wedding and, since Mary's husband was now the captain of a steam-ship and as Eliza would be meeting her grandchildren and their families for the first time, it was only right that she should be appropriately dressed. The last thing she wanted was to let Mary down.

It was a long, tiring day but they returned in good spirits, carrying so many parcels that it was difficult to see where they were going. Eliza was wearing a long coat with a high, ornate collar over a pale blue, ribbed velvet skirt; her blouse was made of dark blue chiffon. The feathers on her huge velvet hat were so bountiful that she had to manoeuvre with care when she boarded the train.

Two trunks were necessary for all the clothes and equipment needed for the journey - Eliza wasn't sure what the weather would be like in Connecticut. What gave her as much pleasure as anything was that, at last, she could give her parasol an airing. It would have looked ridiculous in Dowlais and she hadn't had the nerve to use it in Pontypridd but, away from home, it would give her confidence and was just the thing on board the ocean liner where she would be the mother-in-law of the captain.

David and Gwen were married at the end of May. After the wedding breakfast they left for a long weekend at the Castle Hotel in Brecon - the cost being Eliza's present. Idris was to escort his grandmother down to Cardiff station the following day and see her on to the train for Paddington, where Mary would be waiting to meet her. Elizabeth was going to spend a week with Mair and William. Eliza considered that she had organised things pretty well. She didn't sleep much the night before the journey but was up at five o'clock and, after a large breakfast, dressed in her new clothes. Before leaving the house she put on a pair of silk gloves.

"Grandma, you do look a toff," Elizabeth said.

"I feel like a toff today! I wish you were coming with me, that would make everything perfect, but there you are. You'll be starting off on an adventure of your own next week in Miss Jones's Academy."

"I'll write and tell you all about it."

"Mind you keep all the letters I send because I shall want to read them myself when I come home. Idris! Are you ready?" Eliza called up the stairs. "It's almost time to start."

When they reached the station, Myfanwy, Eluned, Mair and William were waiting to greet them.

"What are you all doing here?" Eliza cried. "We said our goodbyes at the wedding yesterday!"

"You didn't think we would let you go without so much as a wave, did you?" Eluned answered.

"Well, this is nice of you all," Eliza said, feeling her eyes getting moist.

William grinned. "Give my warmest greetings to Mary. I had a high regard for her father, as you well know."

Eliza kissed him. "So did I. I'm looking forward to meeting his grandchildren."

"The train is coming!" Myfanwy cried, grabbing one of Eliza's hat-boxes.

"I can't believe this is happening," Eliza said, looking flustered.

Idris took the luggage and found seats in an empty compartment, where Eliza lowered the window and leaned out. By the time the guard blew his whistle, tears were streaking down Eluned's cheeks. William stood between her and Myfanwy, with his arms around their shoulders. Elizabeth walked alongside the train until she could go no further. She stood at the end of the platform, enveloped in steam, and remained lost in thought for a while after the train left. Eventually, she drew herself up and walked back to the others.

At seventeen, she was quite tall. Her hair was pinned in soft folds on top of her head in a style that suited her; her colouring and the smoothness of her skin she had inherited from her father's side of the family but her habit of throwing her head back when she laughed reminded Eluned of Eliza. In fact, although the two didn't resemble each other, many of their mannerisms were alike and William thought that their temperaments were similar.

"I'm determined not to be sad that grandma has gone," she said when she rejoined her relatives. "She deserves a holiday."

"I like the way you have done your hair," Myfanwy said. "You look quite grown up."

"I put it up for the first time this morning and I'm going to wear it up from now on," she said.

"Today seems to mark the beginning of a new stage in life for everyone in your family, it seems," William said.

"I suppose it does. I am looking forward to it, beginning straight away by staying with you and Aunt Mair."

Chapter 18

The *Ladies Dressmaking Academy* was owned by a Miss Harriet Jones, a lady of indeterminate age; she might have been a well-preserved fifty-five or a mature, dignified thirty-five, being excellently corseted and coiffeured, and endowed with an enviably proportioned bosom which preceded the rest of her torso by a good six inches. Her long, beaked nose resembled that of a Leghorn hen, while her teeth would have been more appropriately assigned to a squirrel or a rabbit.

Miss Jones was a tall woman and since she piled her hair on top of her head she towered over most of the apprentices and the majority of her clients. She wore pince-nez, sometimes near the end of her nose but, more often she carried them in her hand, using them to express her varying moods or to hide her feelings, to emphasise a point, to gain time or save time or convey messages that were too painful for a lady of breeding to put into words. Only rarely, it seemed, were they used as an aid to her vision.

Her relationship with the ladies who patronised her establishment varied according to their social standing; those with a title or related to landed gentry, however remotely, could order gowns which were totally unsuited to their figures or height, while those below the salt were guided by her own tastes, which were impeccable.

"I was talking to a titled lady only the other day," she would say. "She chose this material," or "Lady Rose would never have stripes going round her waist. Now, this is what they are wearing in Paris this season," even though the farthest she had ventured from Pontypridd was Taff's Well.

Miss Jones didn't have a great deal of contact with her apprentices - that task was undertaken by the Manageress, Mrs Morris, a short, motherly individual in her early forties who regularly quoted Miss Jones; the very name was enough to establish discipline when Mrs Morris felt unable to control the high-spirited girls. Miss Jones dealt with clients, did the accounts and ordered materials but was apt to appear without notice anywhere in the building; on those occasions her eyes missed nothing. She would make no comment at the time but convey her criticism or approval via Mrs Morris later, thereby maintaining an aura of remoteness worthy of a lady of her distinction. Another fact reinforced the gap between her and her staff - she was English and staunchly Church of England.

Elizabeth arrived at seven o'clock on June 1st, 1877. After taking a deep breath she pulled the brass door-bell at the side of the imposing front door, which was opened by a girl of her own age who grinned and stood aside.

"Hello! You the new one? I'm glad to see you, I can tell you. The first thing you have to do is clean this brass," she said, pointing to the embellishments on the door. "I had to do it last week. Go upstairs, you'll find Mrs Morris there. She's not bad," the girl added in a whisper. "What's your name?"

"Elizabeth Williams. What's yours?"

"Mattie Harries. Didn't you used to work in the bread shop in Taff Street?"

"Yes. When we lived there."

After Mrs Morris welcomed her and explained the rules, Elizabeth was conducted around the premises by Mattie, entering shyly into each room where the other apprentices looked up and nodded as she was introduced. She saw the fitting-room, the sewing-rooms, the ironing-room and the door of Miss Jones's office, which was indicated in a low voice.

"You won't be doing any sewing for a long time. You have to light the fire, boil the rice for when someone scalds themselves, pick up pins and scraps, sweep the floors, go out for more ribbon or cotton and worst of all, heat the irons and clean them and carry them to the people who are doing the pressing," Mattie explained.

"I didn't know there were so many different sorts of irons," Elizabeth said.

"Some are for doing lace fichus and ruffs - those small rounded ones; these have charcoal put in them, that's another job you will be doing, lighting the charcoal first thing after lighting the fire. Then you've got to wrap these bricks in flannel, they go inside the big irons over there. The worst one of all is this one by here - it's so heavy you can hardly carry it, it doubles me up. It's for pressing thick outdoor materials."

Mattie was enjoying herself, feeling superior as she aired the knowledge that she had amassed in the previous week; she knew how she had felt on her first day. "I bet you never saw one like this before - it's for pressing ribbed velvet, that's why it's got these notched lines underneath, see? Now, come into the big sewing-room and look in the cupboards."

She led Elizabeth through a corridor into a room where six girls sat at a long table stitching various articles of clothing. "This is Elizabeth Williams," she announced, going over to a large double wardrobe on one side of the room, flinging the doors open and extending her arm. "Now there's a sight for you! Just look at this stuff. The silk is for making chemisettes - you put a layer of chiffon over it; this guipure lace is for decorating the bodices of evening gowns. There's tulle for ruffles, feathers for boas, and valencienne lace for trimmings, the galatea is for drawers and combinations."

Elizabeth gasped. "I never saw such lovely material. Aw! I'm going to like it here."

"What do you think of this?" called one of the other girls, whose knees were covered with an expanse of nainsook and silk. "It's part of the trousseau for Miss Alexandra Bartie-Jones. This is one of the nightdresses. We have to make another sixteen!"

"Sixteen nightdresses?" echoed Elizabeth.

Mattie giggled. "That's nothing, you wait! She's having ten petticoats, six merino combinations, twelve chemises...." The girls interrupted her, chanting in turn. "Eight under-bodices, four corsets, four knickers in alpaca, serge, satin and silk; twelve pairs of drawers, two tea-gowns, an opera cloak, a going-away outfit, six day-dresses and a mourning dress, just in case. Well, you never know."

They dissolved into laughter which brought Mrs Morris into the room. "What is all this noise? Miss Harries, it's time you got on with some work. Take Miss Williams to the kitchen, more hot irons are needed and the floor needs sweeping."

"Yes, Mrs Morris,"

As the pair of them made their way downstairs, Mattie continued the list in a whisper. "Twelve blouses, four washing dresses, six jackets, five skirts and handkerchiefs galore!"

"That's enough clothes to last a lifetime!" Elizabeth said. "There's no sense in it!"

"According to Mrs Morris it isn't an extravagant trousseau! Some ladies have a lot more."

"It's all marvellous!"

"You won't like the ironing roster - trudging back and forth carrying hot irons for the Seniors. Woe betide you if the iron is dirty! And it must be the exact temperature for the material; that takes a lot of learning. It mustn't be too hot or too cold. It's dirty work and you get worn out with spitting."

It was a long tiring day. When Elizabeth reached home at half-past eight, she threw her shawl over the back of the rocking-chair and sat down with a groan.

"How did it go? Have you enjoyed it?" Gwen asked.

Elizabeth stretched her feet out and closed her eyes. "It was wonderful. You should just see those beautiful materials from all over the world. And twenty-five different sorts of irons, would you believe?"

"What did you have to do all day?" her father asked.

"Polish the brass on the front door, light the charcoal, sweep the floors five times, pick up pins, go out to the draper's for silk thread, and buy a loaf of bread for Mrs Morris from the bread shop." Her voice dropped. "It was strange going in there again."

By Saturday, Elizabeth had lost her tiredness and felt so at home in the Academy that she might have been there for years. Her father noticed her blossoming and gaining confidence as the weeks sped by.

It was during her apprenticeship that a large choir was formed from all the chapels in the town, in order to enter for the Eisteddfod in

Cardiff. Three contraltos from Sardis were chosen, including Elizabeth and her friend Dolly Lewis. Dolly's father referred to his wife as Mammy, his wife referred to him as Daddy and so did everyone else; people had long forgotten their Christian names. They were known as Mammy and Daddy Lewis and since they referred to their only daughter as 'Our-Dolly-by-here' that name stuck as well.

Every Tuesday and Saturday, Elizabeth and Our-Dolly-by-here teamed up with Dai Davies, 'Fat Onllwyn' and Gerald Edwards, the son of Educated Edwards, so called because he had the irritating habit of falling to his knees during Prayer Meetings to give thanks for the fact that he was better educated than most people, having attended Southampton Training College for three months. It would have been more appropriate had he given thanks for the fact that his son had a God-given tenor voice.

Forty-five people were selected for the choir. Each week, at rehearsals, a different soprano was asked to sing the solo part which occurred in the middle of 'The Kingdoms of the Earth', the test piece. Not until the end of July was it announced that Elizabeth Williams would be the soloist, with Our-Dolly-by-here as stand-in. Excitement ran high.

On the day of the competition the Pontypridd choir spent the morning walking around the eisteddfod, not that they took much in. The contest was due to start at two o'clock in the main tent. Elizabeth looked strained as she entered the marquee where the seven other choirs were assembling; she started swallowing and clearing her throat half an hour before it was her turn to sing. While she waited she listened to the others performing. Some she knew they could beat, a few were good and the choir that sang before them was excellent, much to her concern.

The sopranos led the way into the big tent, followed by the contraltos. Elizabeth's eyes took in the audience as the tenors and baritones lined up behind her; distinguished visitors, civic dignitaries and adjudicators sat in the front row. She lifted her head and tried to forget them as their accompanist took her place at the piano. Mrs Mabel Davies was a born accompanist who knew instinctively when to play softly and when to boost the choir. Unlike many others, she didn't lead or overpower the singers and she wasn't easily satisfied with the pianos which she came across; if they were not properly tuned, she refused to play. Today, she seated herself gracefully at the Steinway.

Mrs Davies was seldom called by her real name. She was the manageress of a draper's shop and it was noticed that she seldom said 'Thank you', it was always 'Thank you, ta.' So, Mrs Thank-you-ta rubbed her palms with a handkerchief before tucking it in her sleeve and looking at the conductor expectantly. Elizabeth forgot her nerves as soon as the opening bars were played and when the time came for her to sing the solo, she closed her eyes, opened her throat and let the sound pour out. Applause drowned the closing notes, when at last the choir could relax. They trooped off the platform, grinning with satisfaction as they returned to the competitors' tent, where they made little effort to control their feelings. They had to sit through two more choirs which Elizabeth felt were not so good as they had been.

"It's that lot from Swansea that bothers me," whispered Dai Davies, wiping the sweat off his forehead.

"Aye! But the soloist wasn't as good as ours," muttered Myfi Benion, her eyes glistening.

The adjudication seemed to last for hours. Each choir was discussed and analysed, each one had good points, it was a very difficult task to award the prize, and so on. Elizabeth squirmed in her seat, making eyes at Our-Dolly-by-here, but at last the announcement came. "We have awarded first prize to the choir from Pontypridd."

Dai Davies and 'Fat Onllwyn' leapt to their feet, grabbing Elizabeth and lifting her up on their shoulders. She was too busy concentrating on maintaining her balance to shout herself, but all around her there were Hurrahs and Bravos, tears and laughter, as she was carried to the platform. The conductor was given forty pounds for the choir; Elizabeth was given five pounds. When she walked off the stage she was embraced by Mrs Thank-you-ta, whose handkerchief was sopping wet with tears.

The Pontypridd choir hung about, basking in their glory. They clustered around the tea-tent, making up for their light lunch, all talking at once; not one of them wanted to leave the scene of their triumph, but by the time they reached Pontypridd station they had at last quietened down. It had been a long, wonderful day which was coming to an end, or so they thought until the train pulled up to the sound of the national anthem being played by the Salvation Army band. The platform was crowded with well-wishers, clapping their backs as they made their way to the street.

When Elizabeth reached Feeder Row she ran into the kitchen and stood in the doorway, grinning. "Dada, I've won five pounds! Can you lend me another ten pounds so I can buy one of those new machines for sewing? A treadle sewing-machine. They are wonderful things - you can make dresses in less than half the time it takes to sew by hand. You should see them in the Academy. If I had one, I'd get work much more easily when my apprenticeship is over."

She knew that her father had to work for two weeks to earn ten pounds but she felt she would never have a better opportunity of melting his heart.

"Whoa there, my girl!" David answered. "Money doesn't grow on trees. Ten pounds?"

"They're being sold at the fair in Berw fields. I'd pay the money back every week when I begin to earn and I'll earn more if I can work faster."

Gwen intervened. "I've heard about those machines but I've never seen one."

"I'd like to help you, I really would, but that's a lot of money. Let me think about it for a few days," her father said.

That night, after Elizabeth had gone to bed, Gwen talked to him. "You know, Elizabeth's grandmother would buy one of those machines, if she were here. I think it's a good idea. Suppose we took in a lodger, that would help."

"How much are lodgers charged?"

"Half-a-crown a week, to include potatoes, on condition they wash every night. Those are the usual terms."

David hesitated.

"A machine would save us money," Gwen continued. "If Elizabeth had one she could make the new curtains we need for the parlour."

Dr William Price convinced David. "Of course Elizabeth must have a sewing machine; it will help her to be independent," he said. "You've read John Stuart Mill. He says it's absolute nonsense the way we treat women as lunatics or slaves. I agree with him. I think women should have the right to vote. In fifty years we shall see women as Members of Parliament and who knows, a hundred years hence we could even have a female Prime Minister."

David smiled indulgently. "Even John Stuart Mill didn't go that far, William."

Elizabeth went for a stroll along the canal bank with Mattie Harries after work on Saturday. Mattie had been given a bonnet for her birthday and arrived at the Academy with it on her head, but as she walked by the gently flowing water on that sultry summer evening she took it off to swipe at the gnats and mosquitoes that swarmed around her.

"Beastly things!" she said. "I come out in great lumps and itch for days afterwards."

"If I'd known we were going to walk here tonight I'd have brought the camphorated smoke-ball that Uncle William gave us. If you rub it on your hands and neck nothing will bite you."

They reached the lock, which was full of water, awaiting a distant barge that was drifting slowly downstream. Elizabeth gazed at the neat vegetable garden at the side of the lock-keeper's thatched cottage, where a man was picking runner-beans.

"I'm hungry," she said in a low voice. "Have you ever tasted fresh runner-beans that have been cooked straight away? A customer gave my grandmother a basketful once and we ate them half an hour later. I'll never forget that meal."

She heard a cry behind her. Mattie was kneeling at the side of the lock, staring at her bonnet which was floating in the water.

"I was after those gnats and it just flew out of my hand!" she groaned. "Aw! My lovely bonnet!"

"It's coming back to the side," Elizabeth told her. "If you wait a minute you could reach it."

They watched in silence.

"Now!" Elizabeth cried.

As Mattie lunged forward she went head first into the lock. Elizabeth screamed with horror as she watched her friend flailing about, and jumped in after her. What happened next was a nightmare that haunted them for the rest of their lives.

They clutched each other, trying to keep their heads above water. The man in the garden tore his coat off and dived some distance away from the hysterical pair, swimming behind them to avoid being dragged under. He was able to get a hand under Mattie's chin but Elizabeth had a vice-like grip on his other arm; he gave her a ferocious kick and grabbed her when she let go.

The lock-keeper hooked the man's shirt with the barge-pole and pulled him slowly back towards the bank. Mattie was hauled out first, then Elizabeth. The man who had saved them both hung on to the side of the lock, getting his breath back. Eventually, he climbed out and bent down with his hands on his knees, looking with disdain at the girls who were spluttering and gasping for air.

"Idiots!" he cried.

The lock-keeper turned Mattie over and started pressing her back with both hands, forcing her to empty her lungs.

"That one fell in but this one deliberately jumped in afterwards!" the rescuer said, grabbing Elizabeth and tipping her face-down over his knee, holding her neck forward while she coughed and heaved.

After a while the lock-keeper sat back. "They should be all right now, Philip."

"Let me go!" Elizabeth shouted, forcing her elbows backwards towards her captor.

He took his hands away and gave her a hefty slap on the rump before removing his knee and letting her fall flat on the ground. She pushed herself up with her hands and glared at her assailant, wiping her face with her sleeve and leaving a trail of mud across it.

"You...you.... how dare you!" she yelled as she scrambled to her feet, her eyes blazing with resentment.

Her tormentor spoke calmly. "I will tell you why, young madam. Your friend fell in, which I take to be accidental, but you put all our lives at risk by your thoughtless behaviour. What did you think you were going to do? You can't swim. I can save one drowning person but to save two who are clinging together is a feat that I won't ever attempt again."

When Mattie started sobbing, the lock-keeper helped her to her feet. "Let's go home, Elizabeth," she cried.

Elizabeth put an arm round Mattie's shoulder and led her away, turning after a few steps to look back. She was enraged to see the man called Philip grinning.

"Life is never dull round here, is it, Roland!" she heard him say.

They hardly spoke on the way to Mattie's house where her mother was appalled by what she saw. "Whatever... how on earth?"

"Don't scold, Mam, please," Mattie said wearily. "We nearly drowned."

"Drowned?"

Elizabeth nodded. "We're lucky to be alive."

"But the canal isn't deep enough!"

Elizabeth looked at the floor.

"My bonnet fell in the lock. I fell in trying to reach it. Elizabeth jumped in to rescue me."

Mrs Harries put her arms round her daughter. "There, there!" she said soothingly, patting her back as she looked at Elizabeth. "You saved Mattie's life! Aw! There's wonderful of you!"

"Well, actually," Elizabeth started to explain.

"My bonnet!" Mattie cried, shaking with sobs. "I lost my bonnet!"

Elizabeth shrugged her shoulders. "I think I'll get home and put some dry clothes on. Don't cry, Mattie *fach*, we're alive. That's all that matters," she said, giving Mrs Harries a tired smile.

David was speechless when Elizabeth appeared in the kitchen doorway.

"Mattie's new bonnet fell in the lock and she fell in after it. She was drowning, Dada! I had to jump in, to save her - I had to!" she spat out.

He stood up shakily. "Come by the fire, child."

"I can't sit down, I'm too wet. I'll go upstairs and get some dry clothes first. Can you throw me that bath towel from the rack?"

"What happened to Mattie?" David whispered as he pulled the towel down.

Elizabeth shivered. "I left her at her mother's. She's all right," she said, going upstairs.

"Gwen is next door, I'll go and get her back."

He turned at the front door. "Your sewing-machine has arrived, by the way. It's in the parlour."

Elizabeth didn't hear him; she was in the bedroom struggling out of her wet clothes.

The lodger arrived the following afternoon. He was a collier in his late twenties, the son of a puddler from Brynmawr, one of eleven children, most of whom had emigrated to America. That much he told Gwen when he arrived; when he had unpacked he came downstairs to the kitchen where he and David assessed each other over a cup of tea.

He was a tall, dark-haired man with a high forehead; his mouth was concealed by a large moustache and, like most colliers, he had one or two small, blue marks on his cheeks as the result of working for years underground, where coal-dust became embedded in the skin. His most compelling feature, however, was the intensity in his eyes.

Elizabeth heard him arriving but stayed in the parlour with the door shut, pedalling away at the sewing-machine. Even when her step-mother opened the door and asked her to join them, she delayed for a good five minutes.

When she paused in the kitchen doorway the lodger got to his feet, looking at her intently.

"This is my daughter, Elizabeth. This is Mr Philip Jones who has come to live with us," David said.

160

Philip Jones stepped forward and took her hand in a firm grip. "How do you do, Miss Williams?"

Elizabeth closed her eyes and screwed up her face. "Aah....haaaa...tishoo!" she sneezed, bending almost double as she pulled a handkerchief from her sleeve with her spare hand and held it over her nose as she nodded.

"Elizabeth had a nasty experience yesterday. A friend of hers fell in the lock and she jumped in and rescued her. They both could have drowned. We are all still in a state of shock."

Elizabeth groaned as she looked at the lodger, her eyes wide with horror.

"Is that so?" Philip Jones said. "How brave!"

Gwen stood up. "I must get ready for chapel. Have my chair by the fire, Elizabeth. You've caught a cold and no wonder."

Elizabeth slumped in the chair and blew her nose noisily as Philip Jones resumed his seat.

"We're proud of Elizabeth, you know," David said. "She was the soloist with the Pontypridd choir when they won first prize at the Cardiff eisteddfod last week."

Philip Jones raised his eyebrows. "A heroine in more ways than one!"

Elizabeth got to her feet. "I must change for chapel too," she said, walking to the door.

"Nonsense!" David said sternly. "You'll stay right here. We don't want you getting pneumonia."

Gwen smiled at her. "Mr Jones has brought us a bag of fresh runner-beans; why don't you cut those up while we are out? We can have them with the cutlets for supper. Will you be going to chapel, Mr Jones?"

"Not tonight, I have some letters to write."

"You'll find an inkstand on the writing-desk in the parlour," David said.

David and Gwen went to chapel, leaving Elizabeth alone with the lodger. As soon as she heard the front door shut, she rounded on him. "I didn't tell them that I rescued Mattie!"

He grinned. "I should hope not."

"I just said that I jumped in after her. That was the truth. I came home soaking wet. I was in no state to describe all the details. In any case...."

Philip Jones raised his hands, still smiling. "There's no need to shout, my little canary."

"How dare you call me a canary!"

He sat back in the chair. "What a magnificent temper! Pray continue while I feed deep, deep upon your peerless eyes."

She banged her fists on her knees. "This is insufferable! Aah...haaa...tishoo!"

He frowned. "All right! I'll be reasonable. Let's have an armistice. Your parents told me that you are an apprentice dressmaker. You can make reparation by mending a shirt of mine. It was ripped at the back of the neck by the barge-pole and you tore the sleeve when you attempted to drown me."

Her eyes narrowed. "I did no such thing."

"Nevertheless, I deserve some recompense."

"This is blackmail!"

"Be careful, Miss Williams. I'll put up with so much and no more."

Elizabeth stood up. "I'm going to do the runner-beans. I'd be grateful if you would go and write your letters in the parlour," she said, with as much dignity as she could muster as she walked out of the room.

The lodger remained in the parlour until Gwen and David returned and although the evening passed without any major incidents, Elizabeth was on edge throughout supper. When David asked Philip Jones where he had obtained the delicious beans, she stiffened and put her knife and fork down, gripping her hands on her lap.

"Friends of mine have a small vegetable garden; I've been staying with them for the past two days while I looked for lodgings," he said, giving Elizabeth a passing glance.

After they had eaten, she escaped to the parlour where she stayed for the rest of the evening.

Chapter 19

A few days later, David was looking forward to a visit from William but Myfanwy arrived instead. She stood in the doorway, about to speak when she noticed the lodger. David introduced them and drew up a chair for her.

"I'm so worried and upset," she said as she sat down, shaking her head. She put her hand to her mouth as her eyes filled with tears.

Gwen put an arm around her shoulders. "Whatever is the matter, Myfanwy *fach*?"

"You know about this cholera in Wood Street; William says it's spreading fast, and.....," she gulped. "Well, now.......Aw! It's too terrible to think about." She burst into tears. "Mair! Mair!"

David's jaw dropped. "You don't mean......"

"William won't let any of us go near her, not even her children. He is there with her by himself."

Elizabeth had been standing by the door. "I'll go and make a cup of tea," she whispered.

Philip Jones followed her to the back kitchen where she stood at the window, with a hand at her mouth, blinking back tears.

He filled the kettle. "Who is Mair?" he asked quietly.

"Aunt Myfanwy's sister."

He put the kettle on the hob. "I know people who have survived cholera. Has your aunt got a good doctor?"

"Uncle William is the best doctor in South Wales," Elizabeth snapped. "Don't tell me you haven't heard of Dr William Price."

"Dr Price is your uncle?" he whispered with disbelief.

She reached for the tea caddy and took a tray from the sideboard. "He and Aunt Mair have been so good to us all. He will be heart-broken. This is terrible news!"

"I'm sorry," he said.

Elizabeth unhooked half-a-dozen cups and put them with the saucers on the tray.

Philip Jones stood frowning for a while. "When you take the tea in, I'll go out for a walk; I want to see some friends anyway and this isn't the time for an outsider to be around."

Elizabeth said nothing.

Mair died that night, leaving William bereft and inconsolable. His children had married and left home; Myfanwy had been living with Eluned's family for some time, having gone there when Eluned's sight began failing. William was left alone, with a woman coming in daily to clean and cook him a meal. The Williams family felt sorry for the broken old man of seventy-seven.

Elizabeth noticed that Philip Jones behaved impeccably towards her for some time after the family bereavement and she was able to relax a little, even finding pleasure in mending his shirt. Any reasonable man would have thrown it away, so badly was it torn, she told herself, but she would show him just how much work had gone into its repair, thereby wiping out some of her indebtedness and perhaps making him feel ashamed of himself.

She was looking forward to leaving the Academy and earning her own living, an exciting prospect in itself but it also would enable her to contribute to the monthly instalments on the sewing machine, which meant that the family could dispense with the lodger, a thought which gave her more than a little satisfaction.

The shirt looked as good as new when it was pressed and folded. Elizabeth left it on a chair in the lodger's room while he was taking his nightly bath in the zinc tub in front of the kitchen fire. She smiled as she imagined his face when he found it.

Philip Jones was more than surprised - he was mortified. The tear at the back of the neck was so delicately stitched as to be almost invisible; a narrow patch extended from the shoulder to the cuff on the sleeve, tapering at each end and double-sewn along the margins, which was made possible by cutting half an inch from both sides of the shirt at the front. It took him some time to deduce this because the new hems were indistinguishable from the old hem at the back. The collar and cuffs had been unpicked, turned inside out and sewn back up again.

He came downstairs and went into the parlour, looking worried. "Miss Williams - this shirt - your repairs, well, they are a work of art but I thought you realised that I was only teasing you; it never occurred to me that you would take this seriously. I was going to throw the old thing away."

Elizabeth enjoyed his discomfort.

"You have even made the frayed cuffs look perfect, and the collar - how? That wasn't part of the arrangement, in any case."

Elizabeth's expression gave no hint of her feelings.

"How can I......"

"Make amends?" she interposed swiftly. "I thought I was making amends for some deep offence that I had caused you, reparation, I think you called it. Well, honour is satisfied, Sir. Now I am very busy and should be glad if you would let me get on with my work."

Elizabeth's first post when she left the Academy was with the Misses Duxham, a haughty pair of spinsters who lived in Dynea. They had obtained patterns from Paris and engaged her on condition that she didn't copy the gowns for anyone else. She worked from eight in the morning until seven at night for one-and-sixpence a day, giving Gwen two shillings a week as rent and her father six shillings for the sewing-machine.

Miss Agatha and Miss Mildred trotted about the town, always side by side, as if tied by an invisible rope. They glided down the street, nodding from a great height to those of the lower classes that they deigned to acknowledge. By the time she left, Elizabeth was referring to them as Miss Agony and Miss Mildew.

She spent the next three weeks working at home for local customers who waited for her services. Looking back, she was glad that she was with her step-mother when a letter from Mary arrived, informing them of her grandmother's sudden death.

Apparently, Eliza had been sitting in Mary's garden reading a letter from Huw. Mary went in to make a pot of tea; when she returned her mother was dead. Eliza hadn't had a day's illness in her life and there had been no hint that she was unwell.

> "She had so enjoyed her journeys across the Atlantic and her stay in Connecticut with her brothers but she seemed impatient to get back to you all.
> For her sake we mustn't be sad. I shall remember her with pride and I know that you share my feelings. I thank God that she spent the last days of her life with me and my family, who loved her.
> Don't mourn her, Elizabeth. She wouldn't want that.

Once more, Gwen helped the family through their grief, not allowing them to hide their feelings. She often referred to Eliza, describing her to Philip Jones at meal-times, telling him what she knew or had heard about. David sometimes prompted her, adding bits of information. One evening they went through the letters in the tin box, reading some of them out loud. Mary's letter was put away with the others and, in time, the pain eased.

Morgan Richards continued to walk Elizabeth home from chapel, Sunday School and singing practice, often staying to tea afterwards, when Elizabeth chose to entertain him in the parlour. She enjoyed accompanying him when he sang love songs that she selected like 'Drink to me only' or duets like 'The Keys of Heaven', especially when she knew that Philip Jones could hear them from the kitchen.

Morgan was upset when Elizabeth told him that she had been given the post of temporary seamstress at Fairfield House, where they had enjoyed carol-singing and the meal in the kitchen afterwards. "Look for me in a basement window when you come there at Christmas time," she said cheerfully.

"It will be wonderful!" she told Gwen. "All those chandeliers and the marble fireplace in the hall, and the work will be easy - Mr Hughes is a widower so I won't have to make any gowns for the lady of the house."

"It will be strange here without you, my girl," her father said.

Gwen saw the bright side of things, as usual. "Well, Philip will keep us company."

Elizabeth didn't approve of the use of the lodger's first name but it hadn't bothered her too much. She had been treating him like an old sock since returning his shirt.

The sewing-room was at the top of the mansion and was fairly quiet during the day, but the maids often called in for a chat and Elizabeth liked the friendly atmosphere in the staff dining-room. The housekeeper, Mrs Bishop, was a pleasant, easy-going sort of person who appreciated the fact that her employer had no wife to dictate to her.

Mr Hughes was a stocky, amiable man who had been quite handsome in his youth. His fondness for whisky, however, had made him somewhat corpulent in middle-age; he claimed that he hadn't seen his feet for years. He had hair like thick grey wire and had accumulated a few lumps and bumps on his face whose main feature was the crimson, pock-marked nose. He was respected by his staff because he was fair and generous, not only to them but to the poor and sick families who lived in the cottages surrounding his estate. Sometimes, when others were busy, Elizabeth was asked to visit these neighbours, taking them bread and cheese or discarded clothing.

Discipline in the house was lax. When Elizabeth was there, two young nephews were staying with Mr Hughes, causing consternation and hilarity amongst the prettier maids by chasing them up and down staircases; if any girl was caught, she would have her bottom pinched and a kiss stolen - this even when Mr Hughes was in the room, if his back was turned.

One morning, Mr Hughes told his nephews that he had to go to London for a few days and wasn't sure when he would be coming back. As soon as he left, the boys announced that they were going to give a staff party, telling the housekeeper to invite staff from surrounding houses as well. The idea was taken up with alacrity.

The boys purloined bottles of claret and brandy from the cellar and helped the butler to make large quantities of punch. The kitchen became a place of frenzied activity as the female staff made chocolate gateaux, sherry trifle, meringues and soufflés. When the staff from other houses arrived at eight o'clock, agog with excitement, lights shone from the chandeliers in the sitting-room, an enormous log fire blazed in the majestic hall fireplace and the scene was set for a unique occasion.

After some undisciplined choral renderings and a few tipsy solos, Rory, the elder of the boys, produced a pair of bagpipes which he had brought with him, his mother being Scottish, while Ian, the younger one, propounded the intricacies of the Highland Fling to his newly-found Welsh friends, lining them up with some difficulty at the start of the proceedings. Mayhem ensued, leaving the great room reminiscent of the morning after the relief of Carthage. Potted palms and scullery maids were strewn across the floor, lying amidst the debris of the battle; the cook was sitting against the wall, her legs protruding under a large picture of Highland cattle, whilst Elizabeth lay dazed under the grand piano, where she had sought refuge.

Suddenly the front doorbell rang. "Someone is trying to get in!" cried the laundry woman.

It took a few seconds for the truth to dawn on most of the guests, but Edwards, the butler, found his wits immediately. "Everybody vanish!" he ordered as he rushed to the door where, on the other side, Mr Hughes was trying to get his key into the lock. In the circumstances it was just as well that the latter was in an inebriated state, having called at the Six Bells on his way home.

When Edwards was sure that the room was empty and the lights dimmed, he removed his weight from the great oak panels and opened the door. "Good evening, Sir. We were not expecting you," he said solemnly.

"Why didn't you answer the bell, Edwards?" Mr Hughes demanded irritably as he stumbled into the hall.

The butler was saved by the sudden appearance of the boys, both of whom were in their dressing-gowns.

"Hello Uncle! Why didn't you let us know you were coming back?" Ian asked in a sleepy voice.

"Have you had a successful visit?" his brother enquired.

Mr Hughes fell slowly forwards into the arms of his nephews, who carried him to bed. They returned to the hall afterwards and collected their guests from some unlikely hiding places, whereupon the revelry continued until six o'clock in the morning. When Mr Hughes emerged for his breakfast the next day, all traces of the night's jollity had been removed. The butler handed him a note from the nephews saying that they had been called home on urgent business.

It was not until a few weeks later that nemesis caught up with the staff. Mr Hughes had visited an old retainer in one of the cottages, staying longer than he had intended, and returning home in an uncontrollable rage.

When he stalked into the hall he astounded the maid. "Get Edwards immediately and the rest of the staff. I want to see the lot of you here within five minutes," he bellowed, following her as she ran to the green baize door, where he shouted at the top of his voice: "All of you, every one."

Elizabeth arrived breathless, having run down three flights of stairs to join the guilty company. Mr Hughes walked slowly up and down in front of the assembled employees, scowling as he did so.

"It has come to my attention, that while I was absent from my home,"

167

he spoke with deliberation, turning his direction now and then and retracing his steps, "my staff, my own trusted people, took advantage of my trust and turned this house into a tavern; a bawdy, drunken rabble ate my food and drank my wine." He paused. "My servants betrayed me, made a mockery of me, even after my return, when I was asleep. They did that to me, even though I have always been kind to them."

He looked at his boots and then up at the ceiling, unsure that he could continue. The women hung their heads; the men stared resolutely ahead, making a quick calculation about the future.

Suddenly, Mr Hughes exploded. "You are sacked. All of you. I want you out of this house," he yelled as he turned towards the front door. "By tonight!" he shouted over his shoulder as he went out, slamming the door behind him.

He stumbled down the drive, sniffing and blinking, and headed straight for the solace of the Llanover Arms, or more precisely, the arms of the barmaid Maggie.

"Whatever is the matter, Hughes *bach*?"

"I've sacked my entire staff. Give me a glass of whisky."

"What did you say?" she asked incredulously, taking off her apron and flinging it on the counter.

"It was no more than they deserved. Do you know what they had the audacity - the brazen cheek - to do while my back was turned, after all these years, after all I've done for them? I have looked after them, I have helped their families, I have been a good employer, I trusted them...."

"Wait a minute, wait a minute," Maggie said. "Come into the kitchen where we can talk. I'll get you a whisky and then you tell me all about it," she added soothingly. "Dilys, take over!" she called up the stairs as they left.

Maggie was taller than her friend Hughes, which was useful at times like this. She put her arms around him, cradling his head in her ample bosom and patting him on the back. Gradually, she was able to piece bits of the story together, learning more each time Mr Hughes came up for air.

"I don't understand how you know about them carrying on all night when you were asleep," she murmured gently.

He frowned and sniffed. "I was told," he spat out.

"You didn't know about any of this until you were told?" she said. "It could be a pack of lies."

"Old Ben told me. His grandson saw all the lights and went to look in through the windows. Then he went and told his mother, who didn't believe him until she went over and saw for herself."

"Aw! It's too bad! What they did was dreadful, simply dreadful."

"It was unforgivable!" Mr Hughes roared.

"You know," Maggie said thoughtfully, "I don't think your servants would have thought of it unless those nephews of yours put them up to it. The servants would have had to do what they were told."

"I shall cut them out of my will, that's what I'll do. The little devils!"

"Those boys deserve to be punished but it doesn't seem fair to sack the servants when it wasn't really their fault. What will become of Edwards and Mrs Edwards and that deaf-and-dumb girl?"

"Serves them right!"

"Come and sit down and drink your whisky. Shall I cook you some dinner?" Maggie asked.

"No, it's all right. I'll get some at home," he said without thinking.

Maggie said nothing for a while, giving the problem thought. Eventually she guided him through to the only possible solution. "Who is going to light the fires tomorrow morning, Hughes *bach*? Who is going to cook for you?"

"I'll get someone else."

"There isn't a lot of time, and folk might not want to work for you when they hear what you've done. No, you acted in haste and I can understand that. I would have been just as angry, but it's not your nature to be unfair or vindictive. You might feel sorry later and after all, they are good staff - you have told me that often."

"Well, I've done it and that's that."

"Hughes *bach*, this isn't you. I have a better idea. Suppose I go and see Mrs Bishop and tell her that you have relented and they can stay. That would be a lot wiser."

He remained silent, pouting like a child.

"Then there will be a meal awaiting you for tonight in a nice warm house; there will be a warming-pan in your bed and you wouldn't have to cook your own breakfast in the morning." She smiled at him. "Even if you find new staff in time, it could take them a long time to get used to your whimsical ways; they wouldn't know you like I do," she said laughing softly as she took his hand and led him out of the room. "Come, those boys aren't worth being upset about. There are more important things in life, aren't there?"

Elizabeth was relieved that she hadn't lost her post, but she developed tonsilitis six weeks later, whereupon Mr Hughes arranged for her to be driven home in a brougham. She stayed in bed for a month and sat by the kitchen fire for another two weeks by which time the permanent seamstress had returned and Elizabeth's services were no longer required.

She did a little sewing for neighbours but hankered after the independence of living away from home and was pleased when she went to work for Mrs Lenox, the wife of the owner of the chain works. After supper in the evenings she and one of the maids used to enjoy walking in the dingle at the bottom of the garden, chasing rabbits around the rhododendron bushes.

Once again though, she went down with tonsilitis and had to leave. She stayed in bed again. It was difficult to swallow, she lost weight and her spirits sagged. Philip Jones once walked three miles after work to buy some fresh fish for her which she refused to eat. When Gwen remonstrated, she merely replied "I didn't ask him to get it for me."

After six weeks in bed, Elizabeth lost the use of her legs. When that happened, her father carried her downstairs to join them for supper each evening. Then he cricked his back at work and had to stay at home himself for a few days. Philip volunteered to carry Elizabeth downstairs and wouldn't take No for an answer.

The first time he came into her room, she clutched her shawl tightly around her as he lifted her up, resenting the fact that his face was within an inch of hers during the process. He seemed quite unconcerned as he pushed the door ajar with one foot and manoeuvred carefully on to the landing.

She was aware of his strength as he took her slowly down the stairs, smiling at her, sarcastically she thought, as he felt for the steps with his feet. She looked everywhere but at him, sighing now and then with affected boredom.

As soon as she recovered, she went down with yet another bout of tonsilitis.

"Things can't go on like this," David told William one evening. "What can be done?"

"She must have her tonsils out. It isn't an operation that can be carried out on the kitchen table. It has to be done under chloroform in hospital. If she were my daughter, I would send her to the Infirmary at Cardiff."

Chapter 20

Elizabeth was nineteen years old when she had her tonsils removed in the infirmary. More than one operation was carried out - in fact, she was taken to the operating theatre every Monday morning for ten weeks, having a bit more cut away each time. She lived in the Women's Ward, unconscious for most of the day on Monday, vomiting half-a-dozen times on Monday night, recovering on Tuesdays, staying in bed till Friday, and starting all over again on the following Monday. At weekends she spent much of her time in the linen-room, where they had a sewing-machine, making clothes for some of the nurses, which relieved the tedium and took her mind off the lurid happenings in the ward.

Her brother Idris, who had left Pontypridd to take a post with a firm of tea importers in Mount Stuart Square, visited her once or twice, bringing exotic gifts such as a sable fur and bottles of expensive perfume from Paris. When she asked him where he had bought them, he told her not to be nosey.

As the weeks wore on Elizabeth became accustomed to the daily routine, to the smell of chloroform that pervaded the building and to the sight of bodies being wheeled away to the mortuary. At night, a lamp flickered fitfully in the middle of the ward, giving a ghostly orange light; she often woke when patients called out in pain or coughed.

When the time came for her to leave, she had become an automaton, doing what she was told, walking with her head down and shoulders bowed. It seemed to her that she had lived in the place for years, that this was reality and her former life a dream. She made no independent decisions, was a passive recipient of all that was meted out, and had become a wraith wandering aimlessly in a gloaming of pain and death.

When they told her that she was fit to be discharged, she became agitated, not recognising the creased and crumpled clothes that were brought to her at eight o'clock one Friday morning. She gave the bottles of perfume away, one to the Sister who looked after them during the day and the other to an old woman who drifted about the place at night, holding a lantern over each patient.

Idris arrived at ten o'clock in a jovial mood. "Right then! I haven't time to hang about; the Guv'nor thinks I'm down on the quayside. What are you looking so glum for, girl?"

Elizabeth stood looking nervously around her. She had said goodbye to the patients she knew, so now there was nothing to detain her.

"Goodbye, Miss Williams," someone called out; a woman in the bed by the door lifted a scrawny hand and waved.

Idris walked quickly into the corridor while Elizabeth followed behind, her eyes darting about as she tried to get her bearings. When she stepped out into the street she shuddered.

"Aw! It's so cold!"

"Don't be daft. It's a lovely spring day! Come on, don't just stand there," he said irritably.

She held her shawl over her mouth to lessen the shock of the fresh air that she breathed in. The world seemed full of ordinary mortals, walking carelessly about. The sight of a horse and cart at the far end of the road made her hesitate while Idris crossed to the other side; she cringed by the wall of the hospital, waiting until she felt safe to move.

By the time they reached the station Elizabeth was exhausted, gasping for air, while Idris was becoming exasperated. He left her sitting in the Ladies' Waiting Room, feeling that he had fulfilled his duties.

"Pull yourself together, for heaven's sake, girl."

Two or three trains passed through the station, filling the place with clouds of acrid yellow smoke, before her train arrived. She asked more than one person if this was the right train for Pontypridd before getting in. At every station she asked the other passengers if they were far from Pontypridd.

"This *is* Pontypridd!" everyone in the carriage shouted when she finally reached her destination.

She stood on the platform, not knowing what to do next. As the number of people around her dwindled, she recognised her step-mother waiting by the ticket-collector, and walked slowly up to her.

"Hello," she said quietly.

"Elizabeth? Elizabeth!" Gwen repeated. "Aw! Just look at you!"

Elizabeth looked at her skirt. "There wasn't time to iron out the creases; I know I look untidy but I couldn't help it."

"It's not your clothes, dear. You're all skin and bones! Aw! How you must have suffered!" Elizabeth was indeed skinny; she weighed less than six stone.

Gwen had been shocked when she saw her step-daughter at the station, but hadn't realised how weak she was. People stared when they saw the young girl leaning against the walls of shops and gasping for breath. Back home in Feeder Row, Elizabeth flopped into the rocking-chair in the kitchen, leant back and closed her eyes. Gwen filled the kettle in silence and put it on the fire. By the time her father came home, however, her breathing had returned to normal and she was able to speak whole sentences without having to pause for breath.

"It's good to see you, Dada."

He kept his feelings under control. "Elizabeth! Home at last! It has been a long time, hasn't it? We haven't seen Idris either since you left. I suppose he put you safely on the train this morning?"

When Philip Jones came in, covered with coal dust, he put his Davy lamp down and smiled, his eyes and teeth gleaming white against his coal-black face. In the circumstances it was impossible to tell what his feelings were as he stood looking at her.

"Hello, Miss Williams," he said quietly.

She nodded slowly.

During supper everyone spoke quietly, putting their knives and forks down gently on their plates; there were gaps in the conversation and they were all ill at ease. The problem was that whenever Elizabeth spoke they could hardly hear her and the thought that she might never sing again was uppermost in their minds.

When she had gone to bed early that night, David wrote to his brother, who lived at the family farm in Pumpsaint, asking if Elizabeth could go and stay there to regain her health and strength. He felt that what she needed now was the peace of the countryside, the pure air, the fresh farm food, and the sunlight that he remembered as a boy in Carmarthenshire. As far as he was concerned, Pumpsaint was a veritable Gilead, where his daughter would become the happy, bouncing girl she once had been.

Elizabeth returned to a semblance of normality only slowly, continuing to eat slops or food that was finely chopped. She didn't bother to protest when Philip Jones took her plate without asking, cutting her meal into tiny pieces before putting it back in front of her. Her voice became slightly firmer and she gained confidence, but was still far from her old self. When her father told her that he had had a letter from his brother inviting her to come and stay for as long as she wanted, she was thrilled. The thought of having the first holiday of her life was as good as any tonic.

David never tired of describing his childhood in Pumpsaint, where his father's smithy had thrived in the old days of the drovers. His bachelor brother and spinster sister lived in the old family farm while his younger brother managed the smithy, a sad place now, without much work.

The stories that intrigued Elizabeth, however, revolved around the 'Wizard of Cwrt-y-Cadno', Dr Henry Harries, and his father, John, a doctor who had studied astrology as a youth. Over the years, surrounded by suspicious country-folk, they exploited their skills in psychology and medicine, with the result that they were both feared in the district. Phenomena like thunder and lightning, floods or fires were thought to occur at their behest; people came to them when their possessions were stolen, to ask the name of the thief. The doctors knew the families in the locality so well, the honest and the dishonest, that it didn't take much guess-work to suggest the answers. The more success they had, the more their reputations grew. Henry advertised his skills as a fortune-teller, consulting his father's brass-bound book which contained maps of the heavens, showing the stars and planets and their relationship to the earth.

David recalled his father telling him about a neighbour whose horse had been stolen. The Wizard 'put his mark on' the thief, saying that the culprit was a man whose nose used to bleed.

"You will see him by the first bridge when you go to Lampeter market," Dr Harries told the neighbour.

Sure enough, the following Saturday, a man was standing near the bridge.

"You stole my horse!" the neighbour cried.

"I never did!"

"You lie, you rogue! Dr Harries has put his mark on you!"

The thief's nose started to bleed. "Aw! You will find the horse in the field behind my house!" he admitted, cringing in terror.

Each evening, when David came home from work, Elizabeth asked for another story. Many of them referred to the medical men's skills as doctors, reminding her of some of her Uncle William's weird remedies.

"An old man in the village had a very bad back. He was bent almost double with pain. His wife consulted Dr Harries who told her to bring her husband and a large sack of potatoes to the field down by the stream after sunset. When the doctor met them there he lifted the sack onto the man's back: 'Start walking round the edge of the field; when you have walked around once, start off again and keep doing that until sunrise!'

When the sun had risen in the sky, the doctor appeared once more. He took the sack off the man's back and told him to stand upright. The man's wife couldn't believe her eyes when she saw her husband standing upright for the first time in months."

"That's a strange tale! It really is," Elizabeth said. "You must tell Uncle William that one."

"Your Uncle Thomas will remember a good many more, no doubt. Dr Henry's son still lives in the old family home at Pant-coy; perhaps you will meet him. Our family has always been friendly with the Harrieses."

"I can't wait to get there."

It was another two months before William considered Elizabeth fit enough to make the journey. She had put on a stone in weight but still had a lot of catching-up to do. She made herself another skirt and blouse while she waited, and her father ordered a new pair of boots for her.

David wrote down instructions for her journey, but repeated them over and over again. "Change at Neath, take the Llandovery train, but get out at Llanwrda. Go to the inn there to wait for the Lampeter mail-coach which stops at Pumpsaint."

Eventually, the morning came when Gwen and Elizabeth set out for the station. Philip Jones insisted on carrying Elizabeth's case.

Gwen repeated advice that had been given many times before. "Eat as much as you can and go to bed early."

"Walk in the sunlight, Miss Williams," Philip said, without a smile.

"And don't come back until you have put on another two stone, mind!" Gwen said.

Elizabeth kept nodding and grinning.

At last the train arrived. Philip found a seat for her in a Ladies' Only

Compartment and put her case on the luggage rack. "I wish I were going with you," he said.

"You think I am incapable of reaching my destination without your assistance, do you?"

He smiled. "Nothing would surprise me! When you return, fighting fit, I look forward to resuming hostilities, if that's what you want, but until then," he paused, "I wish you well."

He stood at Gwen's side as the train moved out. The most ill-fated journey of Elizabeth's life had begun.

The London to Swansea train was three-quarters of an hour late arriving in Cardiff. The wait on the platform seemed interminable but that was nothing compared to the delay after Bridgend, when a break-down held them up for an hour and a half.

"The mail-coach has gone, Miss!" the man at the coaching inn cried. "You have missed it by about twenty minutes. Were you going far?"

Elizabeth looked helplessly from side to side. "To Pumpsaint," she spat out, as if challenging the official to bring the coach back for her. "What can I do now?"

The man scratched his head. "You could stay here until Thursday and then catch the two o'clock coach."

"They expect me tonight. I must get there!"

"It's a long way, must be nigh on eight miles," the man said softly.

Elizabeth stared at him for a moment in silence. "Then I'd better start walking," she announced grimly.

The cart-tracks on the dusty road indicated the route that the coach had taken and, holding her head high, she walked jauntily through the village towards the open countryside, pausing at the outskirts where an old woman in black sat nodding and smiling in a doorway.

"Good day, Ma'am. Could you tell me the way to Pumpsaint, if you please?"

"Pumpsaint is it? Heavens! That's a long way off. Are you going to walk there?"

Yes. I have no choice."

"Well, I never! Pumpsaint indeed! Right you are. Follow this road until you come to a fork, by Bethesda chapel. Turn left there and then, after a few miles, you will see a small path by a spinney. Follow that until you reach a stream - it's a short cut. Walk by the stream until you come to a crossroads where there is a sign for Pumpsaint."

The woman had spoken slowly, pausing after each sentence and eyeing the young girl closely. The child seemed too pale and fragile for such a long journey.

"You have stout boots whatever, young Miss. You will need them."

"Thank you kindly, Ma'am," Elizabeth said quietly as she set off again, this time with a shade less confidence.

It was a warm summer's day. A few white clouds tumbled about in the

175

sky. As she walked along the deserted lane, a willow warbler darted above the hedgerow; bumble bees hovered above the foxgloves that grew in the shade beside the path. She took little notice of them, however, as she concentrated on her situation. "It's early afternoon and it won't be dark until eight o'clock," she told herself. "I have plenty of time."

She stayed in the middle of the uneven dirt track to avoid the ruts made by coaches and carts. The grey chapel of Bethesda grew larger as she approached it, shafts of sunlight striking the plain glass windows. When she reached it, she leant against the wall of the surrounding churchyard to put her case down and undo her boot-laces, tying them up less tightly tightly afterwards. Before continuing the journey she paused to read a headstone:

IN LOVING MEMORY
OF SIÂN JONES
Beloved wife
of
SIÔN JONES
departed this life
June 28th, 1877
aged 20
Nineteen years a virgin,
One year a wife,
Three months a mother
Then I lost my life
R.I.P

Elizabeth sighed and walked on. She followed the left fork and walked along a narrow lane surrounded by hawthorn hedges, watching a buzzard hovering over a distant cornfield. Her spirits lifted as she thought about the family and friends back home where it was difficult for trees to grow, where harassed people tramped the streets at the command of the colliery hooters, where coal-dust fell remorselessly on washing-lines, where any leisure seemed to be a dreary round of soap-suds, hot irons and the everlasting cleaning of boots.

An hour must have passed before she found herself near the spinney, which was perched near the brow of a sloping field. At the bottom of the hill was a flatter piece of ground through which meandered a narrow stream.

When she reached it, she undid her boot-laces and took her boots and stockings off, closing her eyes with relief when she dipped her feet in the water. Angry red patches had appeared on each side of her left foot. "How far have I walked?" she asked herself after a few hours. The sun was lower in the sky and the shadows across the fields seemed longer. The stream looked as though it stretched ahead for miles and although she kept scanning the horizon, there was no sign of a crossroads. She began to count, hoping that the journey would seem shorter, but she gave up after the first thousand, getting angrier with every step.

After another hour the path diverged slightly away from the stream, stretching towards a small hill. She stopped to loosen the boot laces even more before starting to climb. Each time that she thought she had reached the top, there was another slope to be surmounted, and when at last she found herself on the final summit, she gazed with dismay at the flat plain below where the path wound pitilessly on until it was lost in the distant haze. Her toes dug into the hard leather as she made her way slowly down, walking sideways along a zig-zag path to relieve the pressure on her feet.

Until she reached the even ground once more she didn't look up, so failed to notice a low building with a wattle roof, nestling against a bank of hawthorn bushes, and was startled out of her wits by a high-pitched voice.

"What brings you here, my young lady?"

Elizabeth swung round to see a bent old woman carrying a bundle of twigs; her grey hair was matted and her eyes were sunk deep in her face.

"I beg your pardon!" Elizabeth cried. "I didn't see you. I'm sorry."

"Aye, I took care that you didn't. I've been watching you though from afar. What are you doing in these parts, if I might ask?"

"I'm going to Pumpsaint, where my uncle lives. I missed the mail-coach."

"Well, what a long walk you are having to be sure, and with your feet hurting you."

"They are new boots. I put them on for the first time this morning," Elizabeth said miserably.

"So, you will be tired and thirsty; you had better come inside and have a cup of tea with me. I have these twigs for the fire; the kettle will be singing in no time at all. Come on, my dear."

Elizabeth hobbled into the hut, pausing on the threshold to get used to the darkness inside; one small hole in the mud walls let in very little light. In the centre of the earth floor a heap of smouldering embers filled the place with wood-smoke. She sat on a three-legged stool by the fire where her hostess piled on the twigs.

"Now I shall go and get some water from the barrel and then we can have a nice talk," the old woman said, going outside.

Elizabeth looked around. An archway led to an adjoining room which served as a barn and cow house; an open cupboard against one wall contained straw and a pillow. A candle and a bible stood on a low table nearby. The leg of ham suspended from the ceiling over the fire was covered with cobwebs.

"Might I ask your uncle's name?" The old woman asked. "Perhaps I know him."

Again the voice startled her.

"Mr Thomas Williams of Larks Farm."

"I've heard of him. As long as you are in no way related to the Harries

177

family, that is all right."

Elizabeth smiled. "You mean Dr Henry Harries, the Wizard of Cwrt-y-Cadno. My father has told me about him."

"Aye, there's a lot to tell," the woman muttered darkly, as she filled the kettle and hung it on a tripod over the fire. "His father was just as evil. When I was a child we always knew when he was consulting that book and getting in touch with the devil somewhere in the woods in the Cothi valley. A great storm would blow, bending the trees right over; streams overflowed and lightning cracked across the sky." She extracted two cups from a box near the door before continuing. "Folks said Dr Henry used to draw a circle around himself before opening the book to see what the planets foretold. Do you know, he could charm any pain away; he could counteract the effects of witchcraft and summon spirits to appear," she whispered, looking furtively around.

The old crone was enjoying herself, acting out the drama as it unfolded, flinging her hands in the air, narrowing her eyes, spinning round and pointing her gnarled hands to the roof while Elizabeth sipped her tea, enthralled by the performance.

"Dr John Harries even foretold his own death, going up to heaven in a fiery whirlwind like Elijah. When the predicted day came he decided to stay in bed but the house went on fire and he perished. He of all people should have known that you can't defy the planets."

Elizabeth held her cup with both hands. "Never! My father didn't tell me that story."

"I could tell you a lot more. Many things. My own brother's wife - I didn't trust her from the start. She was shifty-eyed. I told him not to marry her but he wouldn't listen. One day he drove some cattle to market and sold them well. He shouldn't have drunk so much afterwards, but there you are. He came home with forty pounds in his pocket and fell asleep without taking his clothes off. When he woke up the next morning, the money had gone."

Elizabeth told herself that she could have named the thief.

Her hostess sucked her lips in over her toothless gums so that her nose reached her chin. "My brother went to see Dr John Harries and do you know what he told him?"

Elizabeth shook her head dutifully.

"When you go home you will find your money back in your pocket and the thief will be bed-ridden for the rest of his life."

When my brother got home, sure enough, the money was in his pocket but his wife was ill in bed. *SHE* was the thief and she was bed-ridden until she died nineteen years later. Now, what do you think of that?"

"That's very strange."

"Well, you be careful if you go anywhere near Cwrt-y-Cadno. I'll say no more. There's bad blood in that family still, I'll warrant, though the present doctor seems to stick to medicine more than devil-worship."

Elizabeth stood up. "I must be on my way. Thank you so much for the tea; I've enjoyed listening to your stories and I feel better for the rest."

They went out into the daylight where Elizabeth picked up her case.

"When you go, watch out for the crow yonder," the old woman said under her breath. "It could be the witch who lives on the other side of the mountain; she turns herself into a crow sometimes but I don't think she will venture much further. Did you not notice how she has been following you?"

Elizabeth frowned. "No."

"Well, turn round now and then to be on the safe side."

"I will. Good day to you, Ma'am, and thank you once again."

"Good day to you, little one."

Elizabeth continued her journey, revived but still picking up her heels to relieve the pain. The sun was sinking over the horizon, glowing red and orange and fading to yellow on either side as she approached the cross-roads where she put the case down at the foot of the sign-post.

PUMPSAINT 2 miles.

It was dusk when she hobbled into the tiny hamlet. Her head was hanging low and she wasn't far from tears. She fixed her eyes on the ground as she struggled against the pain, aware that she must have been a strange sight. A long skirt appeared in front of her and she looked up.

"Can you tell me where Larks Farm is, if you please?"

"Why, yes! It's around the corner," the woman answered eagerly. "Going to the Williamses, are you?"

Elizabeth nodded, too weary to reply. She went on, but when she reached the corner she sank to the ground and pulled her boots off, tying them together and hanging them around her neck. That eased the pain but the ground was uneven and hard. Lights glowing in nearby cottages helped her to see the way forward and with all her energy concentrated on her feet she lurched slowly on, swinging the case from hand to hand.

It was a while before she realised that someone was shouting in the distance. She frowned and stopped, staring ahead without seeing anything, unless, maybe.....yes. Lanterns were swaying in the darkness.

"Elizabeth! Is that you?"

She wiped her face with her sleeve as figures loomed out of the night. Her uncle and aunt were running towards her.

"Elizabeth! We have been so worried!" her aunt cried. "We've been looking for you for hours!"

"You have walked from the coaching inn?" her uncle said incredulously. "What are your boots doing around your neck?"

Elizabeth's stockings were in tatters; blood and dirt mingled with the woollen yarn around her feet. She sniffed and swallowed but could find no words.

"Take this lantern," her uncle told his sister as he dived towards his niece, scooping her up from the ground as she fainted.

When she came to her senses she was sitting in an arm-chair in front of the kitchen fire at the farm, aware of soothing water lapping around her feet, which were immersed in a bowl. "There, there! You will be all right now," her aunt said. "You are here in Larks Farm at last. What a day it has been for us all!"

"What happened to me?"

"You fainted, that's all. Small wonder after all you have been through. Now, would you like a bowl of steaming hot broth?"

"That would be wonderful!" Elizabeth said, letting her head fall back against the cushion that had been put there. She gave a wan smile to her uncle who was sitting on the settle.

"We went out in the pony and trap to look for you, but I suppose you took the short cut by Grannie Bowen's cottage," he said.

"Is she the old woman who lives in a hut? If so, she was very kind. She took me in for a rest and gave me a cup of tea."

Her aunt put the wooden bowl of cawl in Elizabeth's lap and handed her a wooden spoon. "There you are. Eat that up and you will be as right as rain in no time. I am going to boil some rice to wrap round those feet of yours; that will ease the pain. You won't forget today in a hurry, will you!"

"Not if I live to be a hundred."

That night, Elizabeth slept on a feather mattress in a four-poster bed, unaware of the nightjar and the wind blowing through the elm trees; she didn't hear the cockerel at dawn nor the rooks swirling above the farmstead in the morning. The cows had been fetched and milked before she stirred, when her aunt appeared carrying a tray of hot buttermilk, two rashers of bacon, sausages, eggs and a plate of brown bread and butter.

"Hello, there! Are you feeling rested? I've brought your breakfast. Now, mind, eat it all. Your father told us you needed fattening up and we are good at that, here on the farm."

Chapter 21

While her aunt and the dairy-maid, Rosie, went about their tasks Elizabeth spent most of the day sitting by the hearth in the kitchen with her feet on a cushion. The old, half-blind sheepdog Meg slept on a rag rug at her feet. Tinkerbell, the cat, curled up in a shaft of sunlight on the window-sill. The stable door leading out to the farmyard remained open most of the time until the chickens became a nuisance, strutting inside and pecking at bits of dust in between the flagstones. Not long after Rosie shooed them out and shut the bottom half of the door, the pony appeared, sticking his neck through the top half of the door, hoping for some sugar.

The next day, Elizabeth was able to walk around the farmyard with the aid of one of her uncle's walking-sticks. At the far end of the vegetable garden stood the small brick house which had a scrubbed pine seat with three holes of varying sizes in it, useful, Elizabeth thought, if a brood of children lived at the farm. Honeysuckle spilled over the top of one of the white-washed walls, while a large spider's web was draped across the opposite corner.

"Don't bother to walk down the garden before bending down to see if you can see any feet under the door," her aunt told her. "That's what we do."

In the afternoon, Siôn, the farm labourer, brought in a chicken whose neck he had just wrung. He slung it on a table by the door and was about to wield the meat cleaver when he saw Elizabeth staring at him with horror.

"I beg your pardon, Miss," he said, with a grin. "I'll go outside."

When he returned he was carrying the bird minus its head and feet. "There you are, I've brought your supper in."

Elizabeth watched fascinated as Rosie removed the innards and proceeded to wrap the chicken in clay which she scooped up from a bucket. "But it hasn't been plucked!"

"No need to. The feathers come off with the clay when it's cooked," Rosie explained.

While the chicken was being prepared, her aunt made pikelets for their tea. What went in altogether Elizabeth didn't notice but at one stage she saw half-a-dozen eggs and a jug of cream going into the bowl. After being poured on to the bakestone and cooked, each pikelet was dropped into a basin of melted butter.

"If you go on feeding me like this I shall be fat enough to go home next week!" she cried, after supper. "I've never tasted a more delicious chicken. It was so tender."

"Well, you'll be having a treat tomorrow night, I hope," her uncle said. "I'm going fishing with a friend; a tributary of the Teifi flows through his land. With luck you'll taste something that I'm sure you haven't had before - sewin."

"What's that?"

"It's like salmon, only nicer," her aunt told her. "You must have some pheasant before you leave too. Rosie, will you see to that, please?"

As the family sat around the fire afterwards, Rosie lowered the bread-basket from the ceiling and took out a small loaf. Sitting at the kitchen table, she threaded string back and forth through the loaf with a bodkin, leaving loops at each end; every now and then she looked up and grinned at Elizabeth.

"You're wondering what is going on over there, I can see," her uncle said. "Rosie's preparing to catch a pheasant."

Elizabeth frowned. "Well, I couldn't imagine her going out at sunrise with a shot-gun, I must say, but even that makes more sense than - whatever she is doing now."

Rosie got to her feet and went up the kitchen stairs with the loaf in her hand, delighted with the effect she had had on the visitor.

"You may not like this but she'll put the bread on my bedroom window-sill and in the morning Siôn will look for a very dead pheasant lying on the ground," Uncle Thomas said.

"Aw! No! It will have choked on the string!"

Her uncle pursed his lips. "I doubt if it's less painful to be shot and plummet to earth."

"I prefer buying things in the butcher's shop in a town, I think."

Her aunt laughed. "So would Rosie, if the truth be told. She won't eat any animal if she knows which one it is, or was I should say. You see that ham up there? Well, that was Billy; Rosie used to talk to him when she tipped the pig-swill in the sty and she isn't far off tears when she sees Thomas carving him up in slices."

The time Elizabeth spent at Larks Farm that summer was an idyll. She fed the animals, weeded the vegetable garden, picked beans, dug up potatoes, fetched the cows and went delivering milk with Rosie in the early mornings with a wooden yoke over her shoulders, her hands steadying the buckets at her side.

Once a week she went to see her other uncle and his wife who lived next door to the smithy; they always visited the farm on Sunday evenings after chapel. On those occasions, Rosie lit a fire in the parlour, which was rarely used otherwise; the room had a rather dank odour but the jollity of the proceedings made up for its slight air of gloom.

Aunt Anne would sit at the harmonium, which had two keyboards and rows of ivory stops at each side. It wasn't easy to play as the foot pedals had to be kept going non-stop for any sound to emerge.

"Oh, I wonder, Oh I wonder,
will the angels way up yonder
will the angels play their harps
for me?"
They sang with gusto while Aunt Anne perspired; Rosie and Siôn joined in from the kitchen and had better voices than those in the parlour, Elizabeth thought. She tried to sing herself, holding a hand at her throat to no avail, but she smiled whenever someone looked at her. She told herself that it would be easier to accept her loss here on the farm rather than at home where they had heard her sing and knew what it meant to her.
"In the sweet by and by,
we shall meet
on that wonderful shore!"
Elizabeth wished that Morgan was there to share those lamplit evenings in the Carmarthenshire hills.
"There is a happy land,
far, far away."
As far as she was concerned, there was no happier place on earth than the farm, where she would gladly have stayed for ever.

Two pheasants were cooked after hanging up for three weeks. While Rosie covered them with clay, Elizabeth chopped up bacon, prunes and apples which were put in a large pan with half a pound of butter and two bay-leaves. This was put in the oven half an hour before the clay was removed from the cooked birds - a messy business. As soon as they had been cleaned they were added to the pan and turned now and then so that they could brown. When their skins were brittle, they were taken out and put on one side while a pint of cream was added to the juices in the pan. It was a meal to remember.
A week before leaving, her aunt took her to meet the Wizard's son, also called Henry, and his wife Doris. Siôn brought the pony and trap round to the kitchen door and handed the reins to Aunt Anne when she had taken her seat in front. Elizabeth climbed up through the small door at the back and closed the latch as they set off.
It was a perfect day. As they drove away from the farm, sunlight flickered through the Lombardy poplars lining the road; the pony clip-clopped along as if he too was enjoying the outing in the soft balmy air. They went through the village, stopping for a few minutes outside the smithy before going on into the open countryside, past fields of ripening corn which in the distance looked like pocket-handkerchiefs lying on the ground.
Elizabeth was in the yellow muslin dress that she wore at her father's wedding and had borrowed a pale blue bonnet from her aunt for the occasion. She was a very different person from the pathetic creature who had arrived at the farm. Her figure had returned and she made a pretty picture as she swayed from side to side, trying to take everything in so

that she could describe it when she went home.

They had a warm welcome when they reached Pant-coy and although Dr Henry and his wife did all they could to make her feel at ease, Elizabeth was wary at first, recalling Granny Bowen's words of warning. However, it became impossible not to relax when Doris showed her the new coat that she had bought for her husband in Carmarthen.

It was an enormous garment - but then he was a tall man, six-foot-five at least. Doris held it while Henry put it on and then she stood with her back to him while he fastened the coat around the two of them. Since she was only five-foot-one, her head disappeared but her voice could be heard coming from the second button-hole down. Dr Henry was now fat as well as tall, looking comical as he walked around the room on four legs that didn't match.

After that performance, Elizabeth forgot her shyness and enjoyed talking to the doctor, who asked her about Dr William Price. She told him about the remedy for inflammation, which interested him so much he went to get quill and ink to write it down.

After a sumptuous tea of tomato and parsley sandwiches, bread and butter with gooseberry jam, oat cakes, and apple-tart, Elizabeth asked if she could have her fortune told.

"I've heard so much about your family's knowledge of the planets and your grandfather's book."

"Of course Henry will tell your fortune!" Doris announced.

Her aunt joined in. "Go on, Henry! It would mean a lot to Elizabeth."

He smiled. "I don't seem to have much choice in the matter."

Doris cleared the table and covered it with a green velour cloth while Henry produced the book from a small coffer. It was leather-bound, edged with brass and in a pretty battered state. Doris produced the three keys which were needed to open the heavy locks protecting the tome.

"Right! I shall tell this young lady's fortune but not when anyone else is present," Dr Henry said, standing at the door which he held open while the others left.

Elizabeth sat nervously at the table. Dr Henry took a chair opposite her.

"What was the date of your birth?" he asked quietly.

"September 19th, 1860."

Silence followed while the doctor opened the book and fingered through the pages.

"Do you know the hour of your birth?"

Elizabeth bit her lower lip anxiously before suddenly clasping her hands. "Just before four o'clock in the morning! The first words my grandmother said were 'Thank goodness, just in time for me to light the oven'; she always did that at exactly four o'clock."

Dr Henry was unmoved by her outburst and it seemed a life-time before he spoke. Eventually, he sat back and studied her, looking serious.

"Well, there are several probabilities, more possibilities and a few certainties. Let's deal with the certainties, shall we?"

Elizabeth nodded.

"You have survived three grievous losses."

She frowned.

"You will have two husbands."

"Two?" she cried.

"You will rear four children," Dr Henry said, disregarding her reaction. "One will be clever; one will leave you to live far away over an ocean and one will become rich."

They sat in silence while Elizabeth absorbed the information. "Is there any more?" she whispered after a while.

The doctor consulted the book once again. "Your first husband has dark hair and has a mole on his right arm, near the elbow."

Elizabeth relaxed. This was clearly nonsense, but she said nothing, out of politeness, and Dr Henry was taking the matter seriously.

"You will live until the age of seventy-six and die a widow. That's all I am going to tell you."

She took a deep breath. "Well, two husbands! Four children! A long life! It sounds interesting, I must say. Thank you, doctor."

Elizabeth and her aunt left shortly afterwards. As Aunt Anne tugged the reins, Doris blew a kiss but Dr Henry stood in the road until out of sight, looking solemn.

Elizabeth told her uncle and aunt about the prophecy that evening, dismissing it as a harmless piece of fun. "I'm walking out with Morgan and he has light brown hair; we'll get married in time, no doubt."

That night, she smiled as she drifted off to sleep. "Two husbands indeed!" She turned round and settled down again. 'One child will be clever.' Why not all of them? 'One will leave you.' That's a pity. 'One will be rich!' There's lovely!"

She sat up. "What about the other one? There will be four."

She pummelled the bolster before lying on her back and staring at the ceiling.

Half an hour later she got up and walked to the window where she stood looking out over the moonlit farmyard.

'You have survived three grievous losses.'

"Grandma, my mother and.......who else? Nobody that you could describe as a grievous loss."

It was a still clear night. The elms swayed silently at the edge of the field beyond the five-barred gate; an owl hooted from the lichened roof of the hay-loft where Siôn slept. Elizabeth looked at the star shining more brightly than the rest.

As she climbed back into bed she paused. "Of course! It wasn't a person! It was my singing voice!"

She pulled the quilt over her head.

'Your first husband has dark hair and a mole on his arm, near the elbow'

"Hah! So much for the planets!"

Chapter 22

Elizabeth left the farm three days later. Siôn and Rosie waved from the farmyard gate; Aunt Anne, Uncle Thomas and her aunt and uncle from the smithy saw her off in the coach. She took little interest in the journey home, indeed it was difficult to see anything at all for the first ten minutes, as she had to keep blinking away the moisture in her eyes. She felt as if she was leaving a sunlit world of dreams and travelling back to an ordinary place, where hearts were heavier and the skies were not as blue.

"Elizabeth! What a difference! That's better!" Gwen cried when they met at Pontypridd station.

"I've had such a wonderful time. Aunt Anne gave me these for you," she said, handing over a brace of pheasants. "I've got a sewin for Dada - he will be so pleased."

"He hasn't stopped worrying about you. In the beginning he thought you mightn't live, and then, when you stayed for such a long time, he thought you wouldn't come back."

Elizabeth felt a twinge of guilt. No one would know how much she had longed to stay on the farm.

"Morgan Richards called the other day, wanting to know when you were coming home. He was sent over to a branch of the chain works outside Paris in July; he only came back last Tuesday."

David came straight home from work. "It's good to see you, my girl! I knew they would put you right on the farm."

"Dada, how could you ever leave such a beautiful place and come here to live?"

He smiled. "I had to get work, but I'd like a holiday there, to see them all again. Does Thomas still fish for sewin?"

"You are going to have one for your supper."

"Never! Aw! We used to fish together as boys. My word! You are a different girl, isn't she, Gwen? How many cows have they got on the farm now? Is the smithy busy? How are the Harrieses?"

Elizabeth told him about the tea that Doris had provided and about walking about inside Dr Henry's coat. She didn't mention the fortune-telling, but went on to describe how they caught the pheasants and cooked them on the farm.

"I know, they've always done that. Does the pony still put his head through the door for sugar?"

She grinned and nodded. "I think that what I'll miss most is the scent of the herbs in the garden and the earth after a shower of rain, the smell of the pony and the leather of his harness, the honeysuckle and the fresh bread from the stick oven, just like the bread shop, but most of all, the wood-smoke, that wood-smoke everywhere."

David hung on each word.

"I'll miss the animals too. Do you know, they all had a name; there was even a spider called Adam."

When Philip Jones came back at seven o'clock, Elizabeth was standing in the kitchen with her back to the door, gesticulating with her arms as she told Gwen how she had carried her milk-yoke in the mornings. He stood smiling at David, a finger at his lips, listening to the story. She didn't realise he was there until she sat down with a flourish.

"Hello, Miss Williams. You are looking...well. I gather you enjoyed your holiday."

"Yes, thank you," she said politely.

"You are going to have a great meal tonight, Philip," David said. "Have you ever tasted sewin?"

That evening, Elizabeth cooked the sewin and brought it proudly to the table where the others sat waiting. Never had the family had such a feast. Afterwards, David cut the cheese that his sister Anne had sent and put large chunks on everyone's plate.

His face lit up when he tasted it. "Good!" he said. "They still have the old harness in the dairy."

"How did you know? The dairy was spotlessly clean and yet there was this filthy thing hanging on the wall. I didn't like to ask them about it."

Her father grinned. "Did you smell it?"

"It was difficult not to; it was putrid."

"That accounts for the special tang that you can taste; they sell that cheese in the markets for miles around. The harness is one of the most precious things on the farm."

"Well, how strange!" she said. "They didn't eat the pheasants until they smelt like old goats either. Aunt Anne says we should wait for about three weeks - where are we going to hang them here? Not in the parlour, I hope."

As they settled around the fire after the meal, Elizabeth told them a story about the Wizard of Cwrt-y-Cadno that David hadn't heard.

"A young man was suffering from melancholy, sitting in a corner all day long and crying. His family couldn't cheer him up so they went to see old Dr Harries who told them to bring the young man to the stream at midnight where he would meet them. The wizard took the boy down to the water's edge and talked to him for a while; the patient's head was hanging low and he didn't see the doctor pulling a pistol out from under the cloak he was wearing. Without warning, a shot was fired into the night air and the young man was so shocked, he fell into the stream and had to be rescued by his parents.

"'You will feel better tomorrow,' Dr Harries said, and he was right. The young man got better from then on!"

Elizabeth told the story as old Granny Bowen had, acting the part of the patient, his family and the wizard. She didn't see the looks that passed between David and Gwen when they noticed the softness in Philip Jones's eyes as he listened.

David wrote a long letter to the farm late that night, thanking them for the transformation they had wrought in his daughter.

At nine o'clock the next morning the wife of the under-manager at the Great Western colliery called, bringing a roll of material and a pattern for a dress that she wanted made as soon as possible. At ten o'clock Elizabeth was cutting it out on the oak table in the parlour. Life had returned to normal. Every now and then she paused and walked to the window, looking over the railwayline to the rows of houses on the other side. The chimney smoke curling up over the town, and the sad, worried faces of passers-by could not have been more of a contrast with the scenes of the past two months.

Morgan called at the house on Tuesday evening to take her to singing practice. She had forgotten her old routine and didn't know how to handle the situation.

"Hello! Come in a minute while I get my shawl," she said, thinking quickly.

"Aw! There's well you look! Life on that farm did you good."

"I'm going to singing practice with Morgan, mother," she called as they left.

When they had turned the corner, Elizabeth blurted out: "I can't sing any more. When they took my tonsils out - that was the end of my voice."

Morgan stopped and looked at her aghast. She might as well have struck him a blow on the head as far as his reaction was concerned.

"Your voice! Gone?"

"Gone. I've had time to get used to the idea; there are worse things in life. I'll walk with you as far as the chapel. I've been in the house all day and I need some fresh air."

Morgan said nothing for a while, then: "I can't believe this. Are you sure? What do your parents say about it?"

"I haven't discussed it with them, but they have probably guessed."

"They must be upset. It's awful for you."

"Let's talk no more about it. I hear you have been in Paris while I was away. What was that like?"

"But it means that I will only see you after chapel on Sundays! What will we do?" he asked miserably.

Elizabeth was exasperated. "Well, we could go for walks on Mondays or Wednesdays or Thursdays or Fridays," she said, spelling things out for him.

"What if it rains?"

She rolled her eyes. "We can sit in the parlour while my father reads us a story."

They had reached the chapel. "Morgan, have you got a mole on your right forearm?"

He blinked. "A mole? No. Why do you ask?"

"I just wondered, that's all."

When she saw him the following Sunday, he still expressed concern about her voice, upset because she wouldn't be able to go carol-singing that year.

"Please, Morgan, I wish you wouldn't keep reminding me."

"I only wanted to explain that since you couldn't come carol-singing this Christmas I intend cheering you up by taking you to see an opera."

"An opera? Where?"

He grinned. "You know the Omara Opera Company is touring Wales. Well, I've bought two tickets for a performance of *Maritana* at the new Theatre Royal in Cardiff in December," he said proudly.

"Never! That will be wonderful! In Cardiff?" Elizabeth cried. "They say the new theatre is very grand."

"There will be a big orchestra and we have seats in the stalls."

"In the stalls? That must have cost a fortune!"

"A guinea, but it will be worth it."

"Well, that's generous of you, Morgan bach."

"Only six more weeks to wait."

"I'll count the days. What a treat to look forward to!"

Elizabeth stayed at home, making garments for several ladies. Her reputation as a dressmaker had spread, and a queue waited for her return from the farm. She was glad of a continuous flow of orders, but everyone wanted their clothes in a hurry.

"Miss Williams, could you possibly have this ready by Saturday? My son's young lady is coming to tea; she's from a posh family and I don't want to let him down."

"Oh, Miss Williams, I'm on the spot! I have to go to my sister-in-law's funeral on Thursday and I haven't got a rag to wear."

Elizabeth sometimes sat up all night, rushing off with a dress in the morning. A few weeks after coming home, she stayed up long after midnight to finish a satin wedding-dress, which she folded and left on the table in the parlour. She had enjoyed making it for the beautiful seventeen-year-old daughter of Mr Fowler, who had sunk the Maritime colliery. He was a wealthy man. The satin was of the best quality, costing twenty shillings a yard and it had taken two whole days to embroider dozens of seed pearls around the collar and cuffs. She and Mattie were going to watch the bride arriving at the church in two days' times.

It was a stormy night. Rain beat on the window panes and gurgled down the drain-pipes as she got wearily into bed. She put her head on the pillow and imagined Penelope Fowler walking down the aisle. Elizabeth thought that the wedding-dress was the loveliest gown she had ever made, and was proud of it; it was an honour to have been chosen to make it for the wedding of the year in Pontypridd. She drifted happily off to sleep, lulled to rest by a chorus of raindrops.

An hour or so later she woke suddenly, hearing a noise like a train roaring at speed past the back of the house. It was followed by banging in the yard - knocking sounds that occurred at intervals. When she went to the window she saw the casks used for catching rain-water floating around in two or three feet of muddy water, hitting against the kitchen door every so often. It didn't take long to realise that water must be seeping into the house, into the hall and, NO! the parlour! The wedding-dress! She grabbed a shawl and ran downstairs, calling out for her father, but Philip Jones was on the landing before him.

"Don't go any further, Elizabeth!" he said, looking at water swirling around the bottom two steps of the stairs.

"I must rescue the wedding-dress; the water could be near the top of the table," she cried, as she stepped down and waded towards the parlour. Philip Jones followed.

She couldn't get the door open because of the amount of slurry on the floor on both sides but Philip gritted his teeth and leant against it, pushing it slowly inwards. David Williams came downstairs, watched by Gwen, who leant over the banisters.

"If you can open the front door as well, it might help, Sir. We need to shovel some of this muck out," Philip said, pushing the parlour door back far enough to let Elizabeth squeeze through.

"Thank goodness the dress is all right!" he heard her say. "But what if the water gets higher? I must get it upstairs!" When she realised that he was standing behind her she grabbed his hand. "Aw! Please, help me! Please, Philip."

He put a hand over hers. "Of course I'll help you. Tell me what to do."

She picked up an old sheet that needed darning. "Hold your hands out," she said. "I'll drape this over your arms to make sure that we don't get any marks on the satin." She stood by his side. "Now, you stay there while I get my arms under the sheet as well and then.......we can roll the dress on to it."

"What next?"

"I'll move away a bit and lift the train."

He watched and waited.

"So far, so good!" she said.

He frowned. "We still have to get through the door somehow, don't forget."

"Aw!" Elizabeth moaned. "How?"

"Take a step back towards the window. If your father comes in he can move the mud behind the door on this side."

She looked stricken. "Dada! Can you come here and help us to get out?"

"It will be all right, Elizabeth, I promise you it will be all right," Philip said.

She looked at him. "What would happen if the bride couldn't wear this? What about the wedding?"

She closed her eyes as her father brought the spade in and started shovelling mud from one side of the room to the other, while Philip pushed the door further back with one foot.

"You can open your eyes now, little one."

The door was open. Slowly they edged into the hall, holding the dress above their heads.

"I'll go first," Philip said at the bottom of the stairs. "Follow me a step at a time. Don't hurry."

He kicked her bedroom door open and went in sideways. Elizabeth walked round to the window-side of the bed and put her half of the dress on the pillow as Philip lowered the rest.

"The bride will never know how lucky she's been!" Elizabeth whispered. "Philip, I'm so grateful. Thank you."

"It was my pleasure!" he said. "At last you have said my name, twice in fact. That means more to me than any 'thank you'."

She walked back towards the door, hanging her head with embarrassment.

He put a hand under her chin, lifting it slightly. "Look at me, Elizabeth. Are we friends now?"

She smiled and nodded.

"In that case, I'll bring up a bowl of water so that you can wash your feet. Have you seen them?"

She looked down and laughed. "They are no worse than yours!"

The next day the family learnt that a culvert had burst high on the mountain-side, flooding houses lower down. David and Philip worked from morning till night on the yard and the kitchens while Elizabeth and Gwen toiled in the parlour and hall.

"Philip will lose a day's wages, you know," Gwen said, as they scrubbed the parlour floor. "Other lodgers in the street have gone to work. He's the kindest of men; we are lucky to have him living with us."

Elizabeth sat back on her heels and stared at the wall, deep in thought.

When Morgan and Elizabeth arrived back in Pontypridd, after their visit to the opera in Cardiff, it started to drizzle but neither took much notice, being in a trance-like state after the feast of music. Elizabeth was familiar with many of the arias, but hadn't heard the whole work performed with a symphony orchestra. The red velvet curtains, the conductor in evening dress, the glittering jewels, spectacular ball-gowns and the volume of sound when the full orchestra played and everyone on the stage sang had quite overwhelmed her.

It was getting on for half-past-eleven; reflected moonlight quivered in the puddles on the road but the real world seemed drab and ordinary after the radiance of the opera.

When they reached Feeder Row, she sighed. "It's been a wonderful evening, hasn't it?"

"Something to remember for ever," Morgan said, turning up his collar and looking at the sky. "I'd better run. It looks as if it's going to start pelting down."

He looked at her wistfully. "Good night, dear," he said, giving her a peck on the cheek.

She went inside, surprised to see light shining under the kitchen door. Philip Jones was sitting by the fire, his coat slung over the back of the chair and his shirt-sleeves rolled up.

"What are you doing here at this time of night?" she asked.

"I must have fallen asleep," he said as he stood up. "Did you enjoy the opera?"

She stood warming her hands in front of the fire, her thoughts far away. "It was...majestic!"

"Here, let me take your shawl, it's damp. The kettle has boiled once."

"I have never heard such music, so beautifully sung, and the orchestra...well!" She shook her head. "Those trumpets and the clashing cymbals and the harp!" Her eyes were sparkling. "When the soprano sang 'I dreamt that I dwelt in marble halls' I sang the words with her, inside my head.

She sat down, gazing into the fire in a reverie as Philip made tea. "Do you know *Maritana*? Have you ever seen it performed?" she asked absently, not taking her eyes from the depth of the fire.

"Yes, I saw it in the Metropolitan Opera House in New York."

Elizabeth became aware of her surroundings, sitting back in the chair and staring at him. "New York? The Metropolitan!"

"I worked in a colliery in Scranton for some years. I went to the opera the night before I sailed home."

"Why did you come back to Wales?"

"My mother is ill. All my brothers live in America now and have families. Only two sisters are at home; Celia is seventeen and Maggie a year younger. I came back to be near them and help if necessary."

Her shoulders fell as she watched him pouring out the tea. He handed her a cup.

"Thank you."

They sat in silence for a while.

"You go away for a night every three weeks, I've noticed. Is that when you go home to see your mother?" Elizabeth asked.

"Yes, and my sisters. Incidentally, while we're talking about them, they walked eight miles over the mountain to Ebbw Vale to see *Maritana* a month ago. They enjoyed it as much as you have."

She turned to look at the fire again. "I'm sorry about the fish," she blurted out suddenly.

He frowned. "Fish?"

"It was kind of you to walk three miles after work to get it for me, when I was ill," she mumbled with downcast eyes. "I shouldn't have sent it back downstairs."

"The Dover sole! Don't give it another thought. I ate it myself. It was delicious; you missed a treat."

Elizabeth grinned. "I was afraid of that at the time."

He smiled at her.

"Will you go back to America one day?"

"Possibly. It all depends. I'm glad I came back, though - when you are at a distance you worry more about things; when you are where the trouble is, at least you know what's happening." He looked at her. "Yes, I'm glad I came back. Have you found that things happen sometimes as if they were destined?" He picked up the poker and stirred the fire. "Do you know what I mean?"

Elizabeth's cup rattled in the saucer until she slapped a hand on it. "Destined? They can't be." She had turned pale. "I mean.......er......well, how can they?" she stammered in confusion.

"What's the matter, dear? What has upset you?"

"Nothing!" she spluttered as she stood up, put the cup and saucer on the table, and ran out of the room.

She had seen a large mole on his arm, near the elbow.

She spent a sleepless night and found it difficult to concentrate on her sewing next day. It wasn't Philip Jones that she thought about, it was Morgan. She listed his positive qualities in her mind - he was generous, he had a lovely singing voice and perfect pitch, they had had enjoyable times together and, and...what else? She couldn't think of anything. On the negative side - he could be just that little bit boring, he had no imagination, he was an inch shorter than she was and he had an awful mother, but that was hardly his fault.

'Why is he walking me home from chapel?' she asked herself. 'Why not?' 'Because now look what a mess you are in!' 'But I couldn't have known! It's all Philip Jones's fault. No, it's not - it's the wizard's fault. What does it matter whose fault it is - what is to be done about it? I DON'T KNOW! !'

She was tongue-tied when Philip came home from work that day. She stayed in the parlour, knowing that he went straight into the kitchen and washed. Later, she had to help Gwen to get a meal but that was all right because her father was in the kitchen as well. She hardly spoke while they ate and after clearing up she returned to the parlour, where she stayed until she went to bed.

On Sunday, if the others went out of the room, she made an excuse and went out too but matters came to a head on Sunday evening, on the way home from chapel. Morgan had depressed her all day, not that he had done or said anything untoward, at least, until they reached Feeder Row.

"Before you go in, let me tell you something," he said. "I think I'll have saved enough money for us to get married next year. I wanted to tell you before, only my mother told me not to because you got tonsilitis."

It was not a romantic proposal.

"This is so........" she could hardly call it sudden. "Will you let me think about this? Um.. I have so much work to do before Christmas, so many orders, I won't have time to..... well, I would need to make new clothes for myself, wouldn't I?"

Morgan considered her logic and agreed with it. "All right, I shall propose to you on New Year's Eve, on my knees. Don't forget that I love you."

Elizabeth stared after him as he walked away, knowing that she could never marry him. Her hands were at her mouth and she was trembling.

Philip walked down the stairs. "What's the matter, Elizabeth?"

She spun round, looked at him for a second and then closed her eyes. "Nothing, nothing!"

"Something is wrong. Who has upset you?"

"No one!" she groaned as she ran up the stairs.

He stepped out to the street and saw Morgan walking jauntily away with his hands in his pockets. He stood working things out for a while before walking quickly back to the kitchen.

"I'd like a word with you in private," he said quietly to David. "Not now, there isn't time. Tomorrow perhaps, when I come home from work; we could talk in here while the women are in the parlour."

Philip sat hunched in the tub, rubbing his neck with a soapy flannel. "It's hardly appropriate for me to be sitting in a bath-tub when I ask your permission to propose to your daughter, Sir, but I didn't see how else we could be sure of being alone."

David's face lit up as he leaned forward in the rocking-chair. "You want to marry Elizabeth?" he whispered.

"If you agree. I fell in love with her the first day I came to this house. She disliked me for a long time - that was entirely my fault, but now I think at last she might listen to me. When she was so ill, I shared your anxieties; it was difficult not to talk about her and let you know what I felt."

"Well, well! This is great news! I am delighted, my boy. Very pleased indeed, and Gwen will say the same, I'm sure."

"Thank you. The problem is that she has been avoiding me for the past few days. I wish I knew why. Something is worrying her I know, but I can't think what it is. The time has come to let her know my feelings. I'm not sure when, but you had to know in advance."

"Poor Morgan is the problem. He's a nice boy and he has had his chances, but...Gwen says that Elizabeth doesn't love him. I don't think he realises that and neither does she," David said.

"I'm quite sure she doesn't love Morgan," Philip said emphatically.

"It isn't an easy situation. Women are contrary creatures, aren't they?"

Philip smiled. "They can be perplexing at times"

"I can only wish you luck. Poor Philip!"

"And poor Morgan! She has no idea what she's doing to us both, but I feel better that you know my feelings, at any rate. By the way, may we keep this conversation to ourselves?"

"Of course, my boy."

A customer came for a fitting one evening, a few days later; when the session was over, Elizabeth showed her to the door. Philip seized his chance, opening the kitchen door quietly and closing it behind him. He stood waiting in the passage by the side of the grandfather clock. Elizabeth was startled when she turned round and saw him.

"Elizabeth, we must talk. Please don't run away from me," he said, advancing towards her.

She darted into the parlour, which was what he hoped she would do. He followed her in, closing the door behind him.

"I wish I knew why you are avoiding me," he said gently. "Have I done something to upset you?"

She sat at the sewing-machine, looking at the floor. Philip stood leaning against the door, his hands behind him.

"I wouldn't upset you for the world! I fell in love with you as soon as I came to live in this house and I would do anything for you."

Silence followed.

"I hadn't met a woman that I wanted to share my life with until I saw you. I think of you every moment; you have captured my heart and my whole being. You cannot know what anguish you cause me when you shrink from me, when you won't even look at me."

Elizabeth looked out of the window, twisting her hands. "I'm walking out with Morgan," she whispered.

"But you don't love him."

She looked at him in despair.

"Think about all I have said. It's no good running away any more. I shall follow you to the ends of the earth. I will never let you go."

He walked towards the sewing-machine and stood over her. When she lowered her head he bent down and kissed the back of her neck.

"I love you so much; you are dear beyond measure," he whispered, before going out, closing the door quietly behind him.

After he had gone Elizabeth sat quivering, with a hand on her neck where she had been kissed.

When she joined the others in the kitchen a good ten minutes later, Philip looked up and smiled, but said nothing. In fact, Gwen had to do most of the talking during supper, and found it heavy going.

The next evening, when Philip was washing in the kitchen, Elizabeth put her shawl on and told her father that she was going out to see Morgan.

"I'll be back in time for supper, I hope."

David smiled. "Go you, my girl!"

Gwen was strumming at the piano and didn't look round until Elizabeth had gone. When they heard her footsteps fading, David stood up.

"She's gone to tell him!" he whispered. "Poor Morgan!"

"Poor Elizabeth!"

Fifteen minutes later Elizabeth came back with a long face.

"How is Morgan?" Gwen asked.

"I didn't see him. He was out carol-singing. He will be carol-singing every night until Christmas."

Elizabeth made no effort to avoid Philip in the next few days and met his eyes shyly when he spoke to her, but even when they were alone he talked about things in general, making her wonder if the conversation in the parlour had been a dream. Only when he left the house on Christmas Eve did he remind her of it.

He came downstairs holding a suitcase and stood in the hall until he caught her eye. He beckoned her out and walked to the front door where he took her hand, turning it over to kiss her palm.

"I don't want to leave you, God knows I don't but I must go to Brynmawr to see my family. This could be my mother's last Christmas, I'm afraid. You understand?"

She nodded. "When will you be back?"

"I'll be away for three days and, when I come back I'm going to ask you to marry me. Don't say anything now," he added hurriedly, squeezing her hand gently. "When I come back."

He turned to wave at her from the end of the street.

Elizabeth didn't enjoy Christmas that year; the house seemed darker and smaller without Philip. Straight after breakfast on Christmas morning, she set out again to see Morgan.

"What a terrible thing to have to do, on this day of all days!" Gwen said. "I wish she would confide in me. I want to put my arms around her and comfort her."

"Philip will do that when he comes back, Gwen *fach*," David said. "You and I have to stand back in all this. I don't think Philip would want us to interfere and you forget that you are not supposed to know what's going on."

Elizabeth came back trailing her shawl on the ground. "Morgan's got mumps. Uncle William has been to see him and told his mother to keep in him bed for a week and he mustn't have visitors."

She slumped into the rocking-chair by the fire, looking grim.

Chapter 23

It started to snow on Boxing Day, just small flakes at first but by New Year's Eve the valleys had become white winter-meadows, with no sign of coal-dust or grime. David decided that it would be a good idea to have a musical evening on the last night of the year and drew up a list of guests, including Dai Davies, Mattie Harries, Fat Onllwyn, Myfi Benion, Mrs Thank-you-Ta, Gerald Edwards and Our Dolly-by-here. Dilys Ebenezer was always welcome because she could play the violin. It had been taken for granted that Morgan would be present, and it was with relief that Elizabeth had a message from his mother saying that, although he was better, she didn't want him to be out so late at night.

Gwen and Elizabeth made three dozen pikelets, two dozen Welsh cakes and two apple-tarts. David ordered a crate of Thomas and Evans's Corona, containing sparkling lemonade and Dandelion and Burdock, so that they could drink a toast at midnight, as long as visitors brought their own glasses.

No one organised a formal programme, things happened spontaneously. As soon as the first guests arrived, Elizabeth sat at the piano and played a few bars of "Blaenwern" which got people going. Dai Davies was singing before he reached the front door, where David sang as he welcomed latecomers. They went on to "Cwm Rhondda" without pausing, after which Mrs Thank-you-Ta arrived and the men gathered round the piano for the "Anvil Chorus" from *Il Trovatore*. Most of the visitors brought music with them, which David stacked in a pile on the floor by the piano.

When Dai was persuaded to sing "O Isis and Osiris" they found seats or sat on the floor. Philip placed himself on the arm of Elizabeth's chair and stayed there until she got up to fetch tea and Welsh cakes - sustenance was needed following "Myfanwy", "Excelsior" and "The Martyrs of the Arena". By general demand Our Dolly-by-here sang "Y Deryn Pur" after which Myfi sang "On Wings of Song", one of Gwen's favourites.

Elizabeth was delighted when her father and Philip sang "Tenor & Baritone" after which volunteers were sought for the quartet from *Rigoletto*. They all joined in to raise the roof with "Hen Wlad fy Nhadau" before Dilys contributed by playing the violin part in "Panis Angelicus" which Our-Dolly-by here sang beautifully. After that, four guests were selected to render "Brightly Dawns Our Wedding Day". So far 'Fat Onllwyn' had done little but eat, so he was forced to stand up and sing "If with all your hearts".

Elizabeth was alarmed when Philip got to his feet and announced that he and Miss Williams would sing "The Keys of Heaven". She stayed in her seat, protesting about her voice but Philip insisted that she joined him and said her words.

The two of them stood in the middle of the room, waiting for the audience to settle down.

"Madam, will you walk?
Madam, will you talk?
Madam will you walk
and talk with me?"
"No, I will not walk,
No, I will not talk,
No, I will not walk
nor talk with you!"

Elizabeth had no choice but to act her part, which wasn't easy because Philip's antics were causing so much mirth.

"I will give you the keys of Heaven,
Madam, will you walk.........?"
"NO!" she shouted as loudly as she could.
"I WILL NOT!"
"I will give you six white horses..."
"NO!"
"I will give you diamonds and sapphires..."
"NO!"

Philip knelt down for the last verse:

"I will give you the keys to my heart.
Madam, will you walk,
Madam will you talk.
Madam, will you walk and talk with me?"
"YES then, I will walk,
YES then, I will talk,
YES then, I will walk and talk with you."

When the last note sounded, the guests cheered as Philip kissed Elizabeth's hand.

David brought the Corona bottles in and started to fill the glasses while Dai sang Vulcan's song from *Faust*.

Mrs Thank-you-Ta was enjoying herself. "This is a magnificent instrument," she said, stroking the side of the Bechstein.

"There's time for one more!" Gwen cried. "Gerald, we haven't had a solo from you yet. How about "Elen fwyn"?

He walked over to the window and pulled the curtains back. "Right! Let's have a bit of *hiraeth*. Will someone turn the lamps down, please?"

David lit the candles on the piano, as the other lights were dimmed. When a hush had fallen, Gerald stood with his back to the room, looking up at the night sky.

"Do you remember that night, Elen?
Do you remember the stars?
Do you remember me, Elen?
Do you remember, Elen fwyn?"

No one in the land had a sweeter tenor voice and the poignancy of the old song, as he sang it in the darkness, was powerful. Our Dolly-by-here was in tears and the others were so moved that they didn't clap for a few seconds. The reaction was more like the sound the deacons made on Sundays, when the preacher said something particularly apt.

"It's five to twelve!" David Williams shouted. "Has everyone got a glass?"

Dai Davies went out to open the front door so that they could hear the parish clock. Everyone else stood up, grinning at each other in the silence that followed.

As they waited, Philip held Elizabeth's hand and whispered in her ear; she looked up at him, smiled, and nodded. He put his glass on the table, looked across the room and as soon as he caught David's eye, he lifted Elizabeth's hand high in the air, shaking it in both of his, like a referee in a boxing match.

The chimes of the parish clock reached their ears, followed two seconds later by the chiming of the musical clock in the hall. The shouts went up: "Happy New Year! Happy New Year! It's 1880!"

Philip raised his glass and looked at Elizabeth. "Happy New Year, darling!"

She touched his glass with hers. "Happy New Year, Philip."

He bent down and kissed her.

A happy but weary household gathered for breakfast at nine o'clock. When they had finished the meal, Philip brought up the subject of Morgan.

"You must tell him today, dearest."

"Yes, if he's in chapel."

Gwen looked worried. "What if he isn't there?"

No one said anything.

"I can't go to his house and tell him in front of his mother!" Elizabeth cried.

"You could ask his mother if you can go for a walk with him tonight," David suggested.

Philip groaned. "What a ridiculous situation! As soon as we get engaged my sweetheart goes out with my rival!"

"You have nothing to fear, Philip, my boy," David told him, grinning.

"The sooner I tell him the better, but there isn't any hurry, is there," Elizabeth said.

"There certainly is!" Philip said, pulling a piece of paper from his back trouser-pocket. "This is a special licence which I've been carrying around for the past week. We're going to get married next Thursday."

Elizabeth's jaw dropped. "Next Thursday?"

"My mother is longing to meet you and...well, I want her to see you before she dies. I've reserved a room at a hotel in Newport for two nights, so that we can go to Brynmawr on Friday and spend the day with her."

Philip waited anxiously for Elizabeth to return from chapel.

"I didn't see him. His Uncle Elmer arrived from America last week and Morgan took him to the Baptist chapel. They've gone on from there to spend the day with some cousins in Rhydyfelin. Tomorrow night, Uncle Elmer's taking the family out for a meal at the New Inn and Mrs Richards said she's sorry I can't join them; she didn't like to suggest it because she isn't paying. They've asked me to go with them to a lecture which the uncle is giving in Sardis vestry on Wednesday."

"What about Tuesday evening?"

"Morgan goes to singing-practice."

He put a hand to his forehead. "This is awful!"

The family was subdued at lunch but Gwen was unusually tetchy. "It's positively ridiculous for a girl to be going out the night before her wedding, let alone with another man."

David frowned. "We all agree on that, but what else can Elizabeth do? What is this lecture about?"

Elizabeth groaned. "I was hoping you wouldn't ask."

Philip looked up. "Well?"

She swallowed. "Coal," she whispered.

"Coal?" David cried, putting his knife and fork down. His voice rose to a crescendo. "Did you say Coal? An American comes to the valleys of South Wales to give a lecture on *COAL*?"

"I don't believe it!" Philip said.

Elizabeth rolled her eyes.

To be fair to Uncle Elmer, who was employed by a pharmaceutical company currently engaged on the causes of certain skin-infections, he had chosen to lecture on "The Life Cycle of the Female Ringworm" which he claimed was fascinating, but Morgan's mother considered it an indelicate subject, quite inappropriate for Sardis Sunday School vestry when women and children would be present. He had no choice but to give his other talk which went down well back home in Wyoming where he felt like an expert, having been born in Pontypridd and worked in a colliery as a lad.

Elizabeth sat in the front row, flanked by Morgan and his parents. It was a large hall, with a high ceiling. A bright green stripe along each wall, about two-thirds down, separated the yellow ochre above from the chocolate-brown below. In the far corner, sepia photographs of missionaries from the town hung above the fireplace. Three dusty pallets, placed on top of each other, served as a platform where Uncle Elmer stood surveying his audience.

He acknowledged that it might seem strange for a visitor from the United States of America to be talking about coal in a land which exported more of the stuff than any country in the world, but he knew a lot about it, having been born and bred in Wales. Before five minutes had passed, he made his first mistake when he referred to the primeval sludge from which all life had emerged. The faithful, who were on the side of the angels and opposed to Darwin's theory of descent from orang-utangs, were not impressed. One or two moved their chairs noisily and some walked out, at which stage Morgan's mother wished she hadn't forbidden Elmer to tell them about Ringworms, even though the word reproduction might have to be mentioned.

Elizabeth found the lecture tedious, but sat day-dreaming about Philip. She returned to reality when Elmer announced that, as a finale, he was going to conduct a scientific experiment which would leave all those present with a lasting memory of the amazing powers of coal. He picked up a black tin box and placed it on a small table at his side, directly in front of Morgan's mother, which was unfortunate, the way things turned out.

"I have here, inside this ordinary tin box, a few pounds of coal-dust and I'm going to put a small lump of coal from the fireplace inside it. Morgan, perhaps you would assist. My nephew Morgan, and a fine lad he is too, ladies and gentlemen."

Morgan picked up the tongs in the hearth and extracted a piece of lighted coal from the fireplace, carrying it sheepishly over to Uncle Elmer who lifted the lid of the box and said: "Just drop that inside." After Uncle Elmer closed the lid, he stood back and beamed at the audience.

The resulting explosion blew several window panes into the street and filled the vestry with billowing clouds of coal-dust. Fortunately no one was hurt and the minister showed presence of mind by standing up in the darkness to give a vote of thanks, saying he had no idea there was so much to it. Morgan's mother burst into tears when she saw her hat lying on the floor with its Bird of Paradise feathers ruined, and Elmer was in a state of shock, saying he had carried out the same experiment many times back home without any mishap, but as someone pointed out to him, they didn't have Welsh steam coal in Wyoming.

The minister, Mr Morris, decided to dispense with the usual hymn and concluded the meeting by asking for volunteers to scrub the walls down before Sunday. Morgan and Elmer half-carried the distraught Mrs Richards home, while Mr Richards lingered on, apologising for the inconvenience his brother had caused, leaving Elizabeth to make her way back to Feeder Row alone.

She arrived at the kitchen doorway looking as if she had just completed a ten-hour shift at the bottom of the Great Western Colliery. "I didn't have a chance to tell him!" she sobbed.

Half an hour later, rôles were reversed. Philip sat with David and Gwen in the parlour, while Elizabeth enjoyed a good lather in the tub in front of the kitchen fire.

The following morning extraordinary events occurred in the chain works, when a man from the fitting-room appeared to go berserk. He was in the forge when the incident happened. Quite suddenly he started hurling hammers around; one he threw directly into the furnace, another went up into the roof and a third missed another worker's head by inches. Before anyone was injured however, three men grabbed him and threw him to the floor, where one sat on him and held his hands behind his back. The floor manager was sent for.

"Who is this man?"

"Morgan Richards. He came in and asked where David Williams was and when I told him he'd taken the day off to go to his daughter's wedding, he socked me one on the jaw."

Another man took up the story. "I came in afterwards and asked Richards what he was doing at work on his wedding-day and that started it. He just went mad. It's odd, because he is normally a meek and mild man - wouldn't say boo to a goose as the saying goes."

"Let him go. Stand up, Richards. What is going on?"

Within two seconds Morgan was back on the floor, with two men sitting on him.

"Tie him up with those ropes, get him on his feet and take him to the manager's office."

"All right, Richards, you had better start talking. At best you are going to get the sack, but more likely you will spend some years inside Her Majesty's prison - either that or be detained at Her Pleasure, I don't know which is worse. Now get on with it, I haven't got time to waste."

Half an hour later the manager went to see Mr Lenox himself. "Apparently Richards has been courting a woman for six years, saving every penny to get married. He proposed some time before Christmas, but she wanted to wait, so he said he would ask her again on New Year's Eve, but he was ill. He went out with her last night for the first time since he got better and today he finds out that she has gone off to the Registry Office and married someone else. If that is true, Sir, it is a sorry story indeed."

"Why are you telling me all this, Parry? Can you not deal with this domestic problem yourself?"

"He's been throwing hammers about in the forge, Sir, and punched three men. He's lying on the floor of my office with his hands tied at present. He says we can do what we like with him, he doesn't care about anything any more; all he wants to do is murder the man who married his girl. I'll come to the point, Mr Lenox. The only solution is for him to get employment at the chain works outside Paris, where he will be far enough away not to do any damage and where he can cool down and forget this woman. He can get his savings out of the bank to pay for the journey, but he will need a reference."

"Can he speak French?"

"He learnt a few words when the Frenchmen came here last year and he was over there for a month in the summer, but you really don't need any language in the fitting-room. It's so noisy they use sign language, the same one they use in the French works."

"Would you have given him a good reference before today?"

"Without hesitation, Sir. He works hard, he's never late, he's reliable and can do his job under normal stress very well."

Mr Lenox sat back in his chair and looked out of the window.

The Manager kept talking. "The woman in question is the daughter of David Williams, the anchor smith, the one who does Pitman's shorthand."

"You think we should help this man?"

"Yes, Sir. There's no knowing what he might do if he stays in Pontypridd."

"Very well! Write the references straight away, pay him off, find someone to go with him to the bank and then see him on to a train. If he doesn't agree, get the works doctor."

Morgan was half way to Dover as Mr Lenox sat down to dinner at Ynysangharad House that evening.

"Did anything interesting happen at work today, George?" his wife asked from the opposite end of the long mahogany table.

"Nothing out of the ordinary, I don't think. Oh, yes! A poor lad who has been courting a girl for six years and seeing her right up until last night, came to work to find that she went to the Registry Office this morning and married someone else," he said as he took a sip of mulligatawny soup.

"Oh! How wretched for him. How did you come to hear about it?"

"He started hitting other men and throwing hammers about in the forge. Parry talked to him, but instead of sacking him there and then, he asked if he could give the man a reference so that he could go to the Paris works and cool off."

"John Parry is a decent man. I went to see his wife and their new baby last week."

"Parry is irreplaceable."

The butler stood by Mr Lenox holding a silver entrée dish.

"Do you know the family of David Williams, the anchor smith?" Mr Lenox asked as he helped himself to vegetables.

"David Williams? David Williams," she repeated, trying to recall him.

"The one who taught himself Pitman's shorthand; the one who is better read than I am. Go on!"

"Ah! I've heard you mention him. Wait a minute. If his daughter is a dressmaker, she worked here last summer. She was the one you scolded after she and Maisie chased rabbits in the dingle, do you remember? They broke a branch of the white rhododendron."

"Well, she could be the woman involved," Mr Lenox said.

"If it's the same one, she made that exquisite wedding-dress for Penelope Fowler. Well, well! She was a nice girl, as I recall - vivacious, but polite. Would I know the young lad she's jilted?"

"I shouldn't think so. I haven't seen him."

"I am very sorry for him, whoever he is. You should ask Mr Parry to find out if they have taken him on in Paris, dear, you really should. We cannot just consign him to oblivion."

"You are right, my dear, as usual. I shall do that in the morning."

Philip and Elizabeth stood at the window of their room in the Westgate Hotel in Newport.

"I wish you'd known my grandmother, she was the most interesting person," Elizabeth said.

Philip didn't take his eyes off her hair, running his hands through the long strands, watching them fall back against her neck.

"I'm sure she's watching over me at this very moment."

"As I am," he murmured.

He took one of her hands, trying to pull her gently away from the window but she stayed where she was.

"There's something I want to tell you," she said softly. "You know when I went to the farm?"

He waited patiently.

"Well, I had my fortune told by Dr Henry Harries, and do you know what? He told me that my.....husband would be a tall, dark man, with a mole on his arm, by his elbow," she said triumphantly. "I saw the mole on your arm when I came back from the opera."

Philip kissed her forehead, her cheeks, her nose and her neck until she stopped talking and trembled in his arms.

Chapter 24

Philip put his pickaxe against the coal-face and crawled along the floor to join Emlyn and Islwyn who were eating their bread and cheese and arguing about the merits of a strike. He opened his lunch-box and picked up a sandwich that Elizabeth had made for him, smiling as he saw a piece of folded paper underneath it. She was in the habit of sending notes now and then, mostly *billets doux*. Today's message wasn't easy to decipher because beetroot juice had run over the ink and smudged it. He held it sideways near the lamp.

Suddenly, he drew his breath in and shouted: "Boys! I'm going to be a father!"

The others stopped arguing and grinned. "Why didn't you tell us before?" Emlyn asked.

Philip groaned. "I wasn't sure till I read the note that Elizabeth put in my sandwiches."

"Congratulations, Philip," Islwyn said.

Emlyn frowned. "Fancy writing a letter to tell a man something like that."

Philip blinked and read the note again.

"You will be a father before the year is out. I love you. E xxx"

He looked at his friends and repeated the news in a whisper. "Elizabeth is carrying my child!"

He hurried home after work, striding into the kitchen only to find Dr Price standing in front of the fire. Elizabeth sat grinning on the rocking-chair as the men exchanged greetings.

"Elizabeth has told me your good news, Philip. I'm delighted for you both. I know how you must be feeling - I'm to become a father myself again and at about the same time!"

Philip looked at Elizabeth, his eyes softening in his coal-black face. "You were able to take your wife in your arms when she told you, though; it's terrible to come home with filthy hands at a time like this."

"I'll leave you alone at any rate; I want a word with David in the parlour."

William had been rejuvenated when he found another companion to share his life, at the age of eighty. When his son was born, on the same day as Philip's, he was surprised at his reaction. He had fathered many sons but this one, conceived in his old age, he deemed special.

"You are going to grow strong and fearless. I choose you to lead the march of the Druids in the land of my fathers," he murmured as he carried the child slowly around the room, chanting incantations he used at ceremonies at the Rocking Stone. "You shall have a name that no one else bears - I name you Iesu Grist!"

Even the Williams family was shocked. "This time you really have gone too far, William," David said. "It's not fair to the boy, either."

"Think of him as Siôn; that's what we call him at home - the other is only his official name."

Elizabeth and Philip called their first-born Jack. Young Phil arrived eighteen months later but while their children thrived, William's son didn't. When Siôn died at the age of two, his father was crazed with grief. Myfanwy heard that he had been lying face-down inside the Druid's circle all one night.

"Eluned and I are very worried," she told David. "He talks about burning the body of that little boy in a Druid ceremony on the mountain. He's been pushing a cart up the hill by his home for two days now, carrying coal and arranging stones to make a cairn."

David wrung his hands. "He has often told me that he wants to be cremated himself as the Druids were."

"It will be difficult to stop him doing exactly as he likes," Philip said. David nodded.

On the last journey up the hill, the cart contained a gallon tin of paraffin, six pennyworth of wood and, in one corner, a small bundle wrapped in white linen. William placed his son's body underneath the stones that formed the roof of the cairn, poured paraffin over it and lit a match. As the flames took hold, he sat a short distance away, reading out a poem written by an old bard.

> *"My son, child of my hearth, my song,*
> *my one delight before my death,*
> *my knowing poet, my luxury, my jewel*
> *and my candle, my sweet soul and*
> *my one betrayal.*
> *My chick learning my song,*
> *my chaplet of Iseult, my kiss,*
> *my nest. Woe that he is gone!*
> *My lark, my little wizard,*
> *my Siôn, my bow and arrow,*
> *my suppliant, my boyhood.*
> *Siôn, who sent his father*
> *a sharpness of longing*
> *and love. Farewell,*
> *while I remain earthbound,*
> *my merry darling,*
> *my Siôn."*

A handful of neighbours helped two policemen to drag William way. "Leave me! Leave me! I must stay with Siôn. He *SHALL* depart like a Druid!"

But he was put in a cell in Cardiff gaol.

The news spread like wildfire. "He will hang for this," Islwyn told Philip in the colliery.

"He's doomed now," neighbours told Elizabeth as small groups gathered in the street to discuss the news.

David went over to Myfanwy and Eluned. "People are up in arms but I don't see that any law has been broken. William knows that too, otherwise he wouldn't have cremated Siôn so publicly. Don't worry. He'll be home before long and I wouldn't be surprised if he sues the police for wrongful arrest."

William arrived home the following morning.

Elizabeth was supremely happy. Her three-year-old son Jack was a thoughtful, obedient little boy while Phil was like quick silver and always up to mischief; she daren't take her eyes off him for a minute, but he was the image of his father and she doted on him.

She enjoyed going with Philip and the children for picnics in the garden at the back of Lock Cottage on summer afternoons, where they ate raspberry or gooseberry tart made from the fruit-trees growing there. Philip always took care to bolt the gate leading out to the lock. "You never know, my sons could have inherited some weakness from their mother's side of the family!" he told Elizabeth once.

Life on the doorstep in Feeder Row was never dull. Children played hopscotch or noughts and crosses, marking the pavements with chalk. They skipped and shouted and had bare-knuckle fights, life-long pacts were sworn and broken within five minutes, secrets were shared, best friends and enemies laughed and cried and life was good.

Sam's cockle cart was a regular sight:

"Cockles, Kidwelly!
Good for your belly!"

When Elizabeth heard his call she often went out to see whether Sam's peg-leg was inside the cart or hanging outside, to check the weather for the next twenty-four hours.

'Fish alive-o' was another call. The flat fish-cart was always followed by an army of cats; every now and then the fish man would throw a fish-head out to get rid of them but as soon as one lot stayed behind, others would join the parade.

The organ grinder with his monkey, the knife-sharpener with his wheel or the rag-and-bone man, with bags of boiled sweets or goldfish in a bowl, called once a week. Mothers stood in doorways, some with a shawl around a baby, gossiping to neighbours standing next door or across the street.

Philip organised Sunday School treats when children would clamber onto a barge which floated down the canal to a field where everyone got out to play rounders or dance round in circles singing:

"There was a farmer and his wife,
his name was Bobby Bingo!"

When Elizabeth looked back on those carefree days they seemed to be filled with sunlight and laughter. Sometimes she did a little sewing but always at her own pace. Gwen looked after the children once, when she went back and forth to Ffynnon Rhyngyll Farm high on the mountainside. She used to walk to Rhydyfelin where the farmer's son would be waiting on horseback to take her up to the farm and bring her back down with a bundle of clothes to be patched or darned and sheets to be turned sides-to-middle.

"It's wonderful up there where it's quiet and the air is cool and fresh," she told Philip. "When we start out the farm is a little white dot but it gets biggger and bigger as the towns down here get smaller. On the way home, I can see the river winding through the valley."

"I'm not keen on your going up there; you're away from home too long. Why can't the farmer's wife come here to see you?"

"Heavens! She's got seven children to look after. Anyway, I'm patching the last lot of trousers now. Her son could come here to collect them, I suppose."

"Good. And no more dressmaking for a while; you are looking peeky. You know I don't like you working anyway. There's no need for it."

Elizabeth was kneeling on the kitchen floor washing Philip's back as he sat in the tub; the children were in the parlour where David always read them a story at that time of day. It was the only chance that Elizabeth and Philip had to be alone.

"Now, you mustn't be cantankerous while I'm in a delicate state of health, Mr Jones."

Philip groaned. "Elizabeth! Come round here where I can see you. Do you mean...Aw! You are impossible! I learn about Jack by reading a letter at the bottom of a coal-mine, I find a note in my hymn-book about Phil when I am marooned in the gallery at Sardis and now you tell me about another child when I'm sitting in the bath-tub soaking wet!"

She sat on the floor opposite him. "I love you, Philip Jones, even when you shout at me."

She leaned forward and kissed his nose.

Dr William Price's friendship with David continued despite the fact that he had another 'companion' and a growing family. The exhilaration of his law-suit against the police had distracted him from his grief and he was proud of the medals that he had commissioned to commemorate Siôn's cremation. They cost him twopence a dozen; he sold them for threepence each. He came to Feeder Row to show one to David.

"I've had a hundred made. They could become valuable in time, though they will probably be more appreciated in London. A few people there have decided to form a Cremation Society and I've been invited to speak at the inaugural meeting."

"Your fame is spreading, William. I presume the report in the *Times* was responsible."

"Not necessarily. The practice of cremation in this country is inevitable, if the British Isles is not to become one huge graveyard in the next century. The society is being formed to raise money to buy land south of London for a crematorium."

David winced. "A permanent site? A building? For burning bodies?"

"It's a far more natural way of disposing of corpses than burial. I've left instructions for my family to scatter my ashes over the field behind the house so that the plants and flowers will grow more abundantly. Even rogues and criminals would benefit society after their death if the practice became universal."

"I can't agree with you, I'm afraid," David said. "What about 'In my flesh I shall see God'?"

William smiled. "Same thing either way, dear man."

"Let's change the subject - how is your family?"

"They are all thriving. My new son has been named *Iesu Grist the second*. He's a dear little chap."

David sighed. "What is his unofficial name?"

"Taliesin! Tallie for short."

"I wish him well."

Elizabeth's third child was expected in September, but she hadn't been well during the pregnancy and Philip was worried. Her labour was protracted and one morning in July, in the early hours, her child was still-born.

"She was so beautiful, Philip," she sobbed. "We would have had a daughter!"

Philip sat on the bed holding her hand. "I know, I know," he said, closing his eyes.

"Even if we have more children, more daughters, they won't make up for this little one," she gulped, wiping her face with a crumpled handkerchief that was soaked in tears.

Philip stroked her cheek. "Try to get some sleep, sweetheart. I'll turn the lamp lower and sit here with you."

A son born the following year lived for half-an-hour. For months afterwards Elizabeth wandered about the house aimlessly, with vacant eyes. Often, she would get up in the middle of a meal and go into the parlour to cry. Philip's patience was endless. When friends called to see her she told them that a better man never put his feet in shoe-leather.

Philip's joy and relief when Josiah was born two years later was unbounded. The baby was a tiny scrap weighing less than four pounds.

"Who does he look like, do you think?" Elizabeth asked him.

"I'd say he's like my brother Nathaniel in Denver, Colorado."

"Really? What is Nathaniel like?"

Philip smiled. "He is a tall, well-built fellow; women consider him handsome. He's clever, too."

"Why are we calling him after your brother in Ohio, then?"

"I was much closer to him; Nat was eleven years older than me."

Josiah cried every night for the first six months of his life. Elizabeth and Philip were worn out with lack of sleep. When she threatened to throw him out of the window, Philip decided they would take it in turns to get up, not that it made much difference. When it was the turn of one of them to get up every time Josiah cried, the other was always awake.

It wasn't easy for them to whip up enthusiasm for Christmas that year, but Philip looked forward to two days off work when he could snatch some sleep during the day.

On Christmas Eve the family sat round the table for supper, the boys waiting impatiently while their grandfather said grace. He prayed for children who were in a workhouse, for children whose parents didn't have enough money to buy food, for children who were orphans and for anyone who didn't have a family. As soon as he said Amen, eight-year-old Phil gave a whoop of delight and stuck a fork into the sausages that were piled high in a tureen.

After the meal had been cleared, they went into the parlour where a log-fire burned in the hearth. Gwen and David sat on either side of it, Philip sat near the window while Elizabeth sat by the wall opposite her parents, holding Josiah in her arms. The boys sat on the floor in the middle of the room.

A hush fell as they waited for David to read a story. The boys never knew in advance what the Christmas readings would be.

"The Walrus and the Carpenter
were walking hand in hand,"

They all enjoyed that and his account of Christmas at Manor farm, when he acted the parts of Mr Pickwick and Sam Weller with gusto.

"Read some more, read some more, please," the boys cried in vain.

After they had gone to bed and another hour had passed, Elizabeth reckoned it was safe to put the presents on the floor, ready to be found the next morning. Gwen laid two lines of saucers on the floor; Philip put an apple, an orange, a sugar mouse and a new penny on each one.

"I wonder if Josiah is going to let us get some rest tonight," Elizabeth said grimly. "It's your turn to sleep, dear. You look worn out."

David was proud of the ebony walking-stick he had been given when he retired from the chain works where he had been employed for forty-five years. It had a silver plaque with his name on it and had been presented to him by Mr Lenox himself.

He filled his days with reading and looked forward to seeing William once a week, when their arguments sometimes became ferocious. Sadly, these came to an end not long after Christmas. The family learned that in the middle of January, when William was ninety-three years old, he

210

and in the morning, asked for a glass of champagne. When he had drunk it, he said 'Thank you, dear,' and died.

David grieved sorely for his friend, while the rest of the family waited and wondered about the funeral arrangements, if any. Gwen went to see Eluned and Myfanwy to find out if they knew what was to happen and wasn't surprised to learn that William had decreed that he was to be cremated on the same spot as his son.

When the day came, David wore his best clothes and carried his walking-stick as he left the house to call for Eluned and Myfanwy, who accompanied him to Llantrisant. Eluned, whose sight was such now that she could hardly distinguish between day and night, held on to his arm. They joined the crowds who streamed towards the funeral pyre.

Horse-drawn buses and brakes converged from every direction; tents had been erected at the bottom of the hill where cakes and sandwiches were on sale.

"It's like a fair," David said with distaste.

"Fancy not having any hymns!" Eluned said. "What's going on?"

"Nothing really," Myfanwy answered. "Just a lot of smoke on the top of the mountain. A crowd of people are up there, but down here people are just standing about in small groups, like us."

David sighed. "I wish I had argued more with him about this."

Myfanwy smiled. "Would it have made any difference, David?"

"I suppose not," he admitted.

"Can you see anyone we know?" Eluned asked.

"Some I know by sight, but nobody special, unless, wait a minute, two women over there, with a young man. I know that woman's face. Where have I seen her before?"

David told Gwen afterwards that he had never been to a funeral before where nothing happened. Nobody said anything, there were no announcements and no one sang. People just stood in the field and when they tired of hanging about, they drifted away, leaving the smoke on top of the mountain, near a tall pole which had a crescent moon on it - the one that William took with him on Sundays when he conducted ceremonies at the Rocking Stone.

Myfanwy remembered 'that woman's face' before they left, though. She took Eluned up to see her. It was Rhiannon, Mair's daughter, with her sister-in-law and her son. They talked for a long time, which relieved the tension for all of them. Rhiannon had been at her childhood home that morning and seen 'the new family', as she put it.

"They are very nice, as I knew they would be. I like all my father's families, the ones that I've met anyway. It was strange to see the place again, though."

"Yes, it must have been. Do you remember the day your mother and I carried your father away in the trunk?"

Rhianon laughed. "Tch! Will I ever forget it!"

If only William had lived a few weeks longer, no doubt he would have

211

done something about little Josiah, who seemed to be fading away in front of his parents' eyes. The local doctor was quite unable to suggest any remedies. One day Elizabeth waited impatiently on the upstairs landing for the doctor to arrive, eventually going into the front bedroom to look into the street to see if he was coming. She pulled the window down and saw him talking to a neighbour.

She couldn't believe her ears when he pointed to her front door and asked "Isn't the little bugger dead yet?"

In two seconds she was standing at the top of the stairs. "You can go straight back out, Sir. Never set foot in this house again."

Philip sent for another doctor, from Caerphilly, who prescribed a medicine to give with each feed. Within two days Josiah was looking happier and healthier and Elizabeth and Philip had blissful nights of unbroken sleep. He was never a strong child, however, and Philip decided that the time had come to take the family to America, where he felt the environment was altogether better.

"This place is all right for you and me, but I don't want my sons going to work down a coal-mine. It's not only hard work, but it's dangerous, and in the winter, how would you like it if you only saw daylight on Sundays? If the boys grow up in America, they could choose any sort of job and we would have a nice house," he told Elizabeth one night in bed.

"If you think that's the right thing to do then we shall do it, dear. I don't know what mother and Dada will say, mind."

"We can take them with us."

"Aw! They wouldn't want to. Mother has her grandchildren in Swansea and they have the chapel and Aunt 'Luned and Myfanwy."

"Shall I write to my sister in Ohio and ask her to vouch for us?"

"Yes," Elizabeth said, decisively.

Philip made lists of the things that they would take with them. He had always been methodical, doing things quietly and thoroughly. One morning a few days later, Elizabeth took the linen cover off her grandmother's trunk, which was kept at the bottom of the bed in Gwen's room, and went through the contents, putting things that could be thrown away on one side and making a separate pile of items that the family might want to keep.

Eliza's mourning clothes and an eau-de-nil dress with moth-holes in it were there as well as the tin box with her letters. A pair of garters, some handkerchiefs that had never been used, left-over wool from the sampler and at the bottom, in a faded envelope, the letter that Luke Thomas had written before he died.

The trunk was brought downstairs and put in the hall, where Philip packed a few things every evening. They would leave on the 8th of May from Liverpool for a ten-day crossing, but he labelled the trunk a month before that, not wanting any last minute rush. He told the boys about life in America and the experiences he had there before returning to Wales. As the time drew nearer, they became more and more excited at the thought of a new life far away in the land of milk and honey.

Philip came home from work with a cold one day, about three weeks before they were due to leave.

"Well, you had better stay in bed tomorrow," Elizabeth said, "you look rotten."

"I'll see how I feel in the morning."

"I don't want you getting pneumonia and have to cancel everything."

"I'll be all right tomorrow, I expect."

The following morning Philip brought Elizabeth a cup of tea at half-past-five and gave her a kiss before he left. She turned over and fell asleep again, not getting up for another two hours, by which time the tea was cold. After seeing the boys off to school she bathed the baby, made the beds and did a bit of tidying up before going out to get something for Philip's supper. Having assumed that he wasn't going to work, she hadn't prepared a lunch-box for him, so she thought she would buy some lamb cutlets, to make up for it.

As she walked through the town she chatted to several people all of whom seemed to be in a hurry to get away from her; they seemed uncomfortable, their conversation was stilted and she wondered what on earth was wrong with the world. Not one of them could bring themselves to tell her what she obviously didn't know - that a fire had broken out in No.4 seam at the Great Western Colliery and that 150 men were entombed.

All that afternoon she sat in the parlour putting a patch in a pair of Jack's trousers, while David sat by the fire reading. At four o'clock she went to the front door to see if the children were on their way home from school but saw instead the young boy who worked with Philip running up to her. He had his cap in his hand and his face was smeared with tears and coal-dust.

"Mr Jones is all right, Missus. They just brought him up in the cage. He's alive. He sent me to tell you."

"What are you talking about, Billy? What do you mean?"

"There's been a fire in the pit. They've got eighty-six men out. Mr Jones put me and Roy Davies in the cage instead of him. He stayed down for the next cage."

Elizabeth didn't wait to hear any more. Without bothering to get a shawl she ran to the colliery, flying down side-streets, bumping into people as she turned round corners, seeing nothing. Crowds stood around the pit-head, quietly singing the old disaster hymn, its harmonies in the minor key mingling with moans and cries of grief. She pushed her way through to the front where ten stretchers were lying on the ground, some already completely covered with blankets.

"Philip? Philip!"

"Philip Jones is here," a voice said.

She threw herself on the ground where he lay. He was still alive, his eyelids fluttered, but then his head fell sideways into her hands.

"Philip! Philip! Philip!" she screamed. "No! No! Philip!"

Arms lifted her, still screaming, as the blanket was drawn over him and his stretcher was carried away. All the men brought up in his cage died of after-damp, even if they were still breathing when they reached the surface; no more were found alive after that.

At a service in the parlour shortly before the funeral, Elizabeth stood by the coffin with Josiah in her arms so that the minister from Sardis could christen him before his father's body was taken away. Eluned and Myfanwy were there as well as Philip's sisters and their husbands. The two boys were staying in a friend's house for the day. Eleven miners were buried in Glyntâf cemetery that afternoon, each cortége linking up behind another, led by a colliers' choir, singing the colliers' hymn. The family sat in silence hearing the music in the distance at first until the procession stopped at their door. Six colliers came in to take the coffin away. The men of the family went to the graveside; the women stood in the street, which was lined with neighbours, until the singing died away but Elizabeth stayed in the parlour staring at the floor.

Chapter 25

That evening, when the relatives had left, the family sat down to supper; David was about to chide Elizabeth for not putting enough on her plate, until he realised that he couldn't eat much either.

"Dada, after I've put Josh to bed, I want to talk about the future," Elizabeth said quietly. "I'd like us to sit down together and decide how we are going to manage, and I want Jack and Phil to listen so that they will understand."

"I think that would be good. We haven't had a chance to talk amongst ourselves, what with so many people coming and going, day and night," David said.

Elizabeth came downstairs and shut the front door. She smoothed back a few untidy strands of hair and sat down in the kitchen with her hands together over the table.

"Now, I have a lot to say and I want you two boys to listen carefully. Life is going to be different from now on and we have to work out how to manage." She took a deep breath. "I must start working straight away, to earn money to buy food and clothes. That means that grandma will be looking after the house and will need all the help we can give her." She looked at Phil. "Perhaps the most important way of helping is by being good and not causing any trouble."

"That's right," Gwen said emphatically.

Eight-year-old Phil looked round at the family, wondering why all eyes were focused on him.

Elizabeth smiled at him before continuing. "Mrs Davies in West Street called here one day last week and told me she wants a lot of sewing and mending done for her family, so I shall start work tomorrow morning at eight o'clock and finish at six. I shall be paid one and six a day, so, for six days - how much a week will I earn, Jack?"

Her elder son pursed his lips. "I can't work it out in my head."

"Nine shillings. We will be poor, but there's no shame in that," his mother said.

Gwen interrupted. "They say money is pouring into the Disaster Fund; maybe you won't have to work, not all day every day,"

David shook his head. "There are eighty-four widows to have an income for life, as long as they remain widows, and every widow's child under fourteen is to get something."

"Mr Morris told me there were nigh on three hundred children who lost fathers," Elizabeth said.

"Phil and me can help," Jack burst out. "We can take dinners to the chain works!"

Elizabeth looked at her father. The boys had often asked if they could earn a penny every week-day by carrying dinners to men at the chain works, but Philip had forbidden it. He thought that only boys from poor families should do that and he didn't want his children accepting money that could be earned by those who needed it.

"Why not, Dada?" Elizabeth asked.

"Jack has a good idea," David replied.

"You will have to run back home fast afterwards to get your own dinners," Gwen said.

"We will, we will," Phil said.

"So, two pennies for six days is - you can add that up in your head, Jack bach. Twice six is...?"

He grinned. "Twelve."

"And how many pennies in a shilling?" his grandfather asked.

"Twelve!" Phil shouted.

"So, you two can earn a shilling every week for us; it all helps. Another matter: your Auntie Celia in Brynmawr and Auntie Maggie Aberdare, both said that we could go there for holidays whenever we like. Would you two like to go to Brynmawr in the summer holidays?"

They looked at each other warily; they hadn't been away from home before.

"It would help out a lot, because then I can take Josh and go and work for the Gregories in Taff's Well while you are away."

"Who are they?" Gwen asked.

"Anne Gregory was Annie Morgan; we were in school together. Her husband had the foundry on land that was bought to build the railway and they made a lot of money out of it."

"In Hopkinstown," David told Gwen.

"That's right; they have a big house next door to the new foundry. She called last Thursday, I think it was, and said she had work for me, if I wanted it. She will send a pony and trap for us on Monday mornings and bring us back on Fridays; Josh will be looked after in the nursery with Anne's children." Elizabeth sat back. "That's as far as I can work things out for now. Is there anything else that anyone wants to say?"

"Yes," Gwen said. "You are being brave, Elizabeth, but I think it will be easier if we made a new start in a new house, away from all the.....memories."

Elizabeth swallowed and nodded.

"Gwen and I agree about that," David said. "Even if we move to another street it will help, as long as the rent is the same."

"Or less," Elizabeth said.

"Gwen and I will look for another house and I'll put the boys' names on the waiting-list to carry dinners to the chain works."

"So, we'll take one day at a time and if we all pull together we shall manage," Elizabeth said, her voice trailing away to a whisper.

"With God's help," David added.

Elizabeth went to see her first client the next morning. Mrs Davies had four sons - the eldest, Seth, had recently left home to join the Welch Regiment, so the first task was to unpick his old coats and trousers to make them fit his young brothers, who also needed their own trousers patched. Elizabeth brought a bundle of clothes back to Feeder Row and, for the next fortnight, sat in the parlour doing the alterations and darning holes in jumpers and socks as well as sewing sheets sides-to-middle. When she finished at six o'clock each day, she helped Gwen in the kitchen and often did the ironing after midnight.

She was glad to get away from Pontypridd each week in the summer holidays, escaping from the pitying eyes and mumbled sympathy of neighbours and friends, yet being hurt when others crossed the street to avoid talking to her, embarrassed by a situation that they found harrowing. She was treated as one of the family in Anne Gregory's home, and Josiah was looked after by the nanny and nursery maid, with Anne's youngest children while the three older ones ran wild about the place. It wasn't easy to find mending because the children's clothes were thrown away when they no longer fitted and the boys didn't wear patched trousers; sheets were never sewn sides-to-middle. However, Elizabeth made two dresses for Anne and some aprons for the maids.

She was given several shirts and trousers for her own boys, as well as fruit and vegetables from the garden. The Gregories killed a pig once, which Elizabeth took to the local bake-house on Saturday. "Just bring the ham back on Monday and keep the bacon for your family," Anne said. When no more dress-making remained to be done, Elizabeth baked bread and cakes and even papered some bedroom walls. The kindness of the Gregories during those six weeks, the absence of familiar surroundings and faces, even those of her parents, a leisurely routine in a comfortable house and time to play with twelve-month-old Josiah, gave Elizabeth breathing-space to absorb the initial shock of Philip's death.

The boys returned from Brynmawr to a new home in West Street, next door to Mrs Davies, and started carrying meals to the chain works in September. Mr Lenox had decreed that boys whose fathers had died in the colliery disaster were to be given priority on the waiting-list. By that time, Elizabeth was receiving ten shillings a week from the Disaster Fund for herself and her three sons, back-dated to the day of the disaster. David gave lessons in Pitman's Short-hand writing to a young lad from his Sunday School class and Gwen gave piano lessons to a pupil in a nearby street.

The summer of 1892 came and went. So far, the family had managed well.

Every week-day, Jack and Phil ran from school at dinner time to collect a meal from the wife or mother of a man in the chain works. By tradition, these were always put in a basin and carried in a red 'gypsy' handkerchief, tied in a double bow at the top so that it could be easily transported.

"No running, mind!" Phil was told.

Jack was warned on his first day: "Be careful with this - it's broth."

The boys reported to the gate-keeper who told them where to find their recipients. Jack carried a dinner to Mr Simpson in the forge; Phil delivered his basin to Mr Ward in the welding-shop. As long as the dinner hadn't been spilled, they each received a penny.

"Hello, son. What's your name?" Mr Ward asked Phil when he first arrived.

"Philip Jones, from West Street, Sir."

"Thank you, boy. Here's your penny."

Philip's sister Celia, from Brynmawr, turned up the day before Christmas Eve carrying a large goose and presents for the three boys. She had married a master-builder; her sister Maggie, married to a collier in Aberdare, sent Elizabeth a new shawl. Mr Ward and Mr Simpson in the chain works gave Phil and Jack a new penny each, in addition to the usual fee, and Sardis chapel sent a basket of fruit for the family, who had never had so much bounty for Christmas. For Elizabeth, though, the season of good cheer had never been so bleak.

For a long time the behaviour of the two elder boys had been exemplary but, eventually Phil reverted to his old ways. David often stood on the doorstep waiting for him to come back from school. It was no good asking Jack where his brother was because he had received a black eye from Phil the last time he told tales, and knew it was more than his life was worth to divulge incriminating information.

"I can guess where he is, the little imp!" his mother said. "He will have gone swimming in the Berw pool again. He knows I don't like him doing that; the water is filthy!"

On one occasion, Elizabeth left her sewing and went to the Berw pool, looking for him. When Phil saw her striding across the field in the distance, he swam to the shore, grabbed his trousers and ran off in the opposite direction, leaving her to retrieve the rest of his clothes. When he came home, much later, he was sent to bed without any supper and given a sound hiding by his grandfather. Phil promised that he would never swim in the Berw pool again and kept his word; he went swimming in the canal instead and caught typhoid fever.

Elizabeth first became worried when he didn't want to go with Jack to the Sunday School treat. He lay listlessly on the settle, while his brother joined the procession of all the Sunday Schools in Pontypridd, dispersing to have tea in their own chapel vestries after marching through the town. By the time Jack came home, Phil was unconscious.

The doctor advised Elizabeth to let no one but herself into Phil's bedroom. "It's serious. If he lives for twenty-one days, he could pull through; the critical day will be in three weeks' time."

David brought out his copy of Fenner's Family Medicine and read the instructions. "He should be given Fenner's Lung Healers, Fenner's

Fever Cure and Fenner's Cooling Powders."

"I'll get some in the morning. Philip had £3.7.6 left in a box in the chest-of-drawers. I will afford whatever Phil needs."

She bought Calves' Foot Jelly as well and hung a rope of onions over the bedroom door; she put bowls of vinegar and camphor around the room and nursed him day and night. Every day she gave him egg custard, fed him teaspoonfuls of fresh milk and de-seeded black grapes for him.

On the twenty-second day he smiled at her. She walked downstairs and into the kitchen. "He's going to live; he's going to be all right," she told Gwen, shaking her head and bursting into tears. "If anything happened to Phil, if Phil died, I couldn't have gone on."

She faced the prospect of burning Phil's bedding and blankets calmly. "He is alive, he is going to get better - nothing else matters," she told her father, in spite of the fact that only fourpence remained of the savings in the chest-of-drawers.

Jack came home for his meal at mid-day carrying a huge parcel. "The gate-keeper at the chain works asked me to give you this," he told his mother.

Elizabeth frowned. "What is it?"

"I don't know. He wouldn't tell me what was in it nor who sent it."

It was clearly marked: 'Mrs Elizabeth Jones, West Street'.

"Well, it's no good standing there looking at it, open it!" Gwen said. The family watched as Elizabeth untied the string and unfolded the brown paper. She lifted out two blankets, a quilt, a pair of sheets, a pillow and two pillow-cases, holding each item up in silence.

"Who has sent these?" David whispered.

Elizabeth shook her head. "Jack, did Mr Simpson say anything to you about this?"

"No."

"Isn't there a note inside?" Gwen asked.

Elizabeth shook the paper and each article again. "Nothing!"

"It must be someone who knows about Phil's typhoid fever - perhaps it's Mr Ward in the welding shop," David said.

"Ask him tomorrow, Jack. We must write and thank whoever has sent this."

When Phil was up and about, Elizabeth resumed work - at least, she meant to but she slipped in the yard and strained her ankle. The doctor ordered her to stay in bed for six weeks.

"I must work somehow!" she told Mrs Davies-next-door. "If I could borrow an ordinary sewing-machine I could balance it on my lap here, perhaps."

"I don't see how, Mrs Jones. It would have to stand on some sort of table, surely."

Two days later Mrs Davies re-appeared carrying a bed-table. "Look what I've got!" she cried. "My lodger made it for you out of a plank. You put your legs underneath it."

Elizabeth clapped her hands. "That's wonderful! There's kind of him. Now all I need is a machine."

That was lent by Mrs Love, five doors down, and within half-an-hour of its arrival Elizabeth started to make button-holes for Mr Robbins, the tailor, who paid her a penny each for them.

A month later, the gate-keeper at the chain works told Phil to call back to see him before leaving. He was given another large parcel. "Take this to your mother," the man said.

"What's in it?" Phil asked.

"Never you mind."

"Who is it from? Is there any message?"

"Ask no questions and you will be told no lies! Now, off with you!"

"Who sent these?" Gwen asked.

Phil shrugged his shoulders.

They took the parcel upstairs to Elizabeth. This time it contained two overcoats. "They're brand new - they've got Howell's labels in them! They must have cost three pounds each at least! Who can have sent them?"

"Try one on!" Gwen told Phil.

It was a little on the large side. "He'll grow into it before long," Elizabeth said.

"Who does Dada know in the chain works? We must get to the bottom of this."

"The men he knew have retired or left, I should think. Perhaps it's Mrs Lenox; she's wonderfully kind to the families who work there."

"But Dada doesn't work there now. This is a mystery."

And a mystery it remained for a long time.

When she was able to walk again, a different opportunity presented itself, which Elizabeth seized with alacrity. Old Mrs Jenkins Sardis had run a stall in the market for many years, selling cups of tea, cakes and faggots to passers-by, who sat on a bench around the counter while they ate. Now she was seriously ill and wanted someone to carry on in her absence.

Elizabeth enjoyed the job, which she found more interesting than sewing. She paid eight shillings a week rent, made the food at home or in the local bake-house and came home with more money than she made at dress-making. When Mrs Jenkins died some weeks later, her son asked Elizabeth if she would like to take over, giving her the cutlery and crockery stored there. Her spirits rose, but disappointment followed. On the day she took over the thriving little business, an official came to check the situation.

"Mrs Jenkins has died, I hear. Now, you are welcome to replace her but I am sorry to inform you that the rent has to go up. We shall be charging eighteen shillings a week from now on."

"Eighteen shillings! That's ridiculous! I'll be working for four shillings a week! Even when I add the ten shillings from the Disaster Fund, it won't keep body and soul together. Aw! This is cruel."

"That remains the situation, I am sorry. Do you want to run the stall or not?"

"I can't afford to, but God looks after sparrows and he will look after me, even if you don't, Sir."

Elizabeth had cocooned her emotions when Philip died and a formidable woman was emerging from the chrysalis. She proved it when Phil came home from school with a hand over his left ear.

"The teacher boxed my ears because she said I wasn't listening," he said in reply to his mother's question.

Elizabeth was enraged. Phil's hearing had been affected by the typhoid fever and the family knew that he didn't hear half the things they said to him.

The next morning she presented herself in the Headmaster's room, demanding to see the teacher involved. When the young girl arrived, she was told never to repeat her actions or face being reported to the School Board.

Elizabeth's forthright character hadn't gone unnoticed. Mrs Mathews, the chairman of the association of widows receiving money from the disaster fund, called one day. Elizabeth had attended a few meetings when she had the time and energy, but was not one of the leading lights. Mrs Mathews told her that it had been decided to send two representatives to see Mr Godfrey Clarke, the Administrator of the Fund, to present a petition asking for the widows to be given more than the current maximum of ten shillings a week. For some time local newspapers had drawn attention to the considerable sum invested in stocks and shares.

"That's all very well," Mrs Mathews said, "but money is needed now, not later when many children will be working adults."

"I agree."

"I knew you would. The Committee decided that you should accompany me to Talygarn."

"Talygarn?"

"That's where Mr Clarke lives. Can you come with me next Tuesday?"

It wasn't an easy journey; the mansion was a mile away from Llantrisant station, but it was a warm, sunny day and Elizabeth felt honoured to have been chosen to confront Mr Clarke. She found, when she met him, that he was a charming, understanding and sympathetic man who explained that the money had to last for the lifetime of every widow and, as Trustee, he had to guarantee that. They met him in the library, having waited in an oak-panelled hall which had a magnificent marble mantelpiece and glittering chandeliers.

The meeting didn't last long and Mr Clarke rose to his feet after saying that he would do what he could to help them. "Would you like to look around the house and grounds, ladies? Can you stay for lunch first?"

Elizabeth and Dora Mathews had lunch in the servants' hall, after which they were taken on a guided tour of the ground floor by the butler. They marvelled at the gold and white ceilings, the antlers' heads and crossed swords on the walls, the brocade sofas and chairs, the oil-paintings and the view of the wide lawns and rose-gardens through the mullioned windows of the dining-room. In one ornate room a large mirror leant out from the wall so that people could study the ceiling which had taken an Italian craftsman two years to paint. When they had seen the house the butler handed them over to the Head Gardener who took them around the grounds. They were told the names of rare trees and shrubs and shown the vista from the edge of the lake where the lawn dropped away to another lawn twenty feet below. By the summer house they saw the 'Champagne Walk', a narrow path covered with the ends of champagne bottles stuck in concrete, which had taken some years to complete. Before leaving they were shown a panoramic view of the Vale of Glamorgan from the top of a hill.

Elizabeth was pleased when it was announced a few weeks later that each widow would receive an extra half-a-crown a week. This helped but she still had to use all her wits to make extra pennies. She sent Jack and Phil out to collect dandelions and nettles so that she could brew small beer. It sold well for a penny a half-pint in the offices of the Glamorgan Free Press - indeed, she could have sold a lot more there if only she had had the time to make it.

Phil found a job in Ynysybwl, delivering packets of tea on Saturdays for which he was paid ninepence. Jack earned a penny every Friday evening after school when he called at the home of an elderly Jewish man, to attend to his fire.

One evening in late November, Gwen came home after giving a piano lesson, looking puzzled. "There's a man hanging about in the street," she said, waiting for a reaction from someone. "He was there when I went out and he's there again. I've seen him walking past at night before."

Elizabeth shrugged her shoulders. David didn't look up from the newspaper, which was passed on every evening by Mr Davies next door after it had been read. The boys weren't interested.

"Oh, well, I suppose it isn't earth-shattering news, but it's odd," Gwen said. "I wonder who he is."

The two boys didn't always get on together. Jack was a quiet, studious boy, while Phil was a gregarious, impulsive personality always looking for adventure. They had their separate groups of friends, which only mattered when one of them was at a loose end. One day, Jack went off alone to play football, refusing to let Phil go with him. Phil wandered off on his own. An hour later, a group of Jack's friends returned, carrying

Phil in a makeshift stretcher of coats, telling Elizabeth that he had been pelting them with stones from a tree until he fell to the ground. He had dislocated his shoulder.

Hardly a week went by without some sort of trouble or other. When troops were sent to the town during the bitter miners' strike of 1895, they were billeted in the Town Hall, and resented by the community. Elizabeth heard that children used to earn a few coppers by washing-up after the soldiers' meals but she told her boys that they were not to help those who were oppressing miners. However, the minister from Sardis called one evening to ask if Phil was ill, because he hadn't been in chapel for the last two Sundays.

"But he walks to chapel with Jack, Mr Morris, and they walk home together."

"I know where everyone sits, Mrs Jones. Phil hasn't been in the gallery for three weeks now. You sit in the middle on the left-hand side downstairs, not with Phil."

Elizabeth's eyes narrowed. "Leave this with me. I think I can guess what he's been doing and he must be punished for it."

On the following Sunday Elizabeth took Josiah by the hand and left home ten minutes later than Jack and Phil. Instead of turning right for Sardis, she turned left for the Town Hall and asked a soldier on duty if she could speak to her son.

"A few boys are in there, you had better go and look for him yourself."

Elizabeth went in and surveyed the scene, her eyes alighting on Phil who stood at a large sink in his Sunday clothes. She went up to him and tapped him on the shoulder. When he turned round he almost jumped out of his skin.

"Right, young man! Out of here at once! We are going to chapel and I'm going to sit by your side in the gallery, with all the men."

They walked to Sardis in silence. When they went in, Phil begged his mother not to go upstairs with him, but she prodded him in the back and followed him. They were half-an-hour late; every eye watched them make their way to the front row, where men had to move up to make room for them. Elizabeth sat down in triumph and looked at the minister who was about to announce the next hymn, while Phil hung his head in shame. He was mortified at the thought of his friends seeing him sitting with his mother and small brother up there, where no women or tiny children ever sat. Her presence on that memorable Sunday morning ensured that he wasn't absent again.

The strain of the past three years was beginning to tell on the family. David's chest was giving him trouble, which meant that Elizabeth spent a lot on medicines for him and had to get up during the night to boil kettles to leave in his bedroom so that the steam would make made it easier for him to breathe. She was feeling worn out; her eyes ached after ten or twelve hours of sewing and her feet were often swollen. The doctor who saw her once when he came to visit David told her that she ought to have a complete rest, away from Pontypridd, going out in the fresh air and eating plenty of oysters.

"A holiday! Oysters! Doctor, how can I?"

"Well, who will look after the family if you collapse? Who will be the bread-winner then?" he answered.

"I'll think about it," she said, wanting to avoid further lectures. As she shut the front door when the doctor left she noticed someone standing near the lamp-post on the opposite side of the street, but couldn't make out who it was because it was a damp, foggy evening. He was wearing a mackintosh with the collar turned up and she could see the glow of a cigarette that he held in his hand.

"Does that man who hangs around here at night have a beard, Mother?" she called out to Gwen.

"Yes, a pointed beard, like some foreigners have. Why? Is he there again?"

"If it's the same one. Come and look."

David and Gwen went into the parlour and peered out. The man dropped his cigarette, put it out with his foot and walked away.

"How extraordinary!" Gwen said. "It's a bit eerie. Do you think you should go after him, David?"

"I'm not too keen on the idea. I'd rather ask them next door what they make of it."

Elizabeth drew her breath in sharply and put a hand to her throat.

"What's the matter? Do you recognise him?" David asked.

"I know that walk. Aw! The beard is new, but there's no mistaking who it is."

"Who?" Gwen cried.

Elizabeth stared at the man until he disappeared into the mist, then turned round to look at her father. "You both know him; you met him many, many years ago."

David frowned.

Elizabeth whispered. "It's Morgan!"

Chapter 26

The next morning Mrs Davies next door came into the kitchen where David was reading. Elizabeth was working in the parlour and Gwen had gone shopping.

"Mr Williams, I've had a letter from Seth and I can't make it all out. I'd be so glad if you would read it to me."

Seth's regiment had been sent out to South Africa a few months back, much to his mother's concern.

"Of course, Mrs Davies. Come and sit down."

> *Dear Mam and Dada,*
> *Here I am in the boiling sun. I am well, as I hope*
> *you are. Life is not easy here the Bores dont fight fair.*
> *They keep running away instead of standing up to*
> *fight but they turn up all round us at night, When I*
> *feel hungry I take some eggs from a farm and fry*
> *them on a rock it is so hot.*
> *We are lucky to be wearing trowsers them with kilts*
> *have blisters on the back of their knees.*
> *I must go now.*
> *Your loving son,*
> *Seth*

"Aw! I worry about him," Mrs Davies said. "I wish he hadn't gone into the army. What we are doing out there I don't know. Why have they sent our soldiers all that way to fight?"

"We have to protect the Empire, I suppose," David said, handing the letter back. "As Seth points out, it's not an easy war. Our men are fighting local bands of citizens who know the terrain well. The Boers are clever; they hide by day but surround our troops at night and cut off the water supplies. It will be difficult to defeat them. Please God we get some good news soon."

Gwen returned and put her parcels on the table. "Hello, Mrs Davies. How are you?"

"Mr Williams has just been reading me a letter from Seth."

"Didn't he offer you a cup of tea? David *bach*, what are you thinking of!" Gwen said, hanging up her shawl. "Put the kettle on, dear, I'm parched and I'm sure Elizabeth will be ready for a cup."

Mrs Davies leaned forward in her chair. "You know, I think Mrs Jones is working too hard; she's not looking well. She should take a holiday like the doctor ordered."

"The doctor ordered?" David cried. "She never told us."

"Oh, dear! I thought you knew. He told her to get away in the fresh air and eat oysters. I said I'd keep an eye on you both. I know you sleep in the chair here at night sometimes, Mrs Williams, because of those knees of yours and I told Mrs Jones, I said if Mr Williams slept down here as well, it would be easy to boil the kettle to get steam for him, I said."

David and Gwen looked at each other. "You're right, Mrs Davies!" Gwen cried. "Elizabeth needs a rest; you should see how swollen her feet are some days."

"Of course she must have a holiday, if that's what the doctor says. We'll manage perfectly on our own here," David added.

"I told Mrs Jones to get you Kepler's extract of Malt and Cod liver oil, Mr Williams. Mrs Rees, Zion says it's wonderful for the chest."

That evening David took the matter up with Elizabeth. "Mrs Davies was here this morning and spilled the beans, my girl. Why didn't you tell us what the doctor told you?"

Elizabeth sighed. "There's nothing wrong with me, Dada. I'm just tired, that's all."

"David and I have discussed this," Gwen said. "We shall do what Mrs Davies suggests about sleeping down here; I don't know why I didn't think of it before. Now, where shall you go? That's what we have to decide."

"Brynmawr or Aberdare?" David asked. "Shall I write to Celia or to Maggie?"

Elizabeth and the boys enjoyed a holiday in Aberdare. It began at the station there where Aunt Maggie awaited them in a cab. Josiah squealed with delight as the pony pranced along, and didn't want to get out at the end of the journey. Maggie's daughter was engaged to the cab-driver and his boss allowed him to take the family for a ride every morning at six o'clock, for a quarter of the normal fare.

Elizabeth felt as if they were landed gentry being taken out for a drive by their coachman, getting as much pleasure out of the experience as the boys did. One day they had to start without Phil, who was always hopeless at getting up. After they had travelled about fifty yards, a man in the street pointed at something behind them. Phil was running after them in bare feet, clad only in his shirt, carrying his boots in one hand and his trousers in the other.

They returned at the end of each drive ready to fall on the breakfast that Aunt Maggie had prepared for them. Every day Elizabeth ate oysters, which were plentiful and cheap in the local market. When she came home, she looked a different person.

"You will never guess who called here while you were away," Gwen said, with a knowing grin.

"I think I can. Morgan. What did he want?"

"He said he wanted to thank your father for the long letter he sent him when you married Philip."

"He's changed," David said. "I found him most interesting. We had a long talk about his life in France and he wanted to know about William and the cremation. He read about it in the French papers."

"How long has he been back here?"

"He has been travelling back and forth for some years apparently," Gwen said. "He's in charge of the welding-shop at the chain works here now."

"Is that a fact!" Elizabeth cried. "Phil, have you seen a man with a beard in the welding-shop when you take dinners to Mr Ward?"

"Yes. He always talks to me. They are all very friendly in there."

Elizabeth nodded. "Jack, have you seen this man in the forge?"

"Mr Richards? Of course. He's one of the bosses. Everybody knows him."

Elizabeth looked at Gwen whose eyes had become as big as saucers. They waited until they were alone before discussing the subject again. Gwen could hardly contain her excitement.

"Now we know the identity of the anonymous benefactor," she whispered. "Fancy that!"

Elizabeth frowned. "And the boys have known Morgan for years. He has been asking them about us for a long time, no doubt."

"Why is it only in the past few weeks that he started walking up the street at night, I wonder."

"Goodness knows."

"Well, your father has told him to call whenever he likes," Gwen said.

"He hasn't! Aw! I wish he had talked to me before doing that. It could be awkward."

"I don't think so, somehow. Morgan seems to have matured, he is more confident, a man of the world you might say. He's been to Florence and Rome and La Scala and the Paris Opera House. You would like the new Morgan."

"Mother, how can you say such a thing after what I did to him! I can't look the man in the face and I don't want to, anyway."

One evening a week later, Elizabeth looked up from the sewing-machine and saw Morgan standing in the doorway.

"Hello, Elizabeth," he said, as if they had never parted. "How nice to see you again. How are you?"

"Morgan!"

"Your father and I talked about this book when I saw him last and I promised to lend it to him. *Cyrano de Bergerac*. I think he'll like it."

Elizabeth hadn't stopped staring at him. He held himself with assurance, the beard surrounding his face was well-trimmed and gave him an air of authority; he certainly looked a man of substance.

"May I come in and talk to you for a while or would I be disturbing you?"

Elizabeth indicated a seat by the fire. "I've almost finished for today," she said nervously. "I must say I'm surprised that you should want to see me after...after all these years."

"We haven't seen each other since January the third, 1880," he said quietly. "That's a long time ago and yet it seems like last week. You were covered in coal-dust, as I recall."

"How is Uncle Elmer?"

Morgan grinned. "He left us shortly after that débacle and hasn't been back to this country since; we have lost touch with him, I'm afraid."

"I'm not surprised. He was for responsible for a lot, wasn't he!"

"Perhaps it's just as well things happened as they did."

Morgan sat back in the chair, seeming perfectly at ease. Elizabeth found it difficult to believe that they were talking so normally.

"I haven't had the pleasure of meeting your son Josiah, but I must congratulate you on Jack and Phil. You can be proud of them."

"I am. That reminds me, we have only just realised that you must have sent the overcoats and the bedding."

He frowned. "I have no family of my own, I have a senior post, I hope you don't think I was being patronising. I wanted to help; it was no more than that."

"Thank you. They were badly needed and we are grateful."

"You have no reason to be, Elizabeth. I am glad we have had this talk. I have always regretted not having said goodbye to you with a smile and I didn't have a chance to wish you well. One of the reasons for hoping to see you now was to do just that. Do you understand? I don't like to think that you have only miserable memories of me."

Her shoulders fell. "You are a generous person, in every way, Morgan. I haven't said how very sorry I was, and still am, for the way you were treated."

"Please! Your father explained the situation when he wrote to me all those years ago. It's over. You were young and I was foolish, so foolish. No blame can be attached to anyone."

Elizabeth smiled and nodded. "Thank you."

He stood up. "There! We've tied up a loose end in our lives. I must give your father this book. I hope I see you before I return to France but if not," he held out his hand and smiled, "Goodbye, Elizabeth. God bless you!" he said.

Elizabeth stood up and gave him her hand. "Goodbye, Morgan," she said quietly.

Jack left school a week later and started work for Mr Bowen the grocer. The hours were long. After closing at eleven o'clock at night apprentices were expected to go out on delivery rounds, often until two o'clock in the morning.

Phil passed the Labour exam two months later, which enabled him to look for work as well. Elizabeth found him a job as an errand boy in a local sweet-shop. The arrangement was that he would start work at eight o'clock and finish when he had delivered all the goods. The errand-boy who had been sacked the previous week used to finish at about four and go home.

Phil earned half-a-crown in his first full-time job and delivered things so quickly that he was back in West Street by two o'clock. The next week, the boss asked him to call at his own home to clean some windows for his wife. Every day after that, Phil was sent off to do domestic chores of one sort or another, and resented the fact that his efficiency had been rewarded in such a way.

One day he arrived home at three o'clock. "Mrs Humphries said I was no good at cleaning windows. She kept saying: 'Look there, boy, and up in the corner, are you blind or what?', and things like that."

"And what did you say," Elizabeth asked.

Phil hung his head. "I told her to clean the windows herself."

Elizabeth found him a job in a local shoe-shop for the same wages, but for much longer hours. On Saturdays, the manager sent Phil out on deliveries after the shop closed at eleven-thirty at night. One night, he came home for his mackintosh before going to the top of the Common to deliver boots to a vicar who wanted them before the service on Sunday. It was a stormy night, with rain lashing the streets.

"You are not going out at midnight in this weather," Elizabeth said grimly. "I'll get you up at half-past-six and you can take the boots to the vicar then."

Phil was sacked on Monday for not getting the boots to the vicar as promised. Elizabeth was so incensed that she asked her father to write a letter of complaint to the Head Office in Cardiff. A week later, a courteous letter was received which explained that it was for the local manager to run the shop as he saw fit, but they were enclosing a week's wages in lieu of notice. The postal order was for three and sixpence. Elizabeth stared at it for some time before reaching for her shawl and going out.

She flung the door of the shop open and went up to the manager, holding the letter and the postal order before his eyes.

"I am waiting for an explanation, Sir!"

The man's face twitched. "Aw! Well, it's like this. My wife has been ill and I needed cash in a hurry - I was going to pay it of course, but it quite slipped my mind."

"Really!" Elizabeth said, holding out her hand.

Phil had been working there for some months and was delighted when his mother came home with eleven shillings in her purse. Elizabeth found another job for him, this time as a lather-boy in the barber's shop. He set off carrying two white aprons that she had made for him, but four days later he said he couldn't bear the smell of beer on the men's breath and refused to go back.

The family held a conference and decided to ask the manager of the

Great Western Colliery if there were any jobs on the surface. It wasn't easy for Elizabeth to walk through those gates, but it was worth the effort. Phil was taken on as an apprentice painter which pleased his mother greatly.

David's breathing problems didn't get any better. He was unable to walk far and became more or less house-bound, sleeping by the fire in the parlour most afternoons while Elizabeth sewed. He looked forward to weekly visits from Morgan who took his library books back and forth for him. Sometimes, Elizabeth didn't see Morgan when he called but could hear her father talking to him in the kitchen.

"I thought he was going back to live in France," she said to Gwen one day.

"He is, eventually, in a few months' time, I think," Gwen said. "They sent him here to get acquainted with every process in this chain works and incorporate some of the new ideas that they've installed in France and then, when he returns to Paris, he could become a deputy manager there, I think. Something like that. He's done very well for himself."

"Yes," Elizabeth said.

That evening Morgan knocked gently on the parlour door before leaving. He put his head around and smiled.

"Hello, Elizabeth! I won't keep you a minute, I promise. I've got tickets for *Iolanthe* at the Prince of Wales Theatre in Cardiff next Saturday. Would you like to come with me?"

"*Iolanthe* - the new Gilbert and Sullivan opera?"

"Yes. I thought you'd like it. When were you last in a Cardiff theatre?"

Elizabeth threw her head back and laughed. "When I went with you sixteen years ago! It was called the New Theatre Royal then, do you remember?"

"Of course. We saw *Carmen*'."

"You mean *Maritana*."

"Are you sure?"

"You said it was something to remember for the rest of your life! I distinctly recall you saying that," Elizabeth said, with a grin.

Morgan looked at her for a moment without saying anything. "Did I? Then I must have seen *Carmen* at L'Opéra Comique. Anyway, how about *Iolanthe*? It's a matinée performance. We could have dinner somewhere afterwards."

"I'd love to. How nice! Thank you, Morgan."

"I'll call for you at about half-past-twelve," he said. "Au revoir!"

Elizabeth was enchanted by the opera, every bit as enraptured as she had been with *Maritana*. After leaving the theatre they crossed the road to gaze at the lighted windows of Howells and David Morgan's department stores before sauntering to the Angel hotel where Morgan had booked a corner table for dinner. The waiter led them to their seats and handed them menus.

"I can't believe this is happening!" Elizabeth said softly. "To be waited on! What a luxury!"

"I hope you're hungry. Let me see, we definitely won't have the onion soup, not in Cardiff; that's only to be had in France. How about oysters?"

"Perfect!"

"Then, fillet steak with pepper sauce?"

"If you recommend it."

Morgan gave the order. "Madam would like the steak medium to well done; I'll have mine rare - no more than two minutes each side."

"Any wine, Sir?"

Morgan looked at Elizabeth. "No, thank you, just a carafe of water, please."

The dining-room was dimly lit by crystal chandeliers but candles on each table shed golden pools of light over the pink table-cloths and illuminated the carnations standing in narrow silver vases.

They lingered over the coffee.

"May I smoke a cigar?" Morgan asked.

"Please do. I remember the smell of cigar-smoke in Fairfield House and Mr Lenox always smoked one after dinner. It reminds me of life in the elegant homes of the gentry. My goodness, that's going back some years!"

"Mr Lenox retired last week; his son has taken his place."

"Is he as nice as his father?"

"Yes, I think so. He has a lot to learn though. The firm in Paris is more up-to-date."

"Where do you prefer working?"

"There are pros and cons for both places but France is my home now. I have friends and, well, family there, you might say."

Elizabeth looked at him.

"I was married some years ago; Madeleine's father has a small farm in Provence."

"You are married?" Elizabeth whispered.

"Madeleine and the baby died; they are buried in the village churchyard, near her home."

Elizabeth sat back. "Morgan *bach*! I am so sorry. How long were you married?"

"About two years. I came back to Wales some months afterwards," he said, blowing a large smoke ring into the air.

"That's so sad!"

"You have known that pain and anguish too."

"Tell me about her," Elizabeth said softly.

Morgan looked into the distance and smiled. "She was eighteen years old when we married. She was tiny, she had golden hair, she was always laughing." He shrugged his shoulders. "What else can I say about her except......she shines for me like the evening star."

Elizabeth's eyes were moist.

"I'm upsetting you, I'm afraid," Morgan said. "Would you like some

231

more coffee? I would."

He called the waiter and they said nothing until their cups had been replenished.

"What about your family here?" Elizabeth asked.

"My mother died many years ago. My father lives with my sister Catherine now. That's where I'm staying."

They drank their coffee in silence until Elizabeth spoke. "A lot of water has passed under the bridge since we were young, hasn't it!"

Morgan smiled at her. "Inevitably."

She sighed. "Well, this has been a wonderful treat, Morgan. I hope when you go back to France you'll remember it was *Iolanthe* we saw today!" she said with a grin.

"I still think it was *Carmen* that the Omara Opera company did, you know," he said, blowing cigar smoke above her head.

They went home and Elizabeth didn't see him again for some weeks.

A pall hung over the country that year; the only news coming out of South Africa was bad. Casualties were mounting without any progress being made. Seth's letters home became more and more gloomy until they stopped altogether. The papers reported that British troops were being surrounded and trapped, not only in one place either. Kimberley, Ladysmith and Mafeking had become household words. People waited for news of a breakout somewhere - anywhere, but none came.

Morgan continued to visit West Street and often stayed for supper. Phil and Jack were impressed that such a revered figure in the chain works should have become a family friend.

On a warm evening in May, Josiah and a group of children stood around the organ-grinder, while a few women gossiped on the corner. Suddenly a boy came running along and shouting at the top of his voice: "Mafeking has been relieved! We have relieved Mafeking!"

In two minutes pandemonium had broken out. Elizabeth ran outside; neighbours poured from every door. Mrs Davies next door stood with her hands at her mouth while tears streaked down her cheeks.

Her lodger, Mr Payne, grabbed Elizabeth's hand.

"Madam, will you join me in the polka?" he asked without waiting for an answer.

He put an arm around her waist and took her along in time with the music from the organ-grinder. "One, two, three and one, two, three", he sang as he guided her round and round.

Others followed suit. Some women linked arms and swayed from side to side singing "Hello, Dolly Gray!" The street filled up as men streamed home from work early; Morgan hurried over to join the festivities and stood grinning as Elizabeth tried to keep pace with Mr Payne's exuberance. To her relief he finally let her go but without warning; she spun backwards, about to fall flat on her back.

Morgan dived towards her and caught her as she fell, holding her in a vice-like grip on the ground. Her grin faded when she saw the look on his face.

"At last you are in my arms," he said. "Oh, God! I'm not going to let this chance pass. Elizabeth, I shall love you till the day I die." His eyes searched hers. "If I promise to stay in Wales, will you marry me now?"

Elizabeth let her head fall back. "Help me up! I don't think I heard you properly."

"Oh, yes, you did. I'm keeping you here until I get an answer this time."

She looked at him and smiled. "I will marry you, Morgan *bach*. I was afraid you weren't going to ask me!"

He kissed her over and over again and they stayed looking at each other, oblivious of the noise in the street and the circle of children who gathered round them whistling and shouting Ooohs and Aaahs!

When Morgan helped her to her feet, Elizabeth saw seven-year-old Josh staring at them. She took his hand. "Let's play 'There was a farmer and his wife' she said. Morgan took his other hand and linked up with the rest of the children, as they walked around in a circle.

"There was a farmer and his wife,
His name was Bobby Bingo!"

The celebrations continued until well after dark. Jack came home at six, when the grocer shut his shop; Phil arrived shortly afterwards. After supper, Elizabeth, Morgan and the boys went to see the bonfire that had been lit near the Rocking Stone. From Brecon down to Penarth Head, on every mountain top above every valley and along the Bristol Channel, answering beacons flickered in the night.